AF564629

Information Archiving

Information Archiving

Dr. Avdhesh Kumar Gupta

Information Archiving

ISBN 978-93-5111-475-8

Published in 2015 in India by

RANDOM PUBLICATIONS

4376-A/4B, Gali Murari Lal, Ansari Road
New Delhi-110 002
Phone : +9111-43580356, 011-23289044, 011-43142548
e-mail: sales@randompublications.com,
info@randompublications.com, randomexports@gmail.com

Type Setting by : Friends Media, Delhi-110089
Printed at : Thomson Press (India) Ltd.

Preface

The rapid growth in the creation and dissemination of digital objects by authors, publishers, corporations, governments, and even librarians, archivists and museum curators, has emphasized the speed and ease of short-term dissemination with little regard for the long-term preservation of digital information. However, digital information is fragile in ways that differ from traditional technologies, such as paper or microfilm. It is more easily corrupted or altered without recognition. Digital storage media have shorter life spans, and digital information requires access technologies that are changing at an ever-increasing pace. Because of the speed of technological advances, the time frame in which we must consider archiving becomes much shorter. The time between manufacture and preservation is shrinking.

While there are traditions of stewardship and best practices that have become institutionalized in the print environment, many of these traditions are inadequate, inappropriate or not well known among the stakeholders in the digital environment. Groups and individuals who did not previously consider themselves to be archivists are now being drawn into the role, either because of the infrastructure and intellectual property issues involved or because user groups are demanding it. Librarians and archivists who traditionally managed the life cycle of print information from creation to long-term preservation and archiving, must now look to information managers from the computer science tradition to support the development of a system of stewardship in the new digital environment.

This book presents an up-to-date description of information archiving, together with a solution for all technical problems identified in the pertinent professional literature. It is designed for archivists, research librarians, and museum curators who need to understand digital technology in order to manage their institutions.

Author

Contents

	Preface	**v**
1.	**Introduction to Digital Archives**	**1**
	Electronic Archiving	2
	Web Archiving	2
	Audiovisual Archives	3
	Preservation of Archives	7
	Access to Digital Archives	8
	Creating Digital Archives	11
	Digitization Technology	18
	Markup Languages	25
2.	**Best Practices in Digital Archiving**	**42**
	Migration of Digital Materials	44
	Converting Information Objects in Digital Form	47
	Certification for Digital Archives	64
	Methods of Web Archiving	65
	Organisation of Library Web Pages	69
	Digital Reference Services	71
	Issues in Web Archiving	79
3.	**Emerging Trends in Information Archiving**	**88**
	Current Trends	89
	Scholarly Journal Archiving	92
	Archive Architecture	100
	Quality Assurance	103
	Levels of Preservation Service	108

Responsibilities of the Archive Staff 111
Role of Stakeholders 112
The Archival Community 113
Preservation Strategies 116
Source Forms 121
Auxiliary Forms 122
Open Archival Information System (OAIS) 122
Preservation Policies and Procedures 128
Archival Storage 133
Planning for Preservation 134
Logical Model for Archival Information 136
Representation Networks 137
Preservation of Archival Description 139
Archiving: An Information Life Cycle Approach 141
4. Digital Contents 147
Management of Metadata 151
Digital Content Service Development Activity 153
Digital Library Framework 161
Model of Digital Libraries 169
5. Access to Information Archives 171
Tasks of Digital Preservation 172
Organizational Commitments 176
Progress in Digital Archiving 178
Access Management 181
Responsibility for Access 188
Open Access Digital Library 193
Access to Repositories 204
Security of Information Archives 206
6. Information Archiving Programmes 212
E-journal Archiving Program 213
New Age Skills for Information Professionals 218

7. Management of Digital Collections **236**

Descriptive Metadata 237

File Naming Systems 239

Issues in Collection Management 240

Hidden Collections and Archives Program 245

8. Challenges of Archival Information **254**

Meeting the Challenge of Digital Preservation 255

Searching and Advertising 258

Customer Service 259

Challenges of Digital Conservancies 262

Commitments of Digital Research Library 264

Electronic Storage Repository 266

Tools and Policies 268

New Insights into Digital Archiving 272

Bibliography **285**

Index **287**

1

Introduction to Digital Archives

An archive is a collection of historical records, as well as the place they are located.Archives contain primary source documents that have accumulated over the course of an individual or organization's lifetime. In general, archives consist of records that have been selected for permanent or long-term preservation on grounds of their enduring cultural, historical, or evidentiary value. Archival records are normally unpublished and almost always unique, unlike books or magazines for which many identical copies exist. This means that archives (the places) are quite distinct from libraries with regard to their functions and organization, although archival collections can often be found within library buildings. A person who works in archives is called an archivist. The study and practice of organizing, preserving, and providing access to information and materials in archives is called archival science.

Archives in colleges, universities, and other educational facilities are typically housed within a library, and duties may be carried out by an archivist or a librarian. Occasionally, history professors may also run a smaller archive. Academic archives exist to preserve and celebrate the history of their school and academic community. An academic archive may contain items such as papers of former professors and presidents, memorabilia related to school organizations and activities, and items the academic library wishes to remain in a closed-stack setting, such as rare books or thesis copies. Access to the majority of these archives is by appointment only. Users of academic archives are often graduate students and those wishing to view rare or historical documents for research purposes. Many academic archives work closely with alumni relations departments to help raise funds for their library or school

Electronic Archiving

Archives can take many forms. However when pertaining to specifically databases there are three main forms, described by new media artist Bill Viola; branching, matrix, and schizo.

In the branching format one option can potentially lead to numerous other options. Imagine a tree diagram, where multiple branches branch off of one branch. The same rule applies here. We start at a single beginning point then are given choices as to what we wish to see next based on topics.

The matrix form is not as linear as the branching form. The matrix structure is like a grid where there is no direct path to follow. An individual has the ability to view any archival information regardless of their previous selection. Thus, it is a non-linear archival structure. The user is only restrained by the amount of content there is to view.

Also referred to as the spaghetti style by Bill Viola, schizo is a form of archives that is completely random. The user has no control over what they are capable of experiencing. Information is presented to them without any preordained trend. There is no restriction due to topics but in return the user has no control over the information being presented to them.

Web archiving

The process of collecting data from the world wide web and preserving it in an archive, such as an archive site, for the web user to see.

Examples of web archives are:

- Side bars
- Blogs
- Calendar
- Tag cloud
- News websites

Some archives defy categorization. There are tribal archives within the Native American nations in North America, and there are archives that exist within the papers of private individuals. Many museums keep archives in order to prove the provenance of their pieces. Any institution or persons wishing to keep their significant papers in an organized fashion that employs the most basic principles of archival science may have an archive. In the 2004 census of archivists taken in the United States, 2.7% of archivists were employed in institutions that defied categorization. This was a separate figure from the 1.3% that identified themselves as self-employed. Another type of archive is public secrets. This is an interactive testimonial in which women incarcerated in the California State Prison System reveal their stories about what happened to them. The function of the archive is to unfold the stories of the women who want to express themselves and want their stories to be heard. This collection of stories includes the women's direct speeches and also a recording of the women saying their speech. The archives of an individual may include letters, papers, photographs, computer files, scrapbooks, financial records or diaries created or collected by the individual – regardless of media or format. The archives of an organization (such as a corporation or government) tend to contain other types of records, such as administrative files, business records, memos, official correspondence and meeting minutes.

Audiovisual Archives

The audiovisual heritage is an important element within the cultural heritage and has achieved prominence in the twentieth century, the first to have been recorded on audiovisual formats. Audiovisuals are not new but have become of increasing importance as art, entertainment and information carriers. In some cases the transmission of sound and visual data has greater value and impact than the printed document—where, for example, there is a literacy or language barrier. Audiovisuals may also be the only suitable records for the oral or sonic transmission of culture and the arts, news and other current items. The spread and development of modern technologies mean an increase in the role of audiovisual data carriers for communication, information and culture. Today's radio and television rely heavily on archive material and it is estimated that more than 60% of radio and television programmes use archival or stock material for programming.

The definitions are still being formulated, but audiovisual materials are to be understood as visual recordings (with or without soundtrack) and sound recordings irrespective of their physical base or recording process. The carrier usually requires a playback device. This definition is meant to cover the maximum number of forms and formats. Audiovisual materials should not be confused with multimedia; the former provide source material for the latter, and multimedia as such are not archival material. Two features of audiovisual materials add an extra dimension to the principles of collection and preservation: a proliferation both of formats and of systems of production and playback. These cause incompatibility problems between formats and systems. Archives have to maintain original playback devices and employ technical staff who know how to use and maintain the machinery. The Recommendation for the Safeguarding and Preservation of Moving Images, adopted by the General Conference of UNESCO in 1980, provides a basic orientation for integrating and protecting audiovisual recordings as part of the cultural heritage of each nation.

Audiovisual archives are storehouses for a large proportion of the social and cultural heritage of the twentieth century. An audiovisual archive is defined as an organization or department of an organization which is focused on collecting, managing, preserving and providing access to a collection of audiovisual media and the audiovisual heritage, applying archival principles. Such archives contain huge treasures of unique material. Archives of audiovisual materials are relatively new, but they have proliferated in the past few decades. The first sound recordings appeared in 1877 and the first sound archive—the Phonogrammarchiv in Vienna—was established as a research archive in 1899, although it was not followed by others until the 1930s. Film appeared in the 1890s and archives began to be established in the 1930s. Photography had appeared earlier in the nineteenth century. Television was originally recorded on film, but video has been the principal material since the later 1960s. Although audiovisual materials have appeared so recently, time is not on their side and the longer we delay in gathering, conserving and preserving the materials, the less we shall be able to retain. It is vital that steps are taken now to collect and manage audiovisual materials properly before their fragile nature takes a further toll. Already much has been lost owing to ignorance, lack of awareness of the dangers and careless handling.

Audiovisual archives vary in type, purpose and function, and until recently most of them were singlematerial archives: moving image (film or television), sound and still-image archives, the latter frequently housed in more conventional archives of print materials. As the technologies converge so do the archives, to unite effort and conserve resources. Some archives take responsibility for all recorded materials, others take smaller bites and combine one or two of the materials. The larger archives cannot always combine materials in one department; the physical techniques required to deal with each material from the point of view of storage, handling and restoration need different expertise and materials are therefore separated by this parameter alone.

Other functions of collection management can be applied to all the materials: documentation and information retrieval, and selection. Storage vaults may have to accommodate more than one material and the resulting environmental considerations will be different from those more stringently applied to individual materials. Alternatively, an archive may decide that it must apply the optimum storage and environmental values which apply to each material: single-material archives are more fortunate in these cases. Academic archives also house audiovisual materials, many in universities for research, and latterly educational materials for distance learning. These may be small and specialized, or have substantial collections and preservation programmes. Specialized or thematic archives concentrate on a particular format, subject-matter or locality, or relate to specific cultural groups. Many examples could be cited, including the following: special events or periods in history; regional interests; specific cultural groups; academic and research disciplines; folklife collections; oral history; world music; and specific organizations.

Many of these archives have developed within larger organizations. Production archives. Film companies, broadcasting companies and record companies maintain archives primarily for use and exploitation by the parent company. Many of these preserve and restore their materials for re-use, but the archives' main obligation is to the parent organization rather than to preserving the cultural heritage. This may be left to a national archive, which obtains a selection of the production company's material by deposit. Other institutions with archival responsibility include museums, cinematheques, videotheques and national libraries. Most of these are more concerned with maintaining stock for exhibition purposes, and originals may be deposited for long-term preservation in a national archive. There are also collections of last resort which attempt to conserve copies of material in usable condition, but seldom retain archival originals or masters.

Audiovisual materials result from a huge level of investment. Consider the costs of a television channel, or a film production or sound recording company. That the material is allowed to deteriorate through lack of funding for conservation is an unforgivable waste of financial resources and human talent. Considering the huge investment in production, the financial resources available for preservation of the material are ludicrously small. Although some archives were established by private means, the ultimate responsibility for the protection and maintenance of a national heritage must lie with the nation itself, and this means government and granting bodies. It is incumbent upon government to ensure that the national heritage is protected for posterity. Archives in organizations such as broadcast associations or film production companies have commercial backing and motivation, and meet costs from their revenue. Once that commercial motive is fulfilled, however, it is generally acknowledged that, as with other records of the national cultural creativity, the cost of maintaining the collection reverts to government and granting bodies. Many valuable collections have disappeared for ever as a result of production company closures or changes in franchise when materials are not taken over by already overstretched archives.

The basic tasks of an audiovisual archive are collection, preservation, documentation and access provision. Methods of collection and acquisition vary, and include the legal or voluntary deposit of collections or individual items, the deposit of in-house productions, donations, special agreements for copying nationally produced materials, and purchase. Other archives collect their own materials in the form of oral or video history programmes, with the purpose of recording cultures, languages and music before they disappear.

Closely allied to acquisition are evaluation, selection and appraisal. The audiovisual archive acquires materials according to a particular remit, balancing new acquisitions against existing stock and the purpose and function of the archive. Storage space and resources being what they are, archives have to select material for preservation on the basis of relevance, uniqueness and quality. Wherever possible an archive should be dealing with original materials, but originals are hard to come by. There is strictly only one original film, video or master sound recording. Such originals seldom survive and there are various forms of tampering with the products—cut/uncut versions, director's/producer's cut, censored and unexpurgated versions. Owners of original material may be reluctant to deposit their master material in an archive until they have no further use for it, by which time the technical quality has deteriorated.

Three elements in audiovisual documents have to be considered in the selection process: the artefact or carrier, the information content and the aesthetic content, particularly with film and sound recordings. The artefact or carrier will designate the form of the audiovisual and influence selection for technical reasons. Can this material be replayed in the collection which acquires it, or is the carrier so esoteric that it has only antique value? Is the carrier in good physical condition or will it need transfer and/or costly restoration before or on receipt, or indeed is the damage irreparable? There are also implications for damage and disaster to the rest of the collection; canker present in one item may spread to others if it is stored untreated and without inspection. Archives have very stringent selection policies. It is widely quoted that archives select less than 2% of the material presented.

Audiovisual archives, therefore, do not have a huge selection of material, but most of it has unique value, and such archives retain more material than many other archives. Some audiovisual collections will include several interpretations of the same work—for example, music recordings—or several records of the same event carried in different documents: a film, video or sound version. Guidelines for archival selection exist, but they are usually those of organizations with their own parameters. Selection of material is dependent upon the function of the archive, the quality of the material and the uniqueness or rarity of the content. Audiovisual archives should concentrate on recordings of national origin. To avoid duplication of effort, material should be offered back to the country of original production or to archives with a more relevant collection remit.

Preservation of Archives

The main function of any archive is to preserve the heritage and the artefacts which make up that heritage. These are the major concerns of audiovisual archives. Many of the difficulties encountered result from the fragility or the volatile nature of the materials. The carriers are the weak link and the materials have to be transferred to other carriers that are more stable, with a longer life expectancy or more up to date. Audiovisual materials are made of polymers, and all polymers decay! Progress is being made to slow this decay and prolong the life expectancy of the carriers and thus the source material, but preservation measures will simply retard deterioration, not prevent it. The life expectancy of audiovisual materials is dependent on chemistry and storage and handling conditions. After 100 years much early film has been lost, especially volatile nitrate. Sound and video recordings are subject to attack from many enemies. No universal panacea has been found and the new technologies of optical disks are as prone to damage as the old. For example, there have been problems with vinegar syndrome producing tape and laser rot affecting optical disks designed to act as storage media for tape materials. Archives must copy material from one format to another to save the content, to overcome the obsolescence of equipment and systems, and to provide copies for research and other uses. There are three steps in preservation work:

— Conservation;
— Preservation ; and
— Restoration.

Wherever possible the original data have to be preserved on the original format for future use by more advanced technologies of transfer and presentation. Guidelines and standards exist and can be adjusted to suit prevailing conditions—hot and humid climates call for different standards of storage and preservation than cold, temperate climates. The American National Standards Institute (ANSI), the International Standards Organization (ISO) and the British Standards Institute (BSI) all publish standards for composition of tape, and for storage environments and conditions. The international audiovisual NGOs also issue guidelines. Digitization is not yet the answer as there may be loss of quality in copying the original, even though clones will retain the quality of the copy. Digitization is often associated with mass storage techniques, but data density techniques are not necessarily reversible—hence the caution of technicians in retaining originals whenever possible.

Access to Digital Archives

If preservation is the primary concern of the audiovisual archive, access is the second. Audiovisual archiving is a culturally motivated activity, intent upon the preservation of the audiovisual heritage because of its intrinsic worth, regardless of commercial potential. Such values are still important, but most archives are now growing faster than the financial resources to support them. There is therefore a certain necessity for archives to generate some income; there is also the public service aspect—that is, to provide access to the people whose heritage is contained within the archive.

Copyright in archive material is usually vested in the owner and respected, but the archive itself requires rights to acquire, copy, use and provide access to the material. Acquisition of material is achieved by some countries through legal deposit arrangements, but this will only cover a small proportion of the material acquired by an archive—that which is published. Much of the material is unpublished. Archives have ad hoc agreements with donors for voluntary deposits but, in the case of some commercial producers, the archive's rights may be severely restricted. Archives are not in competition with producers or owners, and need some rights over material deposited with them, on which they may have spent considerable time, effort and money for preservation and storage. Archives are not simply convenient storehouses, and have to maintain the integrity of the material. Most especially they need rights to copy the material for preservation, access and exhibition purposes, and some rights to retain the material once acquired. Once deposited, archive copies should not leave archive premises but should remain under archive control.

Detailed cataloguing of archive material is essential to provide a permanent, accurate record, especially of the unedited, unpublished material which abounds. Many archives developed their own rules, but an international initiative is now under way to produce ground rules for all audiovisual materials. Ground rules are necessary for the exchange of information in electronic databases—if everyone uses different criteria, then confusion will result and information exchange be retarded. Accurate and rapid information retrieval is the goal of indexing, and essential data elements have to be devised to make this possible, even though each kind of material will have its own set of data elements. Retrieval by subject has been made easier by the introduction of computer techniques and free-text searching—but the terms for description of subject content have to be carefully chosen, based on international thesauri, or data and material will be lost.

As electronic technology develops so the means of transmitting information—printed and audiovisual— are advanced. In a world of incompatible systems (computers are no exception), the search continues for a system capable of access by as wide a public as possible. Work has started to find the lowest common denominator for the transmission of information with the highest common quality, a sort of 'ASCII' code for all information. In addition to information retrieval, archives have to keep detailed technical records—what has happened to the material, its current format, has it been restored, if so on what system, how and why to assist future technicians. The technical record is usually kept separate from the information record. There are many published information tools ranging from catalogues of holdings to discographies and filmographies, but national discographies and filmographies are compiled independently of the archives, because the latter's stock is not comprehensive, even when legal deposit exists, and seldom up to date. Other discographies and filmographies are selective and cover directors, performers or composers.

Audio, film and video archives was carried out by the Library of Congress on behalf of Eastman Kodak. The figures are alarming. Even with the most stringent selection criteria and limited collection resources, the holdings of just 500 archives amounted to 11,175 million feet of film, 8.5 million hours of video, and 44.5 million hours of audio, and there are many more archives than this. A recent studies of audiovisual archives in Europe alone, Map-TV—Film and Television Collections in Europe, identified some additional 1,900 archives and collections for film and television. There are approximately 40,000 radio and television stations around the world, many of which have archives; film archives exist in over eighty countries, and sound archives in fifty countries at a conservative estimate. A large part of audiovisual production will be lost for future generations without greater efforts from the international community to support the establishment and development of audiovisual archives worldwide. Personnel working in audiovisual archives come from many different professions and scientific disciplines, and have long professional experience and on-the-job training. There is a serious gap, however, between the growing importance of audiovisual archives and the provision of professional education, a gap no less wide in developed than in developing countries. Audiovisual archivists need to be specialists with a thorough knowledge of archival principles and the special characteristics of audiovisual materials. There are two main types of audiovisual archivist:

a) collection managers, documentalists and selectors and
b) technical staff, who have to be of a high standard with thorough knowledge of their disciplines.

There are few courses available; most are summer schools and seminars, but some longer courses can be found in existing schools of library and archival studies.

The UNESCO Memory of the World Programme is an attempt to save the cultural heritage, and audiovisual materials cannot be excluded. These materials, however, are among the most vulnerable to destruction. Lost collections are a sad reminder of the ravages of time, chemistry, natural and man-made disasters, wars and conflicts, but fortunately endangered collections are currently being identified by this programme.

Audiovisual archives have set up their own federations: the International Federation of Film Archives (FIAF) was established sixty-eight years ago, the International Association of Sound Archives (IASA) in 1969 and the International Federation of Television Archives (IFTA) in 1977. All have NGO status within UNESCO. Although each has its own constituency and membership structures, the audiovisual NGOs, ICA and the International Federation of Library Associations and Institutions (IFLA) have collaborated since 1979 in a Round Table on Audiovisual Records under the auspices of UNESCO. The Round Table has been responsible for many activities including publications, the development of guidelines and training. It provides an arena for audiovisual organizations to address common issues and improve the recognition and status of audiovisual archives as vital components in safeguarding the cultural heritage. The Round Table has an important subcommittee—the Technical Co-ordinating Committee—which organizes Joint Technical Symposia across its spectrum of interests and provides technical advice and expertise.

In addition to the international NGOs there are several national and regional associations: the Association of Recorded Sound Collections (ARSC) in the United States, the Association of Moving Image Archives (AMIA), with its network of interests in North America and beyond, and the recently formed South-East Asia-Pacific Audiovisual Archives Association (SEAPAVAA). Other closely allied associations include the International Council on Museums (ICOM) and the International Council on Traditional Music (ICTM). Thus many associations are willing to assist if one knows where to look.

Creating Digital Archives

Creating digital archives was one of the earliest areas of computational activity, and has been going on for at least half a century. When combined with an intimate knowledge of the non-electronic source material, readers should be able to decide for themselves which approach—and thus which combinations of hardware and software, techniques and design philosophy—will be most appropriate to their needs and the needs of any other prospective users.

Creating Electronic Texts

Although every functional aspect of computers is based upon the distinctive binary divide evidenced between 1's and 0's, true and false, presence and absence, it is rarely so easy to draw such clear distinctions at the higher levels of creating and documenting electronic texts. Conversely, if you are hoping to produce an electronic text that will have broad functionality and appeal, and the original source contains presentational features which might be considered worthy of note, then you should be attempting to create a very different object—perhaps one where visual fidelity is more important than the absolute accuracy of any transcription.

Deciding to create an electronic text is just like deciding to begin any other type of construction project. While the desire to dive right in and begin building is tempting, any worthwhile endeavour will begin with a thorough planning stage. In the case of digitized text creation, this stage is called document analysis.

Document analysis is literally the task of examining the physical object in order to acquire an understanding about the work being digitized and to decide what the purpose and future of the project entails. The digitization of texts is not simply making groups of words available to an online community; it involves the creation of an entirely new object. This is why achieving a sense of what it is that you are creating is critical. The blueprint for construction will allow you to define the foundation of the project. It will also allow you to recognise any problems or issues that have the potential to derail the project at a later point. Document analysis is all about definition—defining the document context, defining the document type and defining the different document features and relationships.

At no other point in the project will you have the opportunity to spend as much quality time with your document. This is when you need to become intimately acquainted with the format, structure, and content of the texts. One of the first tasks to perform in document analysis is to define the goals of the project and the context under which they are being developed. This could be seen as one of the more difficult tasks in the document analysis procedure, as it relies less upon the physical analysis of the document and more upon the theoretical positions taken with the project. This is the stage where you need to ask yourself why the document is being encoded. It is also important to take into consideration the external influences on the project. Often the bodies that oversee digitization projects, either in a funding or advisory capacity, have specific conditions that must be fulfilled. They might for example have markup requirements or standards (linguistic, TEI/SGML, or EAD perhaps) that must be taken into account when establishing an encoding methodology.

Also, if you are creating the electronic text for scholarly purposes, then it is very likely that the standards of this community will need to be adhered to. Again, it must be remembered that the electronic version of a text is a distinct object and must be treated as such. Just as you would adhere to a publishing standard of practice with a printed text, so must you follow the standard for electronic texts. The most stringent scholarly community, the textual critics and bibliographers, will have specific, established guidelines that must be considered in order to gain the requisite scholarly authority. Therefore, if you were creating a text to be used or approved by this community their criteria would have to be integrated into the project standards, with the subsequent influence on both the objectives and the creative process taken into account.

If the digitization project includes image formats, then there are specific archiving standards held by the electronic community that might have to be met—this will not only influence the purchase of hardware and software, but will have an impact on the way in which the electronic object will finally be structured. External conditions are easily overlooked during the detailed analysis of the physical object, so be sure that the standards and policies that influence the outcome of the project are given serious thought, as having to modify the documents retrospectively can prove both detrimental and expensive.

While you cannot satisfy each desire, trying to evaluate what information might be the most important to your audience will allow you to address the needs and concerns you deem most appropriate and necessary. Also, if there are specific objectives that you wish users to derive from the project then this too needs to be established at the outset. If the primary purpose for the texts is as a teaching mechanism, then this will have a significant influence on how you choose to encode the document. Conversely, if your texts are being digitized so that users will be able to perform complex thematic searches, then both the markup of content and the content of the markup will differ somewhat. Regardless of the decision, be sure that the outcome of this evaluation becomes integrated with the previously determined project objectives.

You must also attempt to assess what tools users will have at their disposal to retrieve your document. The hardware and software capabilities of your users will differ, sometimes dramatically, and will most likely present some sort of restriction or limitation upon their ability to access your project. SGML encoded text requires the use of specialised software, such as Panorama, to read the work. Even HTML has tagsets that early browsers may not be able to read. It is essential that you take these variants into consideration during the planning stage. There might be priorities in the project that require accessibility for all users, which would affect the methodology of the project. However, don't let the user limitations stunt the encoding goals for the document. Hardware and software are constantly being upgraded so that although some of the encoding objectives might not be fully functional during the initial stages of the project, they stand a good chance of becoming accessible in the near future.

The first stage of document analysis is not only necessary for detailing the goals and objectives of the project, but also serves as an opportunity to examine the context of the document. This is a time to gather as much information as possible about the documents being digitized. The amount gathered varies from project to project, but in an ideal situation you will have a complete transmission and publication history for the document. There are a few key reasons for this. Firstly, knowing how the object being encoded was created will allow you to understand any textual variations or anomalies. This, in turn, will assist in making informed encoding decisions at later points in the project. The difference between a printer error and an authorial variation not only affects the content of the document, but also the way in which it is marked up. Secondly, the depth of information gathered will give the document the authority desired by the scholarly community. A text about which little is known can only be used with much hesitation.

While some users might find it more than acceptable for simply printing out or reading, there can be no authoritative scholarly analysis performed on a text with no background history. Thirdly, a quality electronic text will have a TEI header attached. The TEI header records all the information about the electronic text's print source. The more information you know about the source, the more full and conclusive your header will be—which will again provide scholarly authority. Lastly, understanding the history of the document will allow you to understand its physicality. The physicality of the text is an interesting issue—and one on which very few scholars fully agree. Clearly, an understanding of the physical object provides a sense of the format, necessary for a proper structural encoding of the text, but it also augments a contextual understanding.

While the physical object has trained readers to follow a more linear narrative, the electronic document will provide you with an opportunity to develop the variant branches found within the text. Depending upon the decided project objectives, you are free to highlight, augment or furnish your users with as many different associations as you find significant in the text. Yet to do this, you must fully understand the ontology of the texts and then be able to delineate this textuality through the encoding of the computerised object. It is important to remember that the transmission history does not end with the publication of the printed document. Tracking the creation of the electronic text, including the revision history, is a necessary element of the encoding process.

The fluidity of electronic texts precludes the guarantee that every version of the document will remain in existence, so the responsibility lies with the project creator to ensure that all revisions and developments are noted. While some of the documentation might seem tedious, an electronic transmission history will serve two primary purposes. One, it will help keep the project creator(s) aware of what has developed in the creation of the electronic text. If there are quite a few staff members working on the documents, you will be able to keep track of what has been accomplished with the texts and to check that the project methodology is being followed. Two, users of the documents will be able to see what emendations or regularisations have been made and to track what the various stages of the electronic object were.

Defining the document type is a critical part of the digitization process as it establishes the foundation for the initial understanding of the text's structure. At this point you should have an idea of what documents are going to be digitized for the project. Even if you not sure precisely how many texts will be in the final project, it is important to have a representative sample of the types of documents being digitized. Examine the sample documents and decide what categories they fall under. The structure and content of a letter will differ greatly from that of a novel or poem, so it is critical to make these naming classifications early in the process. Not only are there structural differences between varying document types but also within the same type.

Deciding upon document type will give you an initial sense of the shape of the text. There are basic structural assumptions that come with classification: looking for the stanzas in poetry or the paragraphs in prose for example. Having established the document type, you can begin to assign the texts a more detailed structure. Without worrying about the actual tag names, as this comes later in the process, label all of the features you wish to encode. For example, if you are digitizing a novel, you might initially break it into large structural units: title page, table of contents, preface, body, back matter, etc. Once this is done you might move on to smaller features: titles, heads, paragraphs, catchwords, pagination, plates, annotations and so forth. One way to keep the naming in perspective is to create a structure outline. This will allow you to see how the structure of your document is developing, whether you have omitted any necessary features, or if you have labelled too much.

Once the features to be encoded have been decided upon, the relationships between them can then be examined. Establishing the hierarchical sequence of the document should not be too arduous a task—especially if you have already developed a structural outline. It should at this point be apparent, if we stick with the example of a novel, that the work is contained within front matter, body matter, and back matter. Within front matter we find such things as epigraphs, prologues, and title pages. Within the paragraphs can be found quotations, figures, and notes. This is an established and understandable hierarchy. There is also a sequential relationship where one element logically follows another.

Using the above representation, if every body has chapters, paragraphs, and notes, then you would expect to find a sequence of <chapter> then <paragraph> then <note>, not <chapter>, <note>, then <paragraph>. Again, the more you understand about the type of text you are encoding, the easier this process will be. While the level of structural encoding will ultimately depend upon the project objectives, this is an opportune time to explore the form of the text in as much detail as possible. Having these data will influence later encoding decisions, and being able to refer to these results will be much easier than having to sift through the physical object at a later point to resolve a structural dilemma. The analysis also brings to light any issues or problems with the physical document. Are parts of the source missing? Perhaps the text has been water damaged and certain lines are unreadable? If the document is a manuscript or letter perhaps the writing is illegible? These are all instances that can be explored at an early stage of the project.

While these problems will add a level of complexity to the encoding project, they must be dealt with in an honest fashion. If the words of a letter are illegible and you insert text that represents your best guess at the actual wording then this needs to be encoded. The beauty of document analysis is that by examining the documents prior to digitization you stand a good chance of recognising these issues and establishing an encoding methodology. The benefit of this is threefold: firstly, having identified and dealt with this problem at the start you will have fewer issues arise during the digitization process; secondly, there will be an added level of consistency during the encoding stage and retrospective revision won't be necessary; thirdly, the project will benefit from the thorough level of accuracy desired and expected by the scholarly community.

This is also a good time to examine the physical document and attempt to anticipate problems with the digitization process. Fragile spines, flaking or foxed paper, badly inked text, all will create difficulties during the scanning process and increase the likelihood of project delays if not anticipated at an early stage. This is another situation that requires examining representative samples of texts. It could be that one text was cared for in the immaculate conditions of a Special Collections facility while another was stored in a damp corner of a bookshelf. You need to be prepared for as many document contingencies as possible. Problems not only arise out of the condition of the physical object, but also out of such things as typography. OCR digitization is heavily reliant upon the quality and type of fonts used in the text. OCR software is optimised for laser quality printed text. This means that the older the printed text, the more degradation in the scanning results. These types of problems are critical to identify, as decisions will have to be made about how to deal with them—decisions that will become a significant part of the project methodology.

The final stage of document analysis is deciding which features of the text to encode. Once again, knowing the goals and objectives of the project will be of great use as you try to establish the breadth of your element definition. You have the control over how much of the document you want to encode, taking into account how much time and manpower are dedicated to the project. Once you've made a decision about the level of encoding that will go into the project, you need to make the practical decision of what to tag. There are three basic categories to consider: structure, format and content. In terms of structure there are quite a few typical elements that are encoded. This is a good time to examine the structural outline to determine what skeletal features need to be marked up.

Digitization Technology

Digitization is quite simply the creation of a computerised representation of a printed analog. There are many methods of digitizing and varied media to be digitized. Digitizing other formats, audio and video for example, there are many thorough analyses of procedure. Peter Robinson's The Digitization of Primary Textual Sources covers most aspects of the decision making process and gives detailed explanations of all formats. In other words, recommendations for digitizing are constantly changing. As hardware and software develop, so does the quality of digitized output. The price cuts in storage costs allow smaller projects to take advantage of archival imaging standards.

The digitization chain is a concept expounded by Peter Robinson in his aforementioned publication. The idea is based upon the fundamental concept that the best quality image will result from digitizing the original object. If this is not an attainable goal, then digitization should be attempted with as few steps removed from the original as possible. Therefore, the chain is composed of the number of intermediates that come between the original object and the digital image—the more intermediates, the more links in the chain. This idea was then extended by Dr Lee so that the digitization chain became a circle in which every step of the project became a separate link.

Each link attains a level of importance so that if one piece of the chain were to break, the entire project would fail. Regardless of the technology utilised by the project, the results will depend, first and foremost, on the quality of the image being scanned. Scanning a copy of a microfilm of an illustration originally found in a journal is acceptable if it is the only option you have, but clearly scanning the image straight from the journal itself is going to make an immeasurable difference in quality. This is one important reason for carefully choosing the hardware and software. If you know that you are dealing with fragile manuscripts that cannot handle the damaging light of a flatbed scanner, or a book whose binding cannot open past a certain degree, then you will probably lean towards a digital camera.

If you have text that is from an 18th-century book, with fading pages and uneven type, you will want the best text scanning software available. Knowing where your documents stand in the digitization chain will influence the subsequent imaging decisions you will make for the project. The first step in digitization, both text and image, is to obtain a workable facsimile of the page. To accomplish this you will need a combination of hardware and software imaging tools. This is a somewhat difficult area to address in terms of recommending specific product brands, as what is considered industry (or at least the text creation industry) standard is subject to change as technology develops.

There are quite a few methods of image capture that are used within the humanities community. The equipment ranges from scanners (flatbed, sheetfed, drum, slide, microfilm) to high-end digital cameras. In terms of standards within the digitizing community, the results are less than satisfactory. Projects tend to choose the most available option, or the one that is affordable on limited grant funding. However, two of the most common and accessible image capture solutions are flatbed scanners and high-resolution digital cameras.

Flatbed scanners have become the most commonplace method for capturing images or text. Their name comes from the fact that the scanner is literally a flat glass bed, quite similar to a copy machine, on which the image is placed face down and covered. The scanner then passes light-sensitive sensors over the illuminated page, breaking it into groups of pixel-sized boxes. It then represents each box with a zero or a one, depending on whether the pixel is filled or empty. The importance of this becomes more apparent with the discussion of image type below. As a result of their lowering costs and widespread availability, the use of quality flatbeds ranges from the professional digital archiving projects to the living rooms of the home computer consumer.

One benefit of this increased use and availability is that flatbed scanning technology is evolving continually. This has pushed the purchasing standards away from price and towards quality. In an attempt to promote the more expensive product, the marketplace tends to hype resolution and bit-depth, two aspects of scanning that are important to a project but are not the only concerns when purchasing hardware. While it is not necessarily the case that you need to purchase the most expensive scanner to get the best quality digital image, it is unlikely that the entry-level flatbeds will provide the image quality that you need. However, while it used to be the case that to truly digitize well you needed to purchase the more high-end scanner, at a price prohibitive to most projects, the advancing digitizing needs of users have pushed hardware developers to create mid-level scanners that reach the quality of the higher range.

As a consumer, you need to possess a holistic view of the scanner's capabilities. Not only should the scanner provide you with the ability to create archival quality images but it should also make the digitization process easier. Many low-cost scanners do not have high-grade lenses, optics, or light sources, thereby creating images that are of a very poor quality.

The creation of superior calibre images relates to the following hardware requirements:

— the quality of the lens, mirrors, and other optics hardware;

— the mechanical stability of the optical system;

— the focal range and stability of the optical system;

— the quality of the scanning software and many other hardware and software features.

Also, many of the better quality scanners contain tools that allow you to automate some of the procedures. This is extremely useful with such things as colour and contrast where, with the human eye, it is difficult to achieve the exact specification necessary for a high-quality image.

Scanning hardware has the ability to provide this discernment for the user, so these intelligent automated features are a necessity to decrease task time. One of the disadvantages of a flatbed scanner is that to capture the entire image the document must lie completely flat on the scanning bed. With books this poses a problem because the only way to accomplish this is to bend the spine to the breaking point. It becomes even worse when dealing with texts with very fragile pages, as the inversion and pressure can cause the pages to flake away or rip.

A solution to this problem, one taken up by many digital archives and special collections departments, is to digitize with a stand-alone digital camera. Digital cameras are by far the most dependable means of capturing quality digital images. As Robinson explains, They can digitize direct from the original, unlike the film-based methods of microfilm scanning or Photo CD. They can work with objects of any size or shape, under many different lights, unlike flatbed scanners. They can make images of very high resolution, unlike video cameras. These benefits are most clearly seen in the digitization of manuscripts and early printed books—objects that are difficult to capture on a flatbed because of their fragile composition.

The ability to digitize with variant lighting is a significant benefit as it won't damage the make-up of the work, a precaution which cannot be guaranteed with flatbed scanners. The high resolution and heightened image quality allows for a level of detail you would expect only in the original. As a result of these specifications, images can be delivered at great size. A good example of this is the Early American Fiction project being developed at UVA's Electronic Text Center and Special Collections Department. The Early American Fiction project, whose goal is the digitization of 560 volumes of American first editions held in the UVA Special Collections, is utilizing digital cameras mounted above light tables.

They are working with camera backs manufactured by Phase One attached to Tarsia Technical Industries Prisma 45 4x5 cameras on TTI Reprographic Workstations. This has allowed them to create high quality images without damaging the physical objects. As they point out in their overview of the project, the workflow depends upon the text being scanned, but the results work out to close to one image every three minutes. While this might sound detrimental to the project timeline, it is relatively quick for an archival quality image. The images can be seen at such a high-resolution that the faintest pencil annotations can be read on-screen. There are a few tools that are commonly seen in use with many digitization projects. Regardless of the brand of software purchased, the project will need text scanning software if there is to be in-house digitization of text and an image manipulation software package if imaging is to be done. There are a wide variety of text scanning softwares available, all with varying capabilities.

As this software is optimised for laser quality printouts, projects working with texts from earlier centuries need to find a package that has the ability to work through more complicated fonts and degraded page quality. While there is no standard, most projects work with Caere's OmniPage scanning software. In terms of image manipulation, there are more choices depending upon what needs to be done. For image-by-image manipulation, including converting TIFFs to web-deliverable JPEGs and GIFs, Adobe Photoshop is the more common selection. However, when there is a move towards batch conversion, Graphic's DeBabelizer Pro is known for its speed and high quality. If the conversion is being done in a UNIX environment, the XV operating system is also a favourite amongst digitization projects.

Electronic text creation primarily involves the digitization of text and images. Apart from re-keying, the best method of digitizing text is Optical Character Recognition (OCR). This process is accomplished through the utilisation of scanning hardware in conjunction with text scanning software. OCR takes a scanned image of a page and converts it into text. Similarly, image capture also requires an image scanning software to accompany the hardware.

However, unlike text scanning, image capture has more complex requirements in terms of project decisions and, like almost everything else in the digitization project, benefits from clearly thought out objectives. The first decision that must be made regarding image capture concerns the purpose of the images being created. The reason for this is simple: the higher quality the image need be, the higher the settings necessary for scanning.

There are four main types of images: 1-bit black and white, 8-bit greyscale, 8-bit colour and 24-bit colour. A bit is the fundamental unit of information read by the computer, with a single bit being represented by either a '0' or a '1'. A '0' is considered an absence and a '1' is a presence, with more complex representations of information being accommodated by multiple or gathered bits. A 1-bit black and white image means that the bit can either be black or white. This is a rarely used type and is completely unsuitable for almost all images. The only amenable image for this format would be printed text or line graphics for which poor resulting quality did not matter. Another drawback of this type is that saving it as a JPEG compressed image—one of the most prevalent image formats on the web—is not a feasible option.

8-bit greyscale images are an improvement from 1-bit as they encompass 256 shades of grey. It is often used for non-colour images and provides a clear image rather than the resulting fuzz of a 1-bit scan. While greyscale images are often considered more than adequate, there are times when non-colour images should be scanned at a higher colour because the finite detail of the hand will come through distinctly.

Nonetheless, the idea of archival imaging is still discussed amongst projects and funding bodies and cannot be overlooked. There is no set standard for archiving, and you might find that different places and projects recommend another model. However, the following type, format and resolution are recommended:

— *24-bit*: There really is little reason to scan an archival image at anything less. Whether the source is colour or greyscale, the images are more realistic and have a higher quality at this level. As the above example shows, the filesize of the subsequently compressed image does not benefit from scanning at a lower bit-size.

— *600 dpi*: This is, once again, a problematic recommendation. Many projects assert that scanning in at 300 or 400 dpi provides sufficient quality to be considered archival. However, many of the top international digitization centres recommend 600 dpi as an archival standard—it provides excellent detail of the image and allows for quite large JPEG images to be produced.

  The only restrictive aspect is the filesize, but when thinking in terms of archival images you need to try and get as much storage space as possible. Remember, the master copies do not have to be held online, as offline storage on writeable CD-ROMs is another option.

— *TIFF*: This should come as no surprise given the format discussion above. TIFF files, with their complete retention of scanned information and cross-platform capabilities are really the only choice for archival imaging. The images maintain all of the information scanned from the source and are the closest digital replication available. The size of the file, especially when scanned at 24-bit, 600 dpi, will be quite large, but well worth the storage space. You won't be placing the TIFF image online, but it is simple to make a JPEG image from the TIFF as a viewing copy.

This information is provided with the caveat that scanning technology is constantly changing for the better. It is more than likely that in the future these standards will become passé, with higher standards taking their place.

The goal of recognition technology is to re-create the text and, if desired, other elements of the page including such things as tables and layout.

Refer back to the concept of the scanner and how it takes a copy of the image by replicating it with the patterns of bits—the dots that are either filled or unfilled. OCR technology examines the patterns of dots and turns them into characters. Depending upon the type of scanning software you are using, the resulting text can be piped into many different word processing or spreadsheet programs.

It is critical that you anticipate type problems when dealing with texts that have such forms as long esses, sloping descenders, and ligatures. Taking sample scans with the source materials will help pinpoint some of these digitizing issues early on in the project. While the advantages of exporting text in different word processing formats are quite useful if you are scanning in a document to print or to compensate for an accidentally deleted file, there are a few issues that should take priority with the text creator. Assuming you are using a software program such as OmniPage, you should aim for a scan that retains some formatting but not a complete page element replication. In terms of text creation, and the long-term preservation of the digital object, you want to be able to control this markup. If possible, scanning at a setting that will retain font and paragraph format is the best option.

Scanning at a mid-level of formatting will assist you if you have decided to use your own encoding. As you proofread the text you will be able to add the structural markup chosen for the project. Once this has been completed the text can be saved out in a text-only format. Therefore, not only will you have the digitized text saved in a way that will eliminate program-added markup, but you will also have a basic level of user-dictated encoding.

Unfortunately for the text creator, there are still many situations where the documents or project preclude the use of OCR. If the text is of a poor or degraded quality, then it is quite possible that the time spent correcting the OCR mistakes will exceed that of simply typing in the text from scratch. The amount of information to be digitized also becomes an issue. Even if the document is of a relatively good quality, there might not be enough time to sit down with 560 volumes of texts (as with the Early American Fiction project) and process them through OCR. The general rule of thumb, and this varies from study to study, is that a best-case scenario would be three pages scanned per minute—this doesn't take into consideration the process of putting the document on the scanner, flipping pages, or the subsequent proofreading.

Also, there is the concern that a single person typing in material tends to overlook keyboarding errors—and if the staff member is familiar with the source material, there is a tendency to correct automatically those things that seem incorrect. So while in-house digitization is an option, these concerns should be addressed from the outset.

Markup Languages

Markup is most commonly defined as a form of text added to a document to transmit information about both the physical and electronic source. Do not be surprised if the term sounds familiar; it has been in use for centuries. It was first used within the printing trade as a reference to the instructions inscribed onto copy so that the compositor would know how to prepare the typographical design of the document. As Philip Gaskell points out, 'Many examples of printers' copy have survived from the hand-press period, some of them annotated with instructions concerning layout, italicization, capitalization, etc.' This concept has evolved slightly through the years but has remained entwined with the printing industry. There still seems to be some demarcation between the usage of the term for bibliography and for computing, but the boundary is really quite blurred. The leap from markup as a method of labelling instructions on printer's copy to markup as a language used to describe information in an electronic document is not so vast.

Therefore when we think of markup there are really three differing types. The first is the markup that relates strictly to formatting instructions found on the physical text, as mentioned above. It is used for the creation of an emended version of the document and, with the exception of the work of textual scholars, is rarely referred to again. Then there is the proprietary markup found in electronic document encoding, which is tied to a specific piece of software or developer. This markup is concerned primarily with document formatting, describing what words should be in italics or centred, where the margins should be set, or where to place a bulleted list. There are a few things to note about this type of markup. The first is that being proprietary means that it is intimately tied to the software that created it. This does not pose a problem as long as the document will only remain within that software program; and as long as the creator recognises that in the future there is no guarantee that the software will exist.

This is important, as proprietary software formats allow users to say where and how they want the document formatted, but then the software inserts its own markup language to accomplish this. When users create documents in Word or a PDF file, they are unconsciously adding encoding with every keystroke. As anyone who has created a document in one software format and attempted to transfer it to another is aware, the encoding does not transfer—and if for some reason a bit of it does, it rarely means the same thing. The third type of markup is non-proprietary, a generalised markup language. There are two critical distinctions between this markup and the previous two. Firstly, as it is a general language and not tied to a specific software/hardware, it offers cross-platform capabilities. This ensures that documents utilising this style of encoding will be readable many years down the line.

Secondly, while a generalised markup language, as with the others, allows users to insert formatting markup in the document, it also allows for encoding based upon the content of the work. This is a level of control not found in the previous styles of markup. Here the user is able not only to describe the appearance of the document but the meanings found within it.

Proprietary and Non-proprietary Markup

As the name implies, presentational markup is concerned with the visual structure of a text. Depending upon what processing software is being used, the markup explains to the computer how the document should appear. So if the work should be seen in 12 point, Tahoma font, the software dictates a markup so that this happens. Presentational markup is concerned with structure only insofar as it relates to the visual aspect of the document. It does not care whether a heading is for a book, a chapter or a paragraph—the only consideration is how that heading should look on the page. Most proprietary language formats tend to focus solely on presentational issues. To move into descriptive markup would require that the software provide the document creator with the ability to formulate their own tags with which to encode the structure and presentation of the work.

In other words, descriptive markup relates less to the visual strategy of the work and more to the reasons behind the structure. It allows the creator to encode the document with a markup that more clearly shows how the presentation, configuration, and content relate to the document as a whole. Once again, the beneficial effects of thorough document analysis can be seen.

Having a holistic sense of the document, having the detailed listing of critical elements in the document, will exemplify how descriptive markup advances a project. In this case, a non-proprietary language will be the most beneficial, as it will allow the document creators to arrive at their own tagsets, providing a much needed level of control over the encoding development.

In 1985, Adobe Systems created a programming language for printers called PostScript. In so doing, they produced a system that allowed computers to 'talk' to their printers. This language describes for the printer the appearance of the page, incorporating elements like text, graphics, colour, and images, so that documents maintain their integrity through the transmission from computer to printer. PostScript printers have become industry standard with corporations, marketers, publishing companies, graphic designers, and more. Printers, slide recorders, imagesetters—all these output devices utilise PostScript technology. Combine this with PostScript's multiple operating system capability and it becomes clear why PostScript has become the standard for printing technology.

PostScript language can be found in most printers—Epson, IBM, and Hewlett-Packard just to name a few—almost guaranteeing that a high standard of printing can be found in both the home and office. Portable Document Format (PDF) was created by Adobe in 1993 to complement their PostScript language. PDF allows the user to view a document with a presentational integrity that almost resembles a scanned image of the source. This delivery of visually rich content is the most attractive use of PDF. The format is entirely concerned with keeping the document intact, and, to ensure this, allows any combination of text, graphics and images.

It also has full, rich colour presentation and is therefore often used with corporate and marketing graphic arts materials. Another enticing feature, depending on the quality of the printer, is that when a PDF file is printed out, the hard copy output is an exact replication of the screen image. PDF is also desirable for its delivery strengths. Not only does the document maintain its visual integrity, but it also can be compressed. This compression eases on-line and CD-ROM transmission and assists its archiving opportunities.

PDF files can be read through an Acrobat Reader application that is freely available for download via the web. This application is also capable of serving as a browser plug-in for online document viewing. Creating PDF files is a bit more complicated than the viewing procedure. To write a PDF document it is necessary to purchase Adobe software. PDFWriter allows the user to create the PDF document, and the more expensive Adobe Capture program will convert TIFF files into PDF formatted text versions. If the user would like the document to become more interactive, offering the ability to annotate the document for example, then this functionality can be added with the additional purchase of Acrobat Exchange, which serves an editorial function. Exchange allows the user to annotate and edit the document, search across documents and also has plug-ins that provide highlighting ability.

HyperText Markup Language

HyperText Markup Language (or HTML as it is commonly known) is a non-proprietary format markup system used for publishing hypertext on the World Wide Web. To date, it has appeared in four main versions (1.0, 2.0, 3.2, 4.0), with the World Wide Web Consortium (W3C) recommending 4.0 as the markup language of choice.

HTML is a derivative of SGML—the Standard Generalised Markup Language. SGML allows you to create your own markup language but provides the rules necessary to ensure its processing and preservation. HTML is a successful implementation of the SGML concepts, and, as a result, is accessible to most browsers and platforms. Along with this, it is a relatively simple markup language to learn, as it has a limited tagset.

HTML is by far the most popular web-publishing language, allowing users to create online text documents that include multimedia elements (such as images, sounds, and video clips), and then put these documents in an environment that allows for instant publication and retrieval. There are many advantages to a markup language like HTML. As mentioned above, the primary benefit is that a document encoded with HTML can be viewed in almost any browser—an extremely attractive option for a creator who wants documents which can be viewed by an audience with varied systems. However, it is important to note that while the encoding can cross platforms, there are consistently differences in page appearance between browsers.

While W3C recommends the usage of HTML 4.0, many of its features are simply not available to users with early versions of browsers. Unlike PDF which is extremely concerned with keeping the document and its format intact, HTML has no true sense of page structure and files can neither be saved nor printed with any sense of precision. Besides the benefit of a markup language that crosses platforms with ease, HTML attracts its many users for the simple manner with which it can be mastered. For users who do not want to take the time to learn the tagset, the good news is that conversion-to-HTML tools are becoming more accessible and easier to use. For those who cannot even spare the time to learn how to use HTML-creation software, of which there are a limited quantity, they can sit down with any text creation program (Notepad for example) and author an HTML document. Then by using the 'Open File'; tool in a browser, the document can immediately be viewed.

In contrast, the concise guidelines to HTML that are available on-line (and usually as a "help" option from the menu of a Web client) are a good introduction to some of the basic SGML concepts. This is of real value to the user. The notion of marking up a text is quite often an overwhelming concept. Most people do not realise that markup enters into their life every time they make a keystroke in a word processing program. So for the uninitiated, HTML provides a manageable stepping-stone into the world of more complex encoding. Once this limited tagset is mastered, many users find the jump into an extended markup language less intimidating—and more liberating.

However, one of the drawbacks to this easy authoring language is that many of the online documents are created without a DTD. A DTD is the abbreviation for a document type definition, which outlines the formal specifications for an SGML encoded document. Basically, a DTD is the method for spelling out the SGML rules that the document is following. It sets the standards for what markup can be used and how this markup interacts with others. So, for example, if you create an HTML document with a specific software program, say HoTMetaL PRO, the resulting text will begin with a document type declaration stating which DTD is being used.

As it stands now, web browsers require neither a DTD nor a document type declaration. Browsers are notoriously lax in their HTML requirements, and unless something serious is missing from the encoded document it will be successfully viewed through a Web client. The impact of this is that while HTML provides a convenient and universal markup language for a user, many of the documents floating out in cyberspace are permeated with invalid code. The focus then moves away from authoring documents that conform to a set of encoding guidelines and towards the creation of works that can be viewed in a browser. This problem will become more severe with the increased use of Extensible Markup Language, or XML as it is more commonly known. This markup language, which is being lauded as the new lingua franca, combines the visual benefits of HTML with the contextual benefits of SGML/TEI.

However, while XML will have the universality of HTML, the web clients will require a more stringent adherence to markup rules. While documents that comply with the rules of an HTML DTD will find the transition relatively simple, the documents that were constructed strictly with viewing in mind will require a good deal of clean up prior to conversion. This is not to say that HTML is not a useful tool for creating online documents. As in the case of PostScript and PDF, the choice to use HTML should be document dependent. It is the perfect choice for static documents that will have a short shelf-life. If you are creating course pages or supplementary materials regarding specific readings that will not be necessary or available after the end of term, then HTML is an appropriate choice. If, however, you are concerned about presentational and structural integrity, the markup of document content and/or the long-term preservation of the text, then a user-definable markup language is a much better choice.

User-definable Descriptive Markup

A user-definable descriptive markup is exactly what its name implies. The content of the markup tags is established solely by the user, not by the software. As a result of SGML and its concept of a DTD, a document can have any kind of markup a creator desires. This frees the document from being married to proprietary hardware or software and from its reliance upon an appearance-based markup language. If you decide to encode the document with a non-proprietary language, which we highly recommend, then this is a good time to evaluate the project goals.

While a user-definable markup language gives you control over the content of the markup, and thereby more control over the document, the markup can only be fully understood by you. Although not tied to a proprietary system, it is also not tied to any accepted standard. A markup language defined and implemented by you is simply that—a personal non-proprietary markup system. However, if the electronic texts require a language that is non-proprietary, more extensive and content-oriented than HTML, and comprehensible and acceptable to a humanities audience, then there is a solution—the Text Encoding Initiative (TEI).

TEI is an international implementation of SGML, providing a non-proprietary markup language that has become the de facto standard in Humanities Computing. TEI, which provides 'a full set of tags, a methodology, and a set of Document Type Descriptions (DTDs) that allow the detailed description of the spatial, intellectual, structural, and typographic form of a work' Markup is a critical, and inescapable, part of text creation and processing. Regardless of the method chosen to encode the document, some form of markup will be included in the text. Whether this markup is proprietary or non-proprietary, appearance- or content-based is up to you. Be sure to evaluate the project goals when making the encoding decisions. If the project is short-lived or necessarily software dependent, then the choices are relatively straightforward.

Standard Generalized Markup Language (SGML)

The late 1970s and early 1980s saw a consensus emerging that descriptive markup languages had numerous advantages over other types of text encoding. A number of products and macro languages appeared which were built around their own descriptive markup languages—and whilst these represented a step forward, they were also constrained by the fact that users were required to learn a new markup language each time, and could only describe those textual features which the markup scheme allowed (sometimes extensions were possible, but implementing them was rarely a straightforward process).

The International Standards Organisation (ISO) also recognised the value of descriptive markup schemes, and in 1986 an ISO committee released a new standard called ISO 8879, the Standard Generalized Markup Language (SGML). This complex document represented several years' effort by an international committee of experts, working together under the Chairmanship of Dr Charles Goldfarb (one of the creators of IBM's descriptive markup language, GML). Since SGML was a product of the International Standards process, the committee also had the benefit of input from experts from the numerous national standards bodies associated with the ISO, such as the UK's British Standards Institute (BSI).

A great deal of largely unjustified mystique surrounds SGML. You do not have to look very hard to find instances of SGML being described as 'difficult to learn', 'complex to implement', or 'expensive to use', when in fact it is none of these things. People all too frequently confuse the acronym,

SGML, with SGML applications—many of which are indeed highly sophisticated and complex operations, designed to meet the rigorous demands of blue chip companies working in major international industries (automotive, pharmaceutical, or aerospace engineering). It should not be particularly surprising that a documentation system designed to control and support every aspect of the tens of thousands of pages of documentation needed to build and maintain a battleship, fix the latest passenger aircraft, or supplement a legal application for international recognition for a new advanced drug treatment, should appear overwhelmingly complex to an outsider.

In fact, despite its name, SGML is not even a markup language. Instead, it would be more appropriate to call SGML a 'metalanguage'. In a conventional markup language, such as HTML, users are offered a pre-defined set of markup tags from which they must make appropriate selections; if they suddenly introduce new tags which are not part of the HTML specification, then it is clear that the resulting document will not be considered valid HTML, and it may be rejected or incorrectly processed by HTML software (e.g. an HTML-compatible browser).

SGML, on the other hand, does not offer a pre-defined set of markup tags. Rather, it offers a grammar and specific vocabulary which can be used to define other markup languages (hence 'metalanguage'). SGML is not constrained to any one particular type of application, and it is neither more nor less suited to producing technical documentation and specifications in the semiconductor industry, than it is for marking up linguistic features of ancient inscribed tablets of stone. In fact, SGML can be used to create a markup language to do pretty well anything, and that is both its greatest strength and weakness. SGML cannot be used 'out-of-the-box', so to speak, and because of this it has earned an undeserved reputation in some quarters as being troublesome and slow to implement. On the other hand, there are many SGML applications, which can be used straightaway, as they offer a fully documented markup language which can be recognised by any one of a suite of tools and implemented with a minimum of fuss.

SGML provides a mechanism for like-minded people with a shared concern to get together and define a common markup language which satisfies their needs and desires, rather than being limited by the vision of the designers of a closed, possibly proprietary markup scheme which only does half the job. SGML offers another advantage in that it not only allows (groups of) users to define their own markup languages, it also provides a mechanism for ensuring that the rules of any particular markup language can be rigorously enforced by SGML-aware software. For example, within HTML, although there are six different levels of heading defined there is no requirement that they should be applied in a strictly hierarchical fashion; in other words, it is perfectly possible for a series of headings in an HTML document to be marked up as <H1>, then <H3>, followed by <H5>, followed in turn by <H2>, <H4>, and <H6>—all to achieve a particular visual appearance in a particular HTML browser. By contrast, should such a feature be deemed important, an SGML-based markup language could be written in such a way that suitable software can ensure that levels of heading nest in a strictly hierarchical fashion (and the strength of this approach can perhaps become even more evident when encoding other kinds of hierarchical structure, e.g. a <BOOK> must contain one or more <CHAPTER>s, each of which must in turn contain one or more <PARAGRAPH>s, and so on). There is one final, crucial, difference between SGML-based markup languages and other descriptive markup languages: the process by which International Standards are created, maintained, and updated. ISO Standards are subject to periodic formal review, and each time this work is undertaken it happens in full consultation with the various national standards bodies. The Committee which produced SGML has guaranteed that if and when any changes are introduced to the SGML standard, this will be done in such a way as to ensure backwards compatibility.

This is not a decision which has been undertaken lightly, and the full implications can be inferred from the fact that commercial enterprises rarely make such an explicit commitment (and even when they do, users ought to reflect upon the likelihood that such a commitment will actually be fulfilled given the considerable pressures of a highly competitive marketplace).

The essential difference has been characterised thus: the creators of SGML believe that a user's data should belong to that user, and not be tied up inextricably in a proprietary markup system over which that user has no control; whereas, the creators of a proprietary markup scheme can reasonably be expected to have little motivation to ensure that data encoded using their scheme can be easily migrated to, or processed by, a competitor's software products.The SGML standard gives a very rigid definition as to what constitutes an 'SGML document'. Whilst there is no need for us to consider this definition in detail at this stage, it is worthwhile reviewing the major concepts as they offer a valuable insight into some crucial aspects of an electronic text. Perhaps first and foremost amongst these is the notion that an SGML document is a single logical entity, even though in practice that document may be composed of any number of physical data files, spread over a storage medium (e.g. a single computer's hard-disk) or even over different types of storage media connected together via a network.

As today's electronic publications become more and more complex, mixing (multilingual) text with images, audio, and image data, it reinforces the need to ensure that they are created in line with accepted standards. For example, an article from an electronic journal mounted on a website may be delivered to the end-user in the form of a single HTML document, but that article (and indeed the whole journal), may rely upon dozens or hundreds of data files, a database to manage the entire collection of files, several bespoke scripts to handle the interfacing between the web and the database, and so on.

SGML operates on the basis of there being three major parts which combine to form a single SGML document. Firstly, there is the SGML declaration, which specifies any system and software constraints. Secondly, there is the prolog, which defines the document structure. Lastly, there is the document instance, which contains what one would ordinarily think of as the document. Whilst this may perhaps appear unnecessarily complicated, in fact it provides an extremely valuable insight into the key components which are essential to the creation of an electronic document.

The SGML declaration tells any software that is going to process an SGML document all that it should need to know. For example, the SGML declaration specifies which character sets have been used in the document (normally ASCII or ISO 646, but more recently this could be Unicode, or ISO 10646). It also establishes any constraints on system variables (e.g. the length of markup tag names, or the depth to which tags can be nested), and states whether or not any of SGML's optional features have been used. The SGML standard offers a default set-up, so that, for example, the characters < and > are used to delimit markup tag names—and with the widespread acceptance of HTML, this has become the accepted way to indicate markup tags—but if for any reason this presented a problem for a particular application (e.g. encoding a lot of data in which < and > were heavily used to indicate something else), it would be possible to redefine the delimiters as @ or #, or whatever characters were deemed to be more appropriate.

The SGML declaration is important for a number of reasons. Although it may seem an unduly complicated approach, it is often these fundamental system or application dependencies which make it so difficult to move data around between different software and hardware environments. If the developers of wordprocessing packages had started off by agreeing on a single set of internal markup codes they would all use to indicate a change in font, the centring of a line of text, the occurrence of a pagebreak etc., then users' lives would have been made a great deal easier; however, this did not happen, and hence we are left in a situation where data created in one application cannot easily be read by another.

Furthermore, by supplying a default environment, the average end-user of an SGML-based encoding system is unlikely to have to familiarise him- or herself with the intricacies of the SGML declaration. Indeed it should be enough simply to be aware of the existence of the SGML declaration, and how it might affect one's ability to create, access, or exploit a particular source of data. The next major part of an SGML document is the prolog, which must conform to the specification set out in the formal SGML standard, and the syntax given in the SGML declaration. Although it is hard to discuss the prolog without getting bogged down in the details of SGML, suffice it to say that it contains (at least one) document type declaration, which in turn contains (or references) a Document Type Definition (or DTD).

The DTD is one of the single most important features of SGML, and what sets it apart from—not to say above—other descriptive markup schemes. Although we shall learn a little more about the process in the following section, the DTD contains a series of declarations which define the particular markup language which will be used in the document instance, and also specifies how the different parts of that language can interrelate (e.g. which markup tags are required and optional, the contexts in which they can be used, and so on).

Often, when people talk about 'using SGML', they are actually talking about using a particular DTD, which is why some of the negative comments that have been made about SGML are erroneous, because such complaints should properly be directed at the DTD (and thus aimed at the DTD designer) rather than at SGML in general.

Other than some of the system constraints imposed by the SGML declaration, there are no strictures imposed by the SGML standard regarding how simple or complex the markup language defined in the DTD should be. Whilst the syntax used to write a DTD is fairly straightforward, and most people find that they can start to read and write DTDs with surprising ease, to create a good DTD requires experience and familiarity with the needs and concerns of both data creators and end-users. A good DTD nearly always reflects a designer's understanding of all these aspects, an appreciation of the constraints imposed by the SGML standard, and a thorough process of document analysis and DTD-testing. In many ways this situation is indicative of the fact that the creators of the SGML standard did not envisage that individual users would be very likely to produce their own DTDs for highly specific purposes.

Rather, they thought (or perhaps hoped), that groups would form within industry sectors or large-scale enterprises to produce DTDs that were tailored to the needs of their particular application. Indeed, the areas in which the uptake of SGML has been most enthusiastic have been operating under exactly those sorts of conditions—for example, the international Air Transport Authority seeking to standardise aircraft maintenance documentation, or the pharmaceutical industry's attempts to streamline the documentary evidence needed to support applications to the US Food and Drug Administration.

However, as a general rule, if users wish to write their own DTDs, or tweak an SGML declaration, they are entirely free to do so (within the framework set out by the SGML standard)—but the vast majority of SGML users prefer to rely upon an SGML declaration and DTD created by others, for all the benefits of interoperability and reusability promised by this approach.

This brings us to the third main part of an SGML document: namely, the document instance itself. This is the part of the document which contains a combination of raw data and markup, and its contents are constrained by both the SGML declaration, and the contents of the prolog (especially the declarations in the DTD). Clearly from the perspective of data creators and end-users, this is the most interesting part of an SGML document—and it is common practice for people to use the term 'SGML document' when they are actually referring to a document instance. Such confusion should be largely unproblematic, provided these users always remember that when they are interchanging data (i.e. a document instance) with colleagues, they should also pass on the relevant DTD and SGML declaration.

Having identified the features you wish to encode, you will need to find a DTD which meets your requirements. Rather than trying to write your own DTD from scratch, it is usually worthwhile investing some time to look around for existing public DTDs which you might be able to adopt, extend, or adapt to suit your particular purposes. There are many DTDs available in the public domain, or made freely available for others to use, but even if none of these match your needs, some may be worth investigating to see how others have tackled common problems. Although there are some tools available which are designed to facilitate the process of DTD-authoring, they are probably only worth buying if you intend to be doing a great deal of work with DTDs, and they can never compensate for poor document analysis.

Once again, there are many useful tools available to help convert from one markup scheme to another, but if your target format is SGML this may have some bearing on the likelihood of success (or failure) of any conversion process. As we have seen, SGML lends itself most naturally to a structured, hierarchical view of a document's content (although it is perfectly possible to represent very loose organisational structures, and even non-hierarchical document webs, using SGML markup) and this means that it is much simpler to convert from a proprietary markup scheme to SGML if that scheme also has a strong sense of structure (i.e. adopts a descriptive markup approach) and has been used sensibly. However, if a document has been encoded with a presentational markup scheme which has, for example, used codes to indicate that certain words should be rendered in an italic font—regardless of the fact that sometimes this has been for emphasis, at other times to indicate book and journal titles, and elsewhere to indicate non-English words—then this will dramatically reduce the chances of automatically converting the data from this presentation-oriented markup scheme into one which complies with an SGML DTD.

It is probably worth noting at this point that these conversion problems primarily apply when converting from a non-descriptive, non-SGML markup language into SGML; the opposite process, namely converting from SGML into another target markup scheme, is much more straightforward (because it would simply mean that data variously marked-up with, say, <EMPHASIS>, <TITLE>, and <FOREIGN> tags, had their markup converted into the target scheme's markup tags for <ITALIC>).

It is also worth noting that such a conversion might not be a particularly good idea, because you would effectively be throwing information away. In practice it would be much more sensible to retain the descriptive/SGML version of your material, and convert to a presentational markup scheme only when absolutely required for the successful rendering of your data on screen or on paper. Indeed, many dedicated SGML applications support the use of stylesheets to offer some control over the on-screen rendition of SGML-encoded material, whilst preserving the SGML markup behind the scenes. If you are creating SGML documents from scratch, or editing existing SGML documents there are several factors to consider. It is essential that you have access to a validating SGML parser, which is a software program that can read an SGML declaration and a document's prolog, understand the declarations in the DTD, and ensure that the SGML markup used throughout the document instance conforms appropriately.

In order to retain the full 'added-value' of the SGML markup, you might choose to deliver the raw SGML data over the Web and rely upon a behind-the-scenes negotation between your web-server and the client's browser to ensure that an appropriate SGML-viewing tool is launched on the client's machine. This enables the end-user to exploit fully the SGML markup included in your document, provided that s/he has been able to obtain and install the appropriate software.

Another possibility would be to offer a Web-to-SGML interface on your server, so that end-users can access your documents using an ordinary Web browser whilst all the processing of the SGML markup takes place on the server, and the results are delivered as HTML. Alternatively, you might decide to simply convert the markup into HTML from whatever SGML DTD has been used to encode the document (either on-the-fly, or as part of a batch process) so that the end-user can use an ordinary Web browser and the server will not have to undertake any additional processing.

Meanwhile, delivering electronic text marked-up according to another SGML DTD meant that end-users were obliged to obtain suitable SGML-aware tools, and very few of them seemed willing to do this. The creators of XML adopted the following design goals:

1. XML shall be straightforwardly usable over the Internet.
2. XML shall support a wide variety of applications.
3. XML shall be compatible with SGML.

4. It shall be easy to write programs which process XML documents.
5. The number of optional features in XML is to be kept to the absolute minimum, ideally zero.
6. XML documents should be human-legible and reasonably clear.
7. The XML design should be prepared quickly.
8. The design of XML shall be formal and concise.
9. XML documents shall be easy to create.
10. Terseness in XML markup is of minimal importance.

They sought to gain the generic advantages offered by supporting arbitrary SGML DTDs, whilst retaining much of the operational simplicity of using HTML. To this end, they 'threw away' all the optional features of the SGML standard which make it difficult (and therefore expensive) to process.

At the same time they retained the ability for users to write their own DTDs, so that they can develop markup schemes which are tailored to suit particular applications but which are still enforceable by a validating parser. Perhaps most importantly of all, the committee which designed XML had representatives from several major companies which develop software applications for use with the Web, particularly browsers, and this has helped to encourage a great deal of interest in XML's potential. SGML has its roots in a time when creating, storing, and processing information on computer was expensive and time-consuming. Many of the optional features supported by the SGML standard were intended to make it cheaper to create and store SGML-conformant documents in an era when it was envisaged that all the markup would be laboriously inserted by hand, and megabytes of disk space were extremely expensive.

Nowadays, faster and cheaper processors, and the falling costs of storage media (both magnetic and optical), mean that the designers and users of applications are less worried about the concerns of SGML's original designers. On the other hand, the ever growing volume of electronic information makes it all the more important that any markup which has been used has been applied in a thoroughly consistent and easy to process manner, thereby helping to ensure that today's applications perform satisfactorily. XML addresses these familiar concerns, whilst taking advantage of modern computer systems and the lessons learned from using SGML. For example, now that the cost of storing data is of less concern to most users (except for those dealing with extremely large quantities of data), there is no need to offer support for markup short-cuts which, while saving storage space, tend to impose an additional load when information is processed.

Instead, XML's designers were able to build-in the concept of 'well-formed' data, which requires that any marked-up data are explicitly bounded by start- and end-tags, and that all the tagged data in a document nest appropriately (so that it becomes possible, say, to generate a document tree which captures the hierarchical arrangement of all the data elements in the document). This has the added advantage that when two applications (such as a database and a web server) need to exchange data, they can use well-formed XML as their interchange format, because both the sending and receiving application can be certain that any data they receive will be appropriately marked-up and there can be no possible ambiguity about where particular data structures start and end.

XML takes this approach one stage further by adopting the SGML concept of DTDs, such that an XML document is said to be 'valid' if it has an associated DTD and the markup used in the document has been checked (by a validating parser) against the declarations expressed in that DTD. If an application knows that it will be handling valid XML, and has an understanding of and access to the relevant DTD, this can greatly improve its ability to process that data—for example, a search and retrieval application would be able to construct a list of all the marked-up data structures in the document, so that a user could refine the search criteria accordingly. Knowing that a vast collection of XML documents have all been validated against a particular DTD will greatly assist the processing of that collection, as valid XML data is also necessarily well-formed. By contrast, while it is possible for an XML application to process a well-formed document such that it can derive one possible DTD which could represent the data structures it contains, that DTD may not be sufficient to represent all the well-formed XML documents of the same type.

There are clearly many advantages to be gained from creating and using valid XML data, but the option remains to use well-formed XML data in those situations where it would be appropriate. Today's Web browsers expect to receive conformant HTML data, and any additional markup included in the data which is not recognised by the browser is usually ignored. The next generation of Web browsers will know how to handle XML data, and while all of them will know how to process HTML data by default, they will also be prepared to cope with any well-formed or valid XML data that they receive. This offers the opportunity for groups of users to come together, agree upon a DTD they wish to adopt, and then create and exchange valid XML data which conforms to that DTD.

Thus, a group of academics concerned with the creation of electronic scholarly editions of major texts could all agree to prepare their data in accordance with a particular DTD which enabled them to markup the features of the texts which they felt to be appropriate for their work. They could then exchange the results of their labours safe in the knowledge that they could all be correctly processed by their favourite software.

References

Beagrie, N. and Jones, M. (2001), *Preservation Management of Digital Materials: A Handbook*, London.

Carroll, B. & G. Hodge. (1999). "Digital Electronic Archiving: The State of the Art, the State of the Practice." [Online]. Available: http://www.icsti.org/Dig_Archiving_Report_1999.pdf

Hodge, G.M. and Carroll, B.C. (1999), 'Digital Electronic Archiving: The State of the Art and the State of the Practice.' A Report Sponsored by the International Council for Scientific and Technical Information, Information Policy Committee and CENDI, 26 April 1999.

Moore, R., Baru, C., Rajasekar, A. et al. (2000), Collection-Based persistent Digital Archives. *D-Lib Magazine*, March and April 2000.

2

Best Practices in Digital Archiving

For materials stored digitally, users operate on exact images of the original works stored in their local computers. Separating usage from the original in this way, digital technology affords multiple, simultaneous uses from a single original in ways that are simply not possible for materials stored in any other form. Digital technology also yields additional, effective means of access. In full text documents, a reader can retrieve needed information by searching for words, combinations of words, phrases or ideas. Readers can also manipulate the display of digital materials by choosing whether to view digital materials on a screen, store them on their computer or external media, or to print them. Digital technology, however, poses new threats and problems as well as new opportunities. Its functionality comes with complexity. Anyone with a compass (or a clear night to view the position of the stars in relation to true north) could theoretically set up or repair a sundial. Rapid changes in the means of recording information, in the formats for storage, and in the technologies for use threaten to render the life of information in the digital age as, to borrow a phrase from Hobbes, "nasty, brutish and short." Some information no doubt deserves such a fate, but numerous examples illustrate the danger of losing valuable cultural memories that may appear in digital form.

Today, information technologies that are increasingly powerful and easy to use, especially like those that support the World Wide Web, have unleashed the production and distribution of digital information. Such information is penetrating and transforming nearly every aspect of our culture. If we are effectively to preserve for future generations the portion of this rapidly expanding corpus of information in digital form that represents our cultural record, we need to understand the costs of doing so and we need to commit ourselves technically, legally, economically and organizationally to the full dimensions of the task.

Failure to look for trusted means and methods of digital preservation will certainly exact a stiff, long-term cultural penalty. Archivists responsible for governmental and corporate records have been acutely aware of the difficulties entailed in trying to ensure that digital information survives for future generations. Far more than their library colleagues, who have continued to collect and organize published materials primarily in paper form, archivists have observed the materials for which they are responsible shift rapidly from paper objects produced on typewriters and other analog devices to include files created in word processor, spreadsheet and many other digital forms. Early attention to the difficulties in preserving digital information focused on the longevity of the physical media on which the information is stored. Even under the best storage conditions, however, digital media can be fragile and have limited shelf life. Moreover, new devices, processes and software are replacing the products and methods used to record, store, and retrieve digital information on breathtaking cycles of 2- to 5- years. Given such rates of technological change, even the most fragile media may well outlive the continued availability of readers for those media.

Efforts to preserve physical media thus provide only a short-term, partial solution to the general problem of preserving digital information. Indeed, technological obsolescence represents a far greater threat to information in digital form than the inherent physical fragility of many digital media. In the face of rapid technological obsolescence and to overcome the problem of media fragility, archivists have adopted the technique of "refreshing" digital information by copying it onto new media. Copying from medium to medium, however, also suffers limitations as a means of digital preservation. Refreshing digital information by copying will work as an effective preservation technique only as long as the information is encoded in a format that is independent of the particular hardware and software needed to use it and as long as there exists software to manipulate the format in current use. Otherwise, copying depends either on the compatibility of present and past versions of software and generations of hardware or the ability of competing hardware and software product lines to interoperate.

In respect of these factors- backward compatibility and interoperability- the rate of technological change exacts a serious toll on efforts to ensure the longevity of digital information. Digital information today is produced in highly varying degrees of dependence on particular hardware and software. Moreover, it is costly and difficult for vendors to assure that their products are either "backwardly compatible" with previous versions or that they can interoperate with competing products. Jeff Rothenberg, has suggested that there may be sufficient demand for entrepreneurs to create and archive emulators of software and operating systems that would allow the contents of digital information to be carried forward and used in its original format.

Refreshing digital information by copying it from medium to medium and the possibility of maintaining a complex set of emulators describe two distinct points on a continuum of approaches to preserving digital information. However, neither refreshing nor emulation sufficiently describes the full range of options needed and available for digital preservation. Instead, a better and more general concept to describe these options is migration.

Migration of Digital Materials

Migration is the periodic transfer of digital materials from one hardware/ software configuration to another, or from one generation of computer technology to a subsequent generation. The purpose of migration is to preserve the integrity of digital objects and to retain the ability for clients to retrieve, display, and otherwise use them in the face of constantly changing technology. Migration includes refreshing as a means of digital preservation but differs from it in the sense that it is not always possible to make an exact digital copy or replica of a database or other information object as hardware and software change and still maintain the compatibility of the object with the new generation of technology. Even for information that is encoded in a contemporary standard form, forward migration of the information to a new standard or application program is, as anyone knows who has witnessed or participated in such a process, time-consuming, costly and much more complex than simple refreshing. Compounding the technical challenges of migrating digital information is the problem of managing the process in a legal and organizational environment that is in flux as it moves to accommodate rapidly changing digital technologies. Consider, for example, the barriers to decisive preservation action caused by widespread uncertainty about legal and organizational requirements for managing the intellectual property that digital information represents.

Addressing and resolving the legal and practical questions of migrating intellectual property in digital form necessarily involves a complex set of interested parties, including the creators and owners of intellectual property, managers of digital archives, representatives of the public interest, and actual and potential users of intellectual property. In addition, the parties who represent, for example, owners and users of different kinds of intellectual property (e.g., text and other document-like objects, photographs, film, software, multimedia objects) each operate under very different organizational regimes, with different experiences and expectations. Adding to these complexities is the deep uncertainty that these groups face in confronting an increasingly digital world. Owners of intellectual property are unsure about how to price access to their information and worry, given the ease of copying, that the first digital copy of a work they sell may be the only copy they sell. Users of intellectual property are unsure about what rights are conveyed with the use of a particular digital information object and about how much such use is worth. Government representatives seek in the public interest to manage the powerful changes that accompany digital technologies, but are unsure about what levels of influece are available to them and how to generate appropriate public policy.

The state of the copyright law, which was generated and developed in an analog world but is applied in an increasingly digital universe, is itself confusing and uncertain. And all of these concerns are exacerbated by the fact that bits know no borders. The costs and the technical, legal and organizational complexities of moving digital information forward into the future raise our greatest fear about the life of information in the digital future: namely, that owners or custodians who can no longer bear the expense and difficulty will deliberately or inadvertently, through a simple failure to act, destroy the objects without regard for future use.

Repeated anecdotes about the loss of land use information, satellite imagery or census data, even when false or misleading, feed our general anxiety about the future of the cultural record we are accumulating in digital form. And uncertainty and lack of confidence about our will and ability to carry digital information forward into the future exert a major inhibiting force in our disposition to fully exploit the digital medium to generate, publish and disseminate information. Viewed developmentally, the problem of preserving digital information for the future is not only, or even primarily, a problem of fine tuning a narrow set of technical variables. It is not a clearly defined problem like preserving the embrittled books that are self-destructing from the acid in the paper on which they were printed. Rather, it is a grander problem of organizing ourselves over time and as a society to maneuver effectively in a digital landscape.

It is a problem of building-almost from scratch-the various systematic supports, or deep infrastructure, that will enable us to tame anxieties and move our cultural records naturally and confidently into the future. For digital preservation, the organizational effort-the process of building deep infrastructure-necessarily involves multiple, interrelated factors, many of which are either unknown or poorly defined. One of the biggest unknowns is the full impact on traditional information handling functions of distributed computing over electronic networks. The effort to meet the cultural imperative of digital preservation thus requires a complex iteration and reiteration of exploration, development and solution as the relevant factors and their interrelationships emerge and become clearer and more tractable.

And the first task in the effort is not to posit answers, but to frame questions and issues in such a way as to engage the many parties already working in various ways with digital information so that they can help us understand the relevant issues and, within the context of their work, help us identify, define and incorporate solutions that contribute to the larger, common goal of preserving our cultural heritage. Digital archives are distinct from digital libraries in the sense that digital libraries are repositories that collect and provide access to digital information, but may or may not provide for the long-term storage and access of that information. Digital libraries thus may or may not be, in functional terms, digital archives and, in fact, much of the recent work on digital libraries is notably silent on the archival issues of ensuring long-term storage and access.

Conversely, digital archives necessarily embrace digital library functions to the extent that they must select, obtain, store, and provide access to digital information. Many of the functional requirements for digital archives defined thus overlap those for digital libraries. Many traditional libraries, archives and museums, as institutions, have taken and may well continue to assume digital library and archival functions. Certified digital archives will have available to them a critical fail-safe mechanism. Such a mechanism, supported by organizational will, economic means and legal right, would enable a certified archival repository to exercise an aggressive rescue function to save digital information that it judges to be culturally significant and which is endangered in its current repository. The current repository may be a digital library, another digital archives, or some other individual, organizational, public or private source of digital information.

Without the operation of a formal certification program and a fail-safe mechanism, preservation of the nation's cultural heritage in digital form will likely be overly dependent on marketplace forces, which may value information for too short a period and without applying broader, public interest criteria. Such development is necessary for and will contribute powerfully to the overall growth of an information-based society and economy. We can afford to continue and increase economic and social investments in digital information objects and in the repositories for them on the information superhighway if, and only if, we also create the archival means for the knowledge the objects and repositories contain to endure and redound to the benefit of future generations.

Converting Information Objects in Digital Form

Information objects in digital form, like those in other forms, move through life cycles. They are created, edited, described and indexed, disseminated, acquired, used, annotated, revised, re-created, modified and retained for future use or destroyed by a complex, interwoven community of creators and other owners, disseminators, value-added services, and institutional and individual users.

The digital world is still too new for us to describe fully the life cycle of the information objects that do now or will in the future reside there, but what surely unites the community of actors in their various information-based activities is their common purpose in support of the pursuit of knowledge. The pursuit of knowledge is a process in which the emergence of new knowledge builds on and reconstructs the old. Knowledge cannot advance without consistent and reliable access to information sources, past and present. It is the archival function in the system of knowledge creation and use that serves to identify and retain important sources of information and to ensure continuing access to them. How reliable the archival process proves to be in the emerging digital environment hinges on the trustworthy operation of digital archives and on their ability to maintain the integrity of the objects they are charged to preserve.

For digital objects, no less than for objects of other kinds, knowing how operationally to preserve them depends, at least in part, on being able to discriminate the essential features of what needs to be preserved. Digital technologies increasingly serve to integrate information resources. Text, numeric data, images, voice, and video have heretofore resided in print or other analog media for storage and transmission. When they are encoded digitally, either by conversion or at the point of creation, these various kinds of resources share layers of technology-a common means of storage and transmission- that allows them to be brought together and used in both old and new ways. Multimedia and hyperlinked objects on the World Wide Web represent some of the new kinds of information and new ways of knowing in the digital realm that bring together the traditional forms of information and transform their use.

The application of computer hardware and software has also generated other new kinds of information objects, including the products of simulation, remote sensing, computer-aided design (CAD) and geographic information (GIS) systems. These objects come into being and exist as creatures of the digital environment; if nurtured well, digital technologies will certainly beget still other kinds of information objects, which we can now only anticipate.

The processes of preserving digital information will vary significantly with the different kinds of objects-textual, numeric, image, video, sound, multimedia, simulation and so on-being preserved. Whatever preservation method is applied, however, the central goal must be to preserve information integrity; that is, to define and preserve those features of an information object that distinguish it as a whole and singular work. In the digital environment, the features that determine information integrity and deserve special attention for archival purposes include the following: content, fixity, reference, provenance, and context. What digital archives are trying to preserve after all is the intellectual substance contained in information objects. The notion of content, however, is itself a complex idea that operates at several different levels of abstraction. To preserve the integrity of objects in their charge, digital archives must decide at which level, or levels, of abstraction they are defining information content. At the lowest level of abstraction, all digital information objects consist of simple bitstreams of 0s and 1s. One can distinguish objects from one another merely by distinguishing the configuration of bits.

Preserving the integrity of an information object in this sense means preserving the bit configuration that uniquely defines the object. There are various well-established techniques, such as checksums and digests, for tracking the bit-level equivalence of digital objects and ensuring that a preserved object is identical to the original. Defining content as a collection of bits, however, is often too limited and simplistic to be useful. In the digital environment, as we have seen, ideas are typically embedded in particular formats and structures that are dependent on hardware and software technologies subject to rapid change. In addition to character set issues, digital archives must also grapple with the means of representing and preserving textual content embedded in layout and structure. Markup systems, such as implementations of TeX and the Standard Generalized Markup Language (SGML), do exist as platform-independent mechanisms for identifying and tagging for subsequent layout and retrieval detailed structural elements of documents.

The use of TeX and its variants, for example, is relatively common among scholars in some scientific disciplines such as mathematics and computer science, and the federal government and scholarly publishers are increasingly employing the SGML standard in documents that they produce and distribute electronically. Beyond these relatively specialized segments, however, word processing and desktop publishing systems still dominate the market for the creation of documents with complex structure and layout, and the software for such use typically models and stores document structure and layout in proprietary terms. Although software may provide mechanisms for converting documents to common interchange formats, use of such mechanisms often results in the loss or inadequate rendering of content such as page structures and the layout of headers, footers and section headings.

The preservation of images comprises another example of the ways in which content, defined in terms of structure and format, poses integrity problems for digital archives. Image resolution, accuracy of color representation and compression for storage all require attention, but the interaction of these structural factors tends to pit judgments about the quality of content against the need for its efficient archival storage and use. In general, one can express the tradeoffs as follows: the higher the resolution and the richer the color register, the larger the file size and more costly the storage. The use of compression technologies further complicates the equation because the application of some algorithms to reduce space needs may involve an irreversible loss of data. The popular JPEG algorithm, for example, supports "lossy" compression, whereby the greatest degree of compression requires the maximum settings for allowable loss.

At the highest level of abstraction, digital archives define content in a way that transcends the limits of the hardware and software systems needed for reading and interpreting the bits of an information object and for rendering it for use in a specific format and structural representation; that is, they define content in terms of the knowledge or ideas the object contains. Expressed in this way, the preservation challenge for digital archives is to migrate intellectual content using standard interchange algorithms and other appropriate migration strategies so that the ideas available in the end are identical to those contained in the original object. The measure of integrity in the preservation process thus turns, at least in part, on informed and skillful judgments about the appropriate definition of the content of an digital information object-about the extent to which content depends on its configuration of bits, on the structure and format of its representation, and on the ideas it contains-and for what purposes.

The process of identifying and preserving a digital information object as a whole and singular work goes well beyond considerations of content. It also depends, for instance, on the way that the content is fixed as a discrete object. If an object is not fixed, and the content is subject to change or withdrawal without notice, then its integrity may be compromised and its value as a cultural record would be severely diminished.

Outside the digital landscape, business practices, editorial policies, and legal constraints, have created disciplines for fixing information in discrete objects. For example, business records, such as an annual report, a letter of hire or an engineering drawing for the manufacture of a new product, are fixed in the transactions for which they constitute evidence. The acts of production and broadcast establish radio and television programs as discrete objects. And the act of publication marks a specific version or edition of a literary work. In each of these cases, it is virtually impossible to change or withdraw the cultural record that the release of an information object establishes. On the digital landscape, by contrast, it is still relatively easy for a creator to alter or retract previously released information. Such actions can eliminate or overlay significant content and thereby corrupt the record. It is also relatively easy in an on-line environment-and equally confusing for purposes of preserving information integrity-for an author (or user) to make available concurrently multiple representations of what he or she considers to be the same work, providing no definition of a canonical version and viewing all representations as having equal quality and validity.

To address these problems, a wide range of cryptographic techniques, such as watermarking, already exist for various kinds of digital information objects. These could serve well to mark and identify specific, canonical versions and editions of textual, audio and visual works, and to establish trusted, protected channels of distribution for those objects. However, the standards and infrastructure and the policies and practices for applying such techniques to the creation of fixed versions of digital information objects still need considerable development.

Absent such development and the fixity of information that would result, digital archives face considerable challenges in trying to preserve the integrity of digital objects. Some kinds of digital objects present the problem of fixity of information in yet another way. An increasing number of networked information resources are better modeled, not in terms of versions or editions of works, but as continuously updated databases. The financial communities also depend on large, continuously updated databases. There is no natural way to fix these resources at the database level, no natural set of publication points for the objects as a whole. Their integrity, or singularity, as databases resides in the coherence of the database as a whole and in the continuousness of the updates. To preserve the integrity of such information resources, the complete record of changes has to be built into the design of the database and fixed at the record level.

In the absence of such a preservation-oriented design, digital archives may have no choice but to fix the database artificially in time and capture a series of snapshots of its state at periodic intervals as a way of preserving its integrity. Information objects come into being and acquire their distinctiveness in relation to various other objects in an information space. For an object to maintain its integrity, its wholeness and singularity, one must be able to locate it definitively and reliably over time among other objects.Systems of citation, description and classification provide the necessary means of reference so that one can consistently discover, identify and retrieve relevant objects. Such systems traditionally include bibliographies, catalogues, indices, data dictionaries, directory systems, finding aids and the like, all of which collect, assemble and organize references to bodies of work.

Creators of these resources are already extending them with such innovations, for example, as the use of the 856 field in bibliographic records, to incorporate reference to digital objects. Moreover, in the electronic environment, there are also emerging sophisticated tools for automatically gathering and presenting in new kinds of products referential information from textual, image, sound, video and other kinds of digital objects. To meet the test of consistent reference, however, citations to digital objects from these various manually and automatically generated sources must over time reliably identify the works to which they refer. One way of establishing confidence in a reference system is to generate citations in the first place-either manually or automatically-from the self-referential information that a work itself carries with it, perhaps in a header, a digital envelope or some other distinct part of the digital object.

In the digital environment, the problems of documenting provenance through a record of publication are bound up with the problems of fixity, and particularly with issues involved in tracing multiple versions and editions, as described above. Outside the path of publication, however, there are several other channels of information creation and distribution, including tracing the path of migration within their own organization, that digital archives need to document in order to preserve the integrity of digital objects in their custody. First, there is a chain of provenance from individuals, a trail which has comprised a traditional concern of archivists.

Digital information objects acquire the qualities of content, fixity, reference, provenance and context-and thereby their integrity-as they move through a life cycle in a series of relationships with parties, or stakeholders, who have specific interests in their creation, management, dissemination, use or retention. The initial stakeholder in a digital information object is, of course, the creator of its content. Following creation, a digital information object may pass through a series of gateways of increasingly public release and access. Some digital information objects (like videos of family picnics or private journals) may never be released beyond the initial creator; others will be limited to an immediate circle, which may or may not be physically co-located with the creator. Still other objects will be very widely disseminated.

Once a creator fixes a digital information object by releasing it, for either personal or wider use, the object invites various other kinds of stakeholder interests. Depending on the extent of the release and the nature of the object, users and other stakeholders may refer to it, index it or cite it. Still others may acquire, license or otherwise take custody of it to edit and publish it, to invoke it as evidence of a transaction or perhaps, as in the case of scientific data, to study, analyze and report it.

A distributed structure, built on a foundation of electronic networks, places archival responsibility with those who presumably care most about and have the greatest understanding of the value of particular digital information objects. Moreover, such a structure locates the economic and cultural incentives where they are most likely to prompt those preserving digital information to respond with the greatest agility to the changing digital landscape and to the shifting tides of technology.

Effective structures for digital archives in a distributed network will surely take various forms and will include corporations, federations and consortia, each of which may specialize in the archiving of digital information and range over regional and national boundaries. Both informal collaborations (associations and alliances) and formal partnerships among contractors and subcontractors, will also surely arise, in which responsibilities for archiving are allocated among various other interests in digital information.

Moreover, shared interests in, for example, intellectual discipline, in type of information, in function, such as storage or cataloguing, and even interests in the output of information within national boundaries will all form a varied and rich basis for the kinds of formal and informal interactions that lead to the design of particular archival organizations.

In the end, existing archival organizations may successfully adapt their current roles and responsibilities to changing needs, existing archival roles and responsibilities may be redistributed among other kinds of organizations with stakes in digital information, and focused attention on the division of labor in the digital information economy will lead to the emergence and growth of new kinds of archival structures. Whatever the particular structural outcomes may be as stakeholders, new and old, interact and give shape to the distributed network of digital information, distributed responsibility for preserving that information requires commitment at least to the following set of organizing principles:

1. Information creators/providers/owners have initial responsibility for archiving their digital information objects and thereby ensuring the

long-term preservation of those objects. The creator/provider/owner may engage other parties, such as certified digital archives, to take over some or all of the archival responsibility. Libraries and archival organizations may interact with creators/providers as subcontractors for maintaining digital archives during and after the active life of their information objects.

2. Certified digital archives have the right and duty to exercise an aggressive rescue function as a fail-safe mechanism to preserve information objects that become endangered because the creator/provider/owner does not accept responsibility for the preservation function and does not take steps formally to convey responsibility, or because there is no natural institutional home for the objects.

The conditions of creating digital information and giving it a useful life are essentially the same as those required for the information to persist over time. That is, it must be stored and maintained in an accessible form. It is not unreasonable, therefore, to assert, as the first principle does, that initial responsibility for preservation begins with creation of the information and rests with the creator, owner or provider of it. Individuals and public and private agencies already regard such a responsibility as a natural one for their critical internal records.

Creators of knowledge in other spheres depend on past knowledge and regularly acknowledge their responsibility to add to the enduring record when they publish their own ideas and findings. As the properties and usefulness of other kinds of information objects become more widely known, the ability in the digital environment to reuse and repackage these objects may generate revenue or other benefits. Creators, owners or providers of these objects, including some publishers, who may not have otherwise counted long-term preservation among their key responsibilities, may thus be more inclined to do so and may either assume the responsibility themselves or find a qualified partner to do so. Among potential partners, they will likely find libraries, archives or similar agencies, which have specific collection agendas and will seek to take or share responsibility for preserving organized collections of digital materials.

The second organizing principle calls, in effect, for a fail-safe mechanism. A variety of factors-budgetary constraints, reorganization of priorities or focus, change of business, the need to go out of existence, or expiration of copyright- might prompt custodians to neglect, abandon or destroy their collections of digital information. No distributed system of digital archives will afford effective protection of electronic information unless it provides for a powerful rescue function allowing one agency, acting in the long-term public interest of protecting the cultural record, to override another's neglect of or active interest in abandoning or destroying parts of that record.

Digital archives operating normally and those operating in fail-safe mode differ mainly in the rights and obligations they have with respect to rescuing materials that have fallen in jeopardy because a custodian no longer accepts preservation responsibility. Section 108 of the 1976 Copyright Act of the United States defines the rights and obligations for libraries and archives operating normally to preserve copies of printed materials. The proposed revision of the copyright law reserves to libraries and archives similar rights and duties for digital materials.

However, neither in its present form nor in its proposed revision does the Copyright Act provide a legal foundation defining the rights and duties that must come into play to facilitate and encourage an aggressive rescue function. The Copyright Act, in fact, may not provide the best legal and institutional framework for establishing fail-safe mechanisms for digital archives. However, such a framework is urgently needed because we know that one of the greatest dangers to the long life of digital information is the ease with which it can be abandoned and then deliberately or inadvertently destroyed. One appropriate foundation for an archival fail-safe mechanism against this danger might rest in articulating for the various domains of intellectual property-on analogy from the domain of real estate-a definition of the concept of abandonment and of the rights and duties that follow for digital archives operating in fail-safe mode when they can show that present custodians have abandoned, or are in the process of abandoning, culturally valuable objects. Other means of providing a fail-safe mechanism for digital archives also exist, however.

Users of archived information in electronic form and of archival services relating to that information need to have assurance that a digital archives is what it says that it is and that the information stored there is safe for the long term. Appropriate organizations and individuals need to begin now developing such standards and criteria, including standard methods for a repository to declare its existence as a digital archives and therefore its intentions to preserve the contents over which it has custody, and for describing what the archives contains and what services it provides.

The certification process must also address the standards and best practices for other dimensions of archival operation, including selection and accessioning of material, its storage and access and the engineering of the systems environment. Archives cannot save all information objects; they must appraise and select for retention the most valuable items. Selection processes for archives of all kinds—paper and digital-are matters of intellectual judgment about what to include and save and what to exclude. Criteria for such judgments are largely tied to the intrinsic qualities of the material and many of the criteria that have proven useful in the paper world will no doubt translate to and prove equally effective in the digital environment. In general, selection criteria include an appraisal of the content of the object-its subject and discipline-in relation to the collection goals of the digital archives, the quality and uniqueness of the object, its accessibility in terms of available hardware and software, its present value and its likely future value.

Search and retrieval in large universes of diverse digital materials is the subject of very active computer science research, but search and retrieval today against a rapidly expanding universe of materials in all forms-digital, paper, microform—remains difficult, and the relatively primitive systems currently in operation may, in the short term at least, inhibit the effective selection of materials for digital archives. Redundancy of information is also important for effective selection. Selectors need to know before accepting an object where a copy of record is stored and if and where additional copies are distributed either as backup or for more efficient retrieval. In addition, selectors ultimately need to have a rich understanding of the software and hardware dependencies of candidate digital information objects so that they can factor the carrying costs for an object into their overall assessment of its value.

Such understandings remain in relatively short supply in some measure because the educational processes for wedding selection and technical skills still need to be devised and perfected. In larger measure, however, technical understandings are deficient because the digital environment is so immature that the dependencies of information objects on underlying hardware and software are still in many respects unknown. Finally, selection for digital archives must be a continuing process. Given the need to migrate digital information regularly from its hardware and software environment, the stimulus and occasion will recur to reappraise the value of the material being migrated. Materials may lose value over time and may need to be withdrawn and discarded. Hard decisions may also be necessary about how and whether digital objects migrate if changes in a technical environment force alters what is preserved so that it differs in fundamental ways from what existed in the original object.

Digital archives thus need to formulate and implement policies and practices for ongoing appraisal. Once an information object is identified for inclusion in a digital archives, it needs to be accessioned, that is, prepared for the archives. The accession process involves both describing and cataloguing selected objects, including their provenance and context, and securing them for storage and access. Standards for description are well developed for certain kinds of materials that are likely to appear in digital archives, such as monographs and serials. Because of the high degree of standardization, one might reasonably expect such descriptions eventually to accompany the digital object, thus simplifying the accessioning process. For other kinds of materials, such as WWW pages, motion video and multimedia, relevant attributes are less well understood. Standards of description are less well practiced and one cannot reasonably expect satisfactory descriptive material to accompany the digital object.

In all cases, special attention is needed in the accession process to creating, describing and tracking the versions of the object in the digital archives to satisfy the various requirements for display and other forms of access and for long-term storage. If material is to be deaccessioned then public declarations need to be made to that effect, particularly if it is the last known copy, so that rescue efforts by others can proceed if appropriate. In the accession process, selected digital objects also need to be made secure for indefinite future use. A digital archives may need to establish access controls for its information objects and the means for authenticating them to future users. Establishing access controls involves setting terms and conditions for authorized use by specific users or classes of users. For certain extreme cases, such as rescued objects still under intellectual property protection, there may be no authorized uses for certain periods of time except for internal use within the digital archives to ensure that the object will be accessible in the future.

Authentication, which may make use of cryptography, provides verification that a digital object is what it purports to be and contains the contents that the author/creator or publisher originally intended. One of the characteristics of materials in digital archives may need to be that they contain a digital digest or signature that users can independently verify to assure themselves that the object is unchanged from its archival state. The storage operation in digital archives attends primarily to the media level formatting of information objects. Primary considerations include levels of hierarchy and redundancy. In any digital archives, there may be multiple levels of storage graded to levels of expected use and needed performance in retrieval. Little used material may be stored most efficiently off-line, usually in tape format. For objects in high demand, where retrieval time is at a premium, on-line storage in magnetic media may serve best.

In a distributed network, they may need to be stored on-line in multiple locations. An intermediate solution is near-line storage, where information objects may be stored on optical or tape media and loaded in a jukebox. Retrieval time in near-line storage systems suffers by comparison to on-line storage, but is considerably more responsive to user demand than off-line storage. Digital archives may use any or all of these methods. The most sophisticated systems combine the resources so that objects in use or recent use are stored on-line and, as they age from the time of most recent use, they move to near-line storage and then eventually off-line. Another important storage consideration is redundancy. In a system that is completely dependent on the interaction of various kinds and levels of hardware and software, failure in any one of the subsystems could mean the loss or corruption of the information object.

Effective storage management thus means providing for redundant copies of the archived objects as an insurance against loss. Depending on the copyright status of the objects, digital archives may choose to make backup copies on their own or to make arrangements for other sites, which hold the same object, in the network of digital archives to serve as backup, or they may choose to do both. Providing access to digital information in a distributed network environment means above all that digital archives are connected to networks using appropriate protocols and with bandwidth suitable for delivering the information their control. Digital archives have an obligation to maintain the information in a form so that users over the network can find it with appropriate retrieval engines and view, print, listen to or otherwise use it with appropriate output devices.

In the descriptions of the resources they hold, responsible digital archives must provide to their users what they know about the provenance and context of their digital objects so that users can make informed decisions about the reliability and quality of the evidence before them. With respect to access, digital archives also have the responsibility to manage intellectual property rights by facilitating transactions between rights-holders in the information and users and by taking every reasonable precaution to prevent unauthorized use of the material. Because so many of the operational responsibilities of the digital archives- selection, accessioning, storage and access-are functionally identical to those of more traditional permanent repositories, they may successfully extend their scope to include digital materials. Many traditional archives have already embraced digital materials, and libraries and museums are not far behind.

Retaining the information in digital form by copying it onto new digital storage media may be appropriate when the information exists in a "software-independent" format as ASCII text files or as flat files with simple, uniform structures. Several data archives hold large collections of numerical data that were captured on punch cards in the 1950s or 1960s, migrated to two or three different magnetic tape formats, and now reside on optical media. As new media and storage formats were introduced, the data were migrated without any significant change in their logical structure.

Copying from one medium to another has the distinct advantage of being universally available and easy to implement. It is a cost-effective strategy for preserving digital information in those cases where retaining the content is paramount, but display, indexing, and computational characteristics are not critical. As long as the preservation community lacks more robust and cost-effective migration strategies, printing to paper or film and preserving flat files will remain the preferred method of storage for many institutions and for certain formats of digital information. Yet the simplicity and universality of copying as a migration strategy may come at the expense of great losses in the form or structure of digital information. When the access method for some non-standard data changes, one must, in order to migrate them, often eliminate, or "flatten," the structure of documents, the data relationships embedded in databases, and the means of authentication which are managed and interpreted through software.

Computation capabilities, graphic display, indexing, and other features may also be lost, leaving behind the skeletal remnant of the original object.

This strategy is not feasible, however, for preserving complex data objects from complex systems. It is not possible, for example to microfilm the equations embedded in a spreadsheet, to print out an interactive full motion video, or to preserve a multimedia document as a flat file. Another migration strategy for digital archives with large, complex, and diverse collections of digital materials is to migrate digital objects from the great multiplicity of formats used to create digital materials to a smaller, more manageable number of standard formats that can still encode the complexity of structure and form of the original.

A digital archives might accept textual documents in several commonly available commercial word processing formats or require that documents conform to standards like SGML. Databases might be stored in one of several common relational database management systems, while images would conform to a tagged image file format and standard compression algorithms. Changing format as a migration strategy has the advantage of preserving more of the display, dissemination, and computational characteristics of the original object, while reducing the large variety of customized transformations that would otherwise be necessary to migrate material to future generations of technology. This strategy rests on the assumption that software products, which are either compliant with widely adopted standards or are widely dispersed in the marketplace, are less volatile than the software market as a whole. Also, most common commercial products provide utilities for upward migration and for swapping documents, databases, and more complex objects between software systems. Nevertheless, software and standards continue to evolve so this strategy simplifies but does not eliminate the need for periodic migration or the need for analysis of the potential effects of such migration on the integrity of the digital object.

Digital archives will benefit from the widespread adoption of data and communication standards that facilitate reference to digital information objects and enable their interchange among systems. Business needs in many institutions are driving the development and adoption of data standards. Organizations that create, use and maintain Geographic Information Systems (GIS), for example, are trying to reduce data conversion and maintenance costs by creating data that conform to widely accepted standards so that they can be exchanged, reused, or sold. Digital archives must keep abreast of standards developments and make sure that their own technological infrastructure conforms to widely adopted standards.

Planning for long-term preservation is a critical element of digital preservation. To the extent that creators/providers/owners of digital information accept initial responsibility for archiving their objects, they may begin to see the wisdom of incorporating migration paths or other provisions for preservation as an integral part of the process or system that generates digital information. To assist in this educational process, digital archives might work one-on-one with potential donors to develop agreements early in their careers and establish arrangements for regular, on-line deposit of digital materials in a format acceptable to the repository. In government, institutional, and corporate settings, archivists and librarians can issue guidelines and advice for digital preservation and encourage their parent institutions to adopt common usage rules, comply with data standards, and select applications software that supports migration.

The preservation community as a whole needs to work with industry to create information systems and standards that build in archival considerations, such as backward compatibility from the point of initial design. Backward compatibility or migration paths would enable new generations of software to "read" data from older systems without substantial reformatting. Although backward compatibility is increasingly common within software product lines, migration paths are not commonly provided between competing software products or for products that fail in the marketplace. Although standards and migration paths may become commonplace at some future date, a large body of digital material exists today in non-standard formats, and organizations and individuals continue to produce digital materials in formats that will require migration.

Developing "processing centers" that specialize in migration and reformatting of obsolete materials may provide a cost-effective method of digital preservation. Processing centers might provide reformatting services for particular types of materials, such as text, certain database structures, geographic information systems (GIS), or multimedia products. Such centers might maintain older versions of hardware and software to support migration. In US, a national laboratory for digital preservation, modeled after the National Media Laboratory, is another alternative. Feasibility studies and cost/benefit analyses would be necessary to determine the technological, economic, and commercial viability of such processing centers. In addition to managing their operating environment and the migration of information through hardware and software platforms, a third function by which digital archives fulfill their commitment to preserve electronic information is in managing the costs of these activities.

The principal cost factors of the operating environment are those associated with selection, accession, storage, use, migration, property rights transactions, and the systems engineering needed to manage migration and to maintain the digital archives within a distributed network infrastructure. Some costs, like those for hardware and software as well as those for intellectual property if rights are purchased rather than leased, will appear as capital costs and will need to be amortized. Operating costs will vary by the form of the information, by usage and over time. Digital information in full text form will be relatively cheap to store and use compared to other forms, such as image, sound, video and multimedia information. Full-text takes up less space in storage and less bandwidth in transmission than other forms. The modes of usage for full-text are relatively well, though by no means completely, understood, and so the delivery and access software is relatively more stable and less subject to costly turnover than that for information in other forms.

Usage will also substantially affect operating costs. Healthy demand for particular information objects will push the digital archives that provide them shift delivery to more costly on-line storage or to sophisticated and expensive systems of hierarchical storage. The costs of software and intellectual property may also be pegged to demand. Another usage factor affecting costs is the high variability in the kinds of user access devices.

For many types of information objects, modes of access are still closely tied to the type of workstation available to the user. The tradeoff for the digital archives is either to limit access only to "approved" devices or to support multiple platforms and incur the added associated costs in hardware, software, intellectual property and systems engineering. Operating costs will also vary over time. Storage costs will likely continue to decline both absolutely and relative to other cost factors. The costs of access and of managing property rights transactions are relatively high today because the supporting systems are virtually non-existent; these systems are developing very rapidly and their relative costs will likely also fall. The costs of the property rights transactions themselves, however, cannot be reasonably predicted at this stage and the danger is that costs will rise to the point that they become a barrier to access.

In the long run, the cost factor that will most likely determine the success or failure of digital archives is the investment in the systems engineering and infrastructure needed to support highly distributed network-based functions. Migration costs will vary depending on the complexity of the original data objects, the frequency of migration, the extent to which the functionality for computation, display, indexing, and authentication must be maintained, and the need to compensate for acquisition of intellectual property rights. Digital archives may have to compensate for intellectual property rights and may be required to purchase software or site licenses in order to migrate digital information stored in proprietary formats. Planning for migration is difficult because there is limited experience with the types of migrations needed to maintain access to complex digital objects.

When a custodian assumes responsibility for preserving a digital object it may be difficult to predict when migration will be necessary, how much reformatting is needed, and how much migration will cost. There are no reliable or comprehensive data on costs associated with migrations, either for specific technologies and formats or for particular collections.

There is a large array of cost factors to understand for a panoply of differing kinds of digital information objects in which numerous parties have a variety of different kinds of interests. A multidimensional matrix-with present and future stakeholders mapped along one axis, kinds of digital information along a second, and cost factors against a third-might serve well as a framework for systematically assessing the value of digital information and the affordability of preserving it. There is much we need to know before we can fully elaborate an economic framework of this kind, and much to be learned from detailed studies of a wide variety of public and private institutional experiences with preserving digital materials. A number of organizations, including the US, National Aeronautics and Space Administration (NASA), the National Oceanic and Atmospheric Administration (NOAA), and the Inter-university Consortium for Political and Social Research (ICPSR), have relatively long and rich experiences in maintaining huge archives of certain kinds of digital information, and they are increasingly doing so in a distributed environment over electronic networks.

Yet, despite these various experiences, little systematic understanding has yet emerged of the actual costs of digital archiving. As a result, there is almost no sense of the detailed interplay of cost factors that might promote the kinds of specialization, division of labor and competition needed, in turn, to drive digital archives not just to manage costs against a standard of information quality and integrity, but to strive vigorously to lower those costs while maintaining and improving the standard of quality. Components of storage costs in the digital archives include storage device costs-a jukebox, in this model-storage media costs, and the costs of operating and maintaining the storage equipment, and of periodically refreshing the media and migrating the data. The costs of providing access to the digital archives include providing a document server and software for the server that will support client machines on users' desks, maintaining the server and access software and of operating the server, and printing on demand a selected portion of volumes used and of delivering those printed copies to the user.

Certification for Digital Archives

The introduction of electronic journals has transformed scholarly communication in extraordinary ways—making it possible to disseminate research results more quickly, to provide hyperlinked access to cited publications, and to amplify text with images, audio and video files, datasets and software—but it has also created a dilemma for libraries which now license access to rather than own the journals to which they subscribe.

Clearly, a model of collaboration involving scholars, publishers, and librarians is required to ensure that the e-scholarship of today will be accessible to researchers of the future. Long-term preservation of digital information on a scale adequate for the demands of future research and scholarship will require a deep infrastructure capable of supporting a distributed system of digital archives. A critical component of the digital archiving infrastructure is the existence of a sufficient number of trusted organizations capable of storing, migrating, and providing access to digital collections. A process of certification for digital archives is needed to create an overall climate of trust about the prospects of preserving digital information. Certified digital archives must have the right and duty to exercise an aggressive rescue function as a fail-safe mechanism for preserving valuable digital information that is in jeopardy of destruction, neglect, or abandonment by its current custodian.

Equally influential in the development of digital archiving strategies has been the Reference Model for an Open Archival Information System (OAIS), an initiative of the Consultative Committee for Space Data Systems

(CCSDS) which began in 1995. In the case of e-journals, the "relevant decision-makers" include authors, publishers, and librarians. Although the grantees propose several economic models—from charging authors an archiving fee upon publication, to setting up endowments to ensure perpetual funding, to charging publishers for archiving services (charges which would undoubtedly be passed on to subscribers), to charging libraries for access to archived content—no one means of financing digital archiving of e-journals was identified, and in fact, a combination of funding models will most likely be required. Further, whereas smaller publishers have a strong incentive to have their electronic content archived, larger commercial publishers are reluctant to provide potential archives unrestricted access to their electronic content, fearing loss of control over presentation as well as loss of future revenues. On the other hand, libraries are reluctant to delegate e-journal archiving to publishers alone for fear that bankruptcies or mergers or simply a publisher's decision that it is no longer economically beneficial to support a particular journal could result in loss of access to the scholarly record.

One of the most controversial issues addressed by the grantees concerned when and how archived journals might be accessed. As the academic and publishing communities have moved into the twenty-first century with ever-increasing reliance on digital content, the infrastructure for preserving this content has not yet been created. The goal is to develop all of the technical and organizational infrastructure elements necessary to ensure the longevity of important scholarly e-resources. At a practical level this includes developing a business model that can support the ongoing work of the archive; establishing relations with producers of electronic content, with librarians, and with scholars; and developing the technical and content management infrastructure necessary to support a trusted archive of electronic materials.

Methods of Web Archiving

Web archiving is the process of collecting portions of the World Wide Web and ensuring the collection is preserved in an archive, such as an archive site, for future researchers, historians, and the public. Due to the massive size of the Web, web archivists typically employ web crawlers for automated collection. The largest web archiving organization based on a crawling approach is the Internet Archive which strives to maintain an archive of the entire Web. National libraries, national archives and various consortia of organizations are also involved in archiving culturally important Web content. Commercial web archiving software and services are also available to organizations who need to archive their own web content for corporate heritage, regulatory, or legal purposes.

Web archivists generally archive all types of web content including HTML web pages, style sheets, JavaScript, images, and video. They also archive metadata about the collected resources such as access time, MIME type, and content length. This metadata is useful in establishing authenticity and provenance of the archived collection.

Remote Harvesting

The most common web archiving technique uses web crawlers to automate the process of collecting web pages. Web crawlers typically view web pages in the same manner that users with a browser see the Web, and therefore provide a comparatively simple method of remotely harvesting web content. Examples of web crawlers frequently used for web archiving include:

— Heritrix

— HTTrack

— Wget

On-demand

There are numerous services that may be used to archive web resources "on-demand", using web crawling techniques:

WebCite, a service specifically for scholarly authors, journal editors and publishers to permanently archive and retrieve cited Internet references (Eysenbach and Trudel, 2005).

Archive-It, a subscription service, allows institutions to build, manage and search their own web archive.

Hanzo Archives offer commercial web archiving tools and services, for corporate heritage, regulatory compliance, litigation-support, and electronic discovery.

Website-Archive.com offer a subscription based service that captures screen-shots of pages, transactions and user journeys using real browsers. Screen-shots are stored and can be either viewed online or downloaded in a monthly archive. It is based on the same technology as the functional and cross browser testing service from Cloud Testing.

Iterasi Industrial strength web archiving application that can create high fidelity archives of any webpage for the corporate, legal and government industries.

PageFreezer Archive, browse and search websites, comply with Records Management Laws and provide strong legal evidence.

Database Archiving

Database archiving refers to methods for archiving the underlying content of database-driven websites. It typically requires the extraction of the database content into a standard schema, often using XML. Once stored in that standard format, the archived content of multiple databases can then be made available using a single access system. This approach is exemplified by the DeepArc and Xinq tools developed by the Bibliothèque nationale de France and the National Library of Australia respectively. DeepArc enables the structure of a relational database to be mapped to an XML schema, and the content exported into an XML document. Xinq then allows that content to be delivered online. Although the original layout and behavior of the website cannot be preserved exactly, Xinq does allow the basic querying and retrieval functionality to be replicated.

Transactional Archiving

Transactional archiving is an event-driven approach, which collects the actual transactions which take place between a web server and a web browser. It is primarily used as a means of preserving evidence of the content which was actually viewed on a particular website, on a given date. This may be particularly important for organizations which need to comply with legal or regulatory requirements for disclosing and retaining information.

A transactional archiving system typically operates by intercepting every HTTP request to, and response from, the web server, filtering each response to eliminate duplicate content, and permanently storing the responses as bitstreams. A transactional archiving system requires the installation of software on the web server, and cannot therefore be used to collect content from a remote website.

Registration Services

Registration services provide persistent identifiers to concepts or objects. They often serve up metadata about metadata. Examples of this include Dublin Core extensions, and the OpenURL formats of digital objects.

Physical or digital items can also be registered, and cataloguing services such as OCLC's offer that sort of registration and control. A similar service is associating identifiers with names agents, such as people and institutions, such as name authority services.

Searching Services

Search services are all familiar to us. Some sort of search string is typically mapped to a list of records. Searching Web services put this basic functionality in XML wrappers to make it available to higher-level programs the user interacts with. The leading example of this in digital libraries is the Z39.50 work on SRU/SRW. Rather than having to understand BER and ASN.1, programs interact in XML over HTTP. In this case, the main reason not to change over from classic Z39.50 is probably the investment in the current systems. Newly designed systems would find SRU/SRW much easier to implement and use.

Resolution Services

Resolution services come in many different flavours. Typically, they map from identifiers to data. An example might be a service that accepts an ISBN and returns bibliographic data about the items that ISBN is associated with. Other examples include mapping controlled names to metadata about the people identified, and mapping a subject class number to a textual description of that class.

Navigation Services

It is possible to create Web services that facilitate the navigation through a set of links. Of course, the Web itself is an example of general network movement using links, but more specialized services may also be of use.

Decomposition Services

There are a number of decomposition services appearing. Decomposition services offer the possibility of applying concentrated knowledge and expertise to these problems and making them widely available. These services might be as simple as identifying individual names from a list of names or breaking a class number into its constituent parts, to the more complex problems of exposing the structure of a document or identifying letters/words/sentences within an image.

Enhancement Services

Digital library systems could use any number of enhancement services. An important enhancement are normalization services, such as adding controlled forms of names to metadata containing uncontrolled forms, or adding classification numbers selected on the basis of the text of a document. If links can be identified within metadata records it would also be possible to expand incomplete data. OCLC does that now internally in some of our online services where tables of contents and cover art are added to book catalogue records for display. Web services are a way this type of information could be integrated into distributed and disparate services at less cost than maintaining and integrating all the data locally.

Transformation Services

Many of the above services offer some sort of 'transformation,' so there is overlap between types of services. Transformation services operate at a higher level than many of the other services, e.g. translating the syntax of metadata records from MARC21 to MARC-XML. Somewhat harder to accomplish is the translation of a Dublin Core record (in whatever format) into MARC-21 or between classification systems. At the high-end of these services might be natural-language translations.

Organisation of Library Web Pages

Library web pages are focused mainly on individual libraries and the resources and services they offer. Consequently, with rare exceptions web access hosted by libraries is not designed to serve as a general entry point for the larger world of web-accessible resources. Neither are the multitude of individual library web pages equal to a single, widely known, dependable beginning place for research in the web environment. For this reason, library users and librarians in search of web-based information turn instead (and are sometimes directed through library web pages) to search engines or information services created by what may be referred to in the new parlance as information. A number of recently created content providers may also be counted among the information.coms, including netlibrary.com, questia.com, and several ebook providers. With the availability of what already numbers several dozen information.coms, one might reasonably ask whether research libraries should bother taking concerted action to get into the web information portal business. After all, the information.coms offer a variety of different formats and approaches to finding information, and our constituencies are accustomed to using them.

Developing a scholars portal would undoubtedly be a complex and expensive undertaking and would require concerted action on a scale that has been difficult to achieve, let alone sustain, within the research library community. Letting a thousand flowers bloom, it turns out, has always been easier than cultivating a garden. Such services do not plumb to the depths of information ordinarily reached by researchers in subject disciplines. Conceptually, one might say that information.coms are horizontal rather than vertical information retrieval services. So except for the most straightforward types of inquiries, their ability to facilitate what the academy considers in-depth research is extremely limited.

In the best of all possible web-based worlds, the subject library of the future might be conceived of as a highly customized, narrowly focused search engine adapted to the character of publications and research habits of a discipline. This is not, however, the nature of current information.coms and there is no evidence yet that one or more will evolve in this direction. Indeed, the largest drawback of all may be precisely that information.coms in general have not been designed with the particular needs of the research community in mind. Rather, for good business reasons, they appear focused on broad customer bases and the most common information-seeking activities of the general public. This may simply be a necessary condition for success with commercial enterprises.

More limited niche markets are certainly not prohibited in the commercial world, and indeed, some are beginning to appear in the education sector. At this time, however, the information.coms with an education focus are aimed more at providing content than web searching and are still able to offer only small and basic collections as gauged by research library standards. In addition, these and other information.coms are proprietary and distinct and are themselves in some need of aggregation for portal access. For instance, while one will occasionally find information on a university web page about how to search the Internet including a listing of search engines, never will one encounter such a listing when accessing an information.com, since it would be self-destructive to promote one's competition. Thus, ironically, the information.com world, while replete with help for web information seekers, in the final analysis adds to the overall complexity of the situation.

There are other more proactively positive reasons that ARL, along with strategic partners, should undertake to build a scholars portal. One may be simply that there is arguably no other agency (or group of agencies) with the breadth of awareness, the information, the skills, and the objectivity to succeed at doing so. This is not meant to be a grandly arrogant statement but rather to point out the unique character of the research library community: the libraries themselves, those who operate them, their not-for-profit status, and the potential resident therein for making sense of the world's largest unmanaged database, the World Wide Web. In other words, research librarians can likely create a scholars portal better than anyone else.

Digital Reference Services

Digital reference is the provision of reference service over the Internet. The term for digital reference has taken many forms: digital, virtual, chat, on-line and real-time, to mention a few of the more popular names. Distributed reference services, captures best the notion that the modern day library, to a great degree, is a web-based learning environment. The lines between on and off-campus students and courses are blurring as technology is incorporated into all aspects of education.

Digital reference differs from traditional reference in two fundamental ways. First, there is a disconnect between the user and the physical space of the library. Second, digital reference creates artifacts of the exchange between librarian and user. That is, the transaction can be recorded in terms of the content of the interaction, the resources used, the time it took, the time of day it took place, the librarian involved, the general location of the user and a number of other quantifiable variables. On many library Web sites, the user is hard-pressed to identify the staff, whose names, if they're there, are five levels down. The human factor is still important. Although the Library turnstile counts and circulation figures have shot up from last year, many students opt to do much of their research away from the Library or campus. The Library's considerable investment in electronic resources, as well as the growth in size of distance and web-based learning methods, has meant a steady increase in the use of licensed databases, library catalogue and other resources, from home, office, student residences and the labs. The culture created by the pervasive use of the Web is one of convenience and speed.

To address these realities, the Library has developed a number of proactive, innovative and flexible approaches to providing reference services. In addition to email reference, the Library offers online library research tutorials, web-based subject guides, an FAQ page, and a telephone call centre. The buzz in the digital reference world is about providing "high tech with high touch." The software acquired is in fact not considered chat but web call centre software and it differs from chat platforms in a number of ways. The most significant difference is the ability to co-browse web pages while conversing (chatting) via text with the user.

The librarians considered this feature important because it gives us the ability to assist users "inside" licensed databases. The software acquired is called VRD—Virtual Reference Desk, and is a product of the company Library Systems and Services Incorporated (LSSI). LSSI is unusual in the web based call centre business in that it is a company made up of librarians and has supported the library community for the past 20 years in the provision of automation based products and services. While web call centre software is a relatively new activity for the company, the product has become tremendously popular in the library community.

Library and information service managers now have a wide set of computer-based solutions from which they can select the best mix of services to meet the needs of their customers. Phrases such as 'the electronic library' and 'digital libraries' are beginning to appear in the literature. Collier and Arnold define the electronic library as 'a managed environment of multimedia materials in digital form, designed for the benefit of its user population, structured to facilitate access to its contents and equipped with aids to navigation of the global network'. The Electronic Libraries (e-Lib) Programme in the United Kingdom, which resulted from a study (known as the Follett Report) into various crises affecting academic libraries, is funding sixty or so projects covering the areas of document delivery, electronic journals, on-demand publishing, digitization, training and awareness, and access to networked resources.

In the United States the National Science Foundation (NSF) and other agencies have funded six institutions to work on the Digital Libraries Initiative. Berry describes some of the work in progress and gives a definition from the University of Michigan Digital Library Project: 'a digital library is the generic name for federated structures that provide humans both intellectual and physical access to the huge and growing worldwide networks of information encoded in multimedia digital networks'.

The parallel developments of computer processing speed, storage facilities, multimedia and telecommunications now enable access from one workstation to huge information resources worldwide. The traditional view of a library as a store of information held locally is being eroded as the library becomes a gateway to information resources worldwide. This, of course, has huge implications for library users, information providers, librarians and information scientists. The first electronic digital computer, ENIAC, was completed in Philadelphia in 1946, but all commands had to be input separately. Early computers were huge, expensive, complicated machines that consumed a lot of electricity, generated a lot of heat, needed specialist operators and were used for processing data in specialist laboratories. Their size, complexity and cost meant that they were not used for any library or information work until the mid-1960s, when transistors replaced the original valves.

By then codes had been developed so that text could be input, stored and output on these computers with the individual characters being translated into strings of binary digits. Very large scale integration of the electronic components that comprise any computer has resulted in a huge increase in the power available and a decrease in the cost of processing. The 1980s saw the development of the microcomputer, which enabled many libraries and information units to acquire their own computer systems. By the mid-1990s Personal Computers (PCs) have become commonplace in libraries and information units worldwide, and many people also have PCs at home. These PCs may be used for what has become known as 'edutainment', where educational packages which parents hope will improve their children's education are used, as well as encyclopedias on CDROM and games, of which a large number are available.

With the development of the information superhighway many of these domestic PCs can now link to the Internet to access information sources that previously were only available in a library or information centre. Many professionals, including doctors, pharmacists, veterinary surgeons and lawyers, now have PCs on their desks. The battery-powered 'laptop' computer is a portable device that can be used when travelling on trains and planes. The speed with which the processor carries out basic instructions (measured in millions of instructions per second (mips) or given as a frequency and measured in megahertz (MHz)) and the amount of main store that can be accessed are factors used to describe a processor. The earliest computers processed up to 10,000 instructions per second and there has been continuous increase in this speed so that current PCs have a processing speed of thousands of mips. Intel is a major manufacturer of processors and in mid-1996 it announced plans for a 200 MHz Pentium processor which means that it will operate at two to three times the speed of current Pentiums. The main memory of any computer is used to store information that is currently being processed. The earliest computers were capable of storing only 1,000 to 8,000 characters of information.

The amount of store has increased continuously over the years with a parallel decrease in costs. The most common form of memory can be written to as well as read from, and is referred to as RAM (Random Access Memory). The standard PC of today has a RAM of about 8, 16 or 32 MB (the unit normally used to refer to storage of one character is a byte; 1,000 bytes are called a Kilobyte or KB, and 1 million bytes are called a Megabyte or MB). A variety of input devices may be attached to a computer to enable information in any form (for example, text, voice, image) to be converted into the appropriate binary codes. For instance the Arab Organization for Standardization and Metrology (ASMO) developed the ASMO 449 for Arabic characters, and the East Asian Character Code is based on work undertaken by the Research Libraries Group (RLG) in the United States for the processing of Chinese, Japanese and Korean ideographic characters.

Unicode is the general name used to refer to the International Standards Organization (ISO) 10646 standard 16-bit code which encompasses the world's principal scripts and has been developed by a consortium involving computer manufacturers such as IBM and Apple, and software developers such as Microsoft, as well as RLG and ISO. A major input device of the 1990s has been the mouse, and its use to 'point and click' at sections of the screen is a common feature of current computer systems. Scanners can also be attached to PCs to input images or graphics. Laser scanners are used to input the information from barcodes on books and borrower cards in circulation systems or from journal issues for serials control systems.

Video scanners can be used as input devices so that a videoconference can be set up over linked PCs with the participants able to see each other, or for medical diagnoses. Touch-sensitive screens allow the user to point directly at, for instance, a particular option from a menu of possibilities displayed. The traditional medium for storing data is based on magnetic materials. Most PCs have a hard disk which is in a sealed cartridge that contains the read/write heads. The capacity of hard disks has increased greatly over the years from about 5 MB in 1980 to as high as 2.5 GB in 1996 (a Gigabyte, or GB, is equal to 1,000 MB). Data can also be input and output on to floppy disk and most workstations have a floppy disk drive capable of reading and writing 3.5 inch diameter disks. Optical storage media have become increasingly popular in recent years and many PCs now have an integral CDROM reader. The price of CDROM technology has dropped dramatically over recent years owing mainly to the popularity of CDROM as the medium for games and entertainment products. The most common output device is the screen or monitor. Many monitors now do not just display text information but can also display the complex graphics and video that have appeared for games in the home computer market, and are also used in multimedia CDROMs.

Speakers can be attached to deliver sound linked to images on the screen so that, for instance, Nelson Mandela's voice or the national anthem of Estonia can easily be heard when using Encarta. Laptop computers use flat screens based on liquid-crystal display technology as this consumes little power. Hard copy printout is still required and there are now many high-quality laser printers available. Again the technology of printers has developed greatly and prices have decreased over the years. Probably the major recent software development for library, information and archive work has been the use of the Windows interface. In the mid-1980s an operating system known as PC-DOS (PC-Disk Operating System) was produced by the American firm Microsoft for IBM to use with its PC.

Many archive and records offices use industry-standard software for their work. Simonson describes the use of general word processing and database management software (that is easily and cheaply available) for archive purposes at the Surrey Record Office in the United Kingdom. He notes that the advent of multimedia computing, networks and the information superhighway places the onus on archivists to find ways of making the information in their custody available electronically. There is also an urgent need for archivists to understand and get involved in the information revolution that is currently taking place, so that a coherent strategy can be developed for managing the electronic archives of the future.

These activities involved the implementation of some form of data communications network. A network used to link equipment over a limited area is known as a local area network or LAN. In many universities around the world there are campuswide LANs that enable students and staff from all over the campus to link to, amongst other things, the library's Online Public Access Catalogue (OPAC). Many libraries and information units have also become involved in providing access to a range of CDROMs via a LAN.

The CDROMs can be attached to a network file server such as SCSI Express. Another approach is to use an optical server which is dedicated to running a group of CDROM drives. Products which provide this facility include CD-Net, CD-Manager and CD-Connection. A final approach, which is beginning to be popular, is to copy the CDROM data to magnetic disks. A major recent advancement in this area has been the development of products such as SilverPlatter's Electronic Reference Library (ERL), which provide the user with a seamless way of accessing CDROM databases, local databases and remote databases.

CDROM has proved to be very useful in many countries. However, bibliographic databases on CDROM do provide users with information on items that may not be accessible locally and so the number of interlibrary loans rises significantly. National or regional networks that link LANs or other computing facilities are known as wide area networks, the major one being the Internet. Often national libraries act as focal points in helping others in a particular country with this activity. The Conference of European National Libraries (CENL) is involved in the development of Gabriel a World Wide Web server—which provides links to sources of information about the services and collections of members of CENL. It developed from work on Web servers carried out at the British Library and the Koninklijke Bibliotheek (KB) in the Netherlands.

The Network of Networks project in Latin America, which is supported by the International Development Research Centre (IDRC), aims to improve the flow of information between eighteen networks in the region by the use of electronic mail, computer conferencing and the distribution of databases on CDROM. Library management (housekeeping) systems typically are integrated packages which include modules for various cataloguing, OPAC, acquisitions, circulation, serials control and interlibrary lending.

Great political changes have taken place in Eastern Europe during the 1990s and this has, amongst other things, opened the market for library systems. Borgman reports on developments related to library automation in Croatia, the Czech Republic, Hungary, Poland, Slovakia and Slovenia. The Regional Library Programme of the Open Society Institute in Budapest, Hungary, was established in 1994 to support, promote and advance the information sciences in Central and Eastern Europe and the Commonwealth of Independent States, and has recommended longterm goals for automated access to library information.

In order to support these goals a series of library automation workshops has been held in various countries of the region. Some of the library housekeeping systems hold records in the Machine-Readable Records (MARC) format whilst others allow for the import and export of MARC-based records. There are a variety of MARC formats available and Campos et al. provide an overview of some of the national MARC formats (for example, CATMARC (Catalonia, Spain) and IndoMARC (Indonesia)) as well as the increasing use of the UNIMARC format.

The concept of an integrated library house-keeping package with the various modules accessing the same bibliographic record is beginning to be replaced by the concept of deintegration, with libraries buying different packages from different suppliers, and mixing and matching to best suit their particular needs. Library house-keeping systems no longer operate in a stand-alone fashion. Libraries which use a system to manage local processing of stock also need to provide their users with access to a range of information services as part of the electronic library; this could include access to networked CDROMs, locally loaded databases, the Internet and so on. The chosen system provides traditional library management functions as well as access to networked CDROMs, local databases, the Internet and (for a trial period) access to OCLC FirstSearch databases.

Some software producers organize for local agents to supply the necessary training and maintenance functions of support. If local support for Western software is poor and/or very expensive there is an argument for the development of local software; examples include the SISPUKOM library management software developed within Malaysia and the INGRID system, based on Informix, developed at Tartu University Library in Estonia. For many years a range of software has been available specifically aimed at information storage and retrieval of textbased information. Examples of such software include BRS/Search, CAIRS, CDS/ ISIS, Cardbox Plus, HeadFast, IdeaList and InMagic. CDS/ISIS is very widely used all over the world as it is available free of charge to nonprofit organizations in UNESCO Member States and exists in a number of language versions. A regular feature on CDS/ISIS is included in Information Development.

For many years textretrieval software was used to process bibliographic data, but recent developments in storage technologies have meant that this software can now be used also for fulltext retrieval purposes. The producers of this software have continued to develop their products and many now run under Windows, can deal with graphical data as well as text data and can be used when creating local CDROMs.

Geographic information systems (GIS) software comprises tools for the collection, analysis, retrieval and display of spatial information. Technologies that integrate the management and analysis of this type of data (from maps, weather satellites and so on) are being used in a variety of ways for environmental studies, global change research, transportation planning, urban planning, marine studies, and so on. As with bibliographic data, there is a need to share resources worldwide and the MARC format is being investigated as one possible solution.

In the United Kingdom the Joint Information Systems Committee (JISC) of the funding bodies for higher education has organized the establishment of centralized databases for the academic community. By charging a university a fixed annual fee, searching becomes 'free at point of use' for researchers, teaching staff and students. The rise in the use of the Internet has been accompanied by the development of commercial, consumeroriented online services. The technique adopted was to provide the searcher with a menu of options on the screen so that an appropriate option could be selected which would then lead to another set of options or to the data. On the positive side, menus can be self-explanatory, easy for the novice searcher and give a structure to the search. However, they may be slow to work through and irritating for frequent searchers. With the major move to a Windows environment, many producers of search systems are developing their software to work in Graphical User Interface (GUI) mode.

When a screen of potentially clickable items is presented it is not always obvious to the novice searcher where to go next in this two-dimensional environment and so there are many aspects of screen design that need to be borne in mind by the interface developer. Schneiderman outlines eight golden rules for any designer of a search interface. Most retrieval software is based on the user combining chosen terms or phrases using the standard Boolean operators AND, OR, NOT in the search statement.

Issues in Web Archiving

The Web is written in 220 languages (although 78 percent of it is in English) by authors from every nation. Ninety-five percent of Web pages are publicly accessible, a collection 50 times larger than the texts collected in the Library of Congress (LC), making the Web the information source of first resort for millions of readers. Nonetheless, the Web is still less than 10 years old, and the economic, social, and intellectual innovation it is causing is just beginning. The Web is growing quickly, adding more than 7 million pages daily. At the same time, it is continuously disappearing. The average life span of a Web page is only 44 days, and 44 percent of the Web sites found in 1998 could not be found in 1999. Web pages disappear every day as their authors revise them or servers are taken out of service, but users become aware of this only when they enter a Universal Resource Locator (URL) and receive a "404-Site Not Found" message.

As ubiquitous as the Web seems to be, it is also ephemeral, and much of today's Web will have disappeared by tomorrow. The implication is clear: if we do not act to preserve today's Web, it will disappear. In the past, important parts of our cultural heritage have been lost because they were not archived-in part because past generations did not, or could not, recognize their historic value. This is a cultural problem. In addition, past generations did not address the technical problem of preserving storage media-nitrate film, videotape, vinyl recordings-or the equipment to play them. They did not solve the economic problem of finding a business model to support new media archives, for in times of innovation the focus is on building new markets and better technologies. Finally, they did not solve the legal problem of creating laws and agreements to protect copyrighted material yet at the same time allow for its archival preservation. The very pace of technical change makes it difficult to preserve digital media. How many people can retrieve documents from old word processing diskettes or even find yesterday's e-mail?

All documents follow a life cycle from valuable to outdated, but then, perhaps, some become historically important. Archivists often rescue boxes of documents as they are being transported from the attic on their way to the dump. But the Web is not stored in attics; it just disappears. For this reason, conscious efforts at preservation are urgent. The hard questions are how much to save, what to save, and how to save it. Every new technology takes a few generations to become stable, so we do not think to preserve the hardware and software necessary to read old documents. Digital documents are particularly vulnerable, since the very pace of technical progress continuously makes the hardware and software that contain them outmoded.

A Web archive must solve the technical problems facing all digital documents as well as its own unique problems. First, information must be continuously collected, since it is so ephemeral. Second, information on the Web is not discrete; it is linked. Consequently, the boundaries of the object to be preserved are ambiguous. Who has the responsibility for collecting and preserving the Web and the resources to do so? The economic problem is acute for all archives. Since their mission is to preserve primary documents for centuries, the return on investment is very slow to emerge, and it may be intangible hence hard to measure. Archives serve the public interest in the very long run, with immediate benefits for only a few scholars. For this reason, they tend to be small and specialized. However, a Web archive will require a large initial investment for technology, research and development, and training-and must be built to a fairly large scale if it is continuously to save the entire Web. New intellectual property laws concerning digital documents have been optimized to develop a digital economy, thus the rights of intellectual property holders are emphasized. Copyright holders have reason for caution, because the technology is so new and the long-term implications of new laws are unknown.

Although the Web is popularly regarded as a public domain resource, it is copyrighted; thus, archivists have no legal right to copy the Web. And yet it is not preservation that poses an economic threat, it is access to archives that might damage new markets. Finding a balance between preservation and access is the most urgent problem to be solved, because if today's Web is not saved it will not exist in the future. When one is building a Web archive these problems translate into three questions: What should be collected? How do we preserve its authenticity? How do we preserve or build the technology needed to access and preserve it? Ultimately, the scope and scale of a Web archive will be determined by the definition of the digital object to be collected-the "Web page." This is not a simple matter. From a user's point of view, a Web page is the image called forth by placing a URL address into a Web reader. This operational definition is necessary but not sufficient, for an archive also must be sure that the document is translated in an authentic manner. In this case, authenticity means that the document must both include the context and evoke the experience of the original. The average Web page contains 15 links to other pages or objects and five sourced objects, such as sounds or images. For this reason, the boundaries of the digital object are ambiguous.

If a Web page is the answer to a user's query, a set of linked Web pages sufficient to provide an answer must be preserved. From this perspective, the Web is like a reference library; that is, it is the totality of the reference materials in which a user might search for an answer. If so, the object to be preserved might include everything on the Web on a given subject at a given point in time, for example, the 2000 election or the World Trade Center terrorist attack. None of these possibilities would be easy to realize, for the Web is not a fixed collection of artifacts. Today, the "surface" Web contains all of the static hypertext markup language (HTML) pages that can be accessed by URLs. Some of the surface Web, especially in the commercial sector, requires passwords or encryption keys; this area might be called the "private" Web. To archive these Web pages would require permission of the owners. The private Web is often encased in security protection services that make copying and preservation doubly difficult. Beyond these problems, surface Web pages are often generated on the fly, customized on demand from databases in the "deep" or "dark" Web.

The deep Web is estimated to be 500 times larger than the surface Web. It includes huge data sources and software code that provides information services for surface Web pages on the fly. The deep Web is the information architecture that produces what we read on the surface; the surface itself exists only as long as a reader is using it. This deep Web cannot easily be archived, since the data are guarded by technical protection services. It is also potentially protected by privacy concerns, since if Amazon.com owns a profile of one's use of information, it is not necessarily available for archiving without his/her consent. Here there are not only tensions between markets and archives but also conflicts between privacy concerns and the interest of history. The ambiguous boundaries of Web objects are also problematic because they are compounds of design elements, including texts, pictures, graphics, digital sound, movies, and code-the list expands as innovation continues. Each of these elements has intellectual property rights attached to it, although they are rarely marked and sometimes impossible to trace. Yet, at least in principle, a digital archive would have to have permission from each of these rights holders. In the words of the US National Research Council's report, The Digital Dilemma: Intellectual Property in the Information Age, "for the digital world, one must sort out and clear rights, even of ephemera".

Even if the Web page could be copied technically and we knew what we wanted to preserve, Web pages are protected by copyright law. Even now there are sophisticated debates about how a Web archive should collect data: Should the default be that copyrighted information is collected and the owner has to opt out; or should it not be collected or disclosed unless the owner actively gives permission ("opts in")? This is a question that may be resolved by legislation or the courts. It is important to remember that the Web is a global document; consequently, there are likely to be many jurisdictions making laws and rules, and enforcement across national borders will be difficult without treaty agreements.

Defining the boundaries of the object to be collected also requires decisions about authenticity and provenance. These decisions must be recorded as part of the archive; the preservation community calls this kind of information "metadata," or information about information, and often builds records of what is in the collection using these metadata. A standard way of recording the metadata must be created to record the historical and technical context in which the document(s) were found. Technologies to reproduce the Web object-however defined-must be preserved, including the hardware and software necessary to access the information in an authentic context or to recreate it. This is difficult in the best of cases. Have we authentically preserved a computer game if we preserve only the graphics, or must we preserve the look and feel of the game in use? Every solution changes the context of information in ways that affect its authenticity. One strategy tries to preserve the original equipment; another uses contemporary technology to emulate the original "look and feel" of the information in use; still another migrates the digital signal to new storage media.

Migration is not just a technical problem. Storage media for digital documents are not yet stable for long-term preservation. Magnetic storage media such as tape and discs eventually deteriorate. Moreover, hardware and software eventually become obsolete, hence very expensive to preserve and operate. A Web archive must migrate from one technical environment to another as generations of technology succeed one another. Nevertheless, under today's law such migration could be a violation of copyright law because it involves copying the signal from one medium to another. These problems are typical of those that occur in the early stages of every innovation, when getting to market quickly is more important than is perfecting the product. Digital information products are not designed for longevity, and even if they were, it is likely they would become obsolete quickly.

As a consequence, the technologies of digital preservation are complex and expensive. The problems are understood far better than are the solutions at this point, but it is already clear that a Web archive will require substantial investment in technological infrastructure and technical research and development, and that commercial entities are unlikely to lead this effort unless there is short term economic value in doing so. Both archives and libraries collect, organize, preserve, and provide access to the documentary record. The distinguishing function of archives is to preserve the integrity of documents for the long run. Preservation for centuries invariably requires new technologies; hence, the Council on Library and Information Resources and other organizations are investigating long-term storage and migration of data.

While the technical problem of preservation is difficult, it is well understood. The problem of access, by contrast, involves legal and economic issues that have not yet been adequately explored. While print archives provide a useful model, the economic and legal environments surrounding print are quite different from those surrounding digital documents.

Inevitably, a Web archive will be a new kind of organization, one that responds to the problems and interests surrounding the Web. It may not be a place at all-it may be a function distributed among institutions over many locations on a global network. The starting point for building a Web archive is to envision organizational strategies to manage this process. Two organizational strategies are emerging-one from the archival and library professions and the other from computer scientists. These strategies are not opposites and are not mutually exclusive, but contrasting them helps frame the strategic choices. An archival catalogue supports high-quality collections built around select themes, saving only the Web sites judged to have potential historical significance or special value, and describing these special qualities in collection records and catalogues that could be searched. This is a fundamental debate about the nature of the Web as a technical object as well. The librarian tends to look at the content of the Web page as the object to be described and preserved.

Digital technology poses new threats and problems as well as new opportunities. Its functionality comes with complexity. Anyone with a compass could theoretically set up or repair a sundial. A digital watch is more useful and accurate for telling time than a sundial, but few people can repair it or even understand how it works. Reading and understanding information in digital form requires equipment and software, which is changing constantly and may not be available within a decade of its introduction. Even newer technology such as 9-track tape is rapidly becoming obsolete. Rapid changes in the means of recording information, in the formats for storage, and in the technologies for use threaten to render the life of information in the digital age as, to borrow a phrase from Hobbes, "nasty, brutish and short." Some information no doubt deserves such a fate, but numerous examples illustrate the danger of losing valuable cultural memories that may appear in digital form.

A large portion of the selected records, however, resided on tapes that the Bureau could read only with a UNIVAC type II-A tape drive. By the mid-seventies, that particular tape drive was long obsolete, and the Census Bureau faced a significant engineering challenge in preserving the data from the UNIVAC type II-A tapes. By 1979, the Bureau had successfully copied onto industry-standard tapes nearly all the data judged then to have long-term value. Though largely successful in the end, the data rescue effort was a signal event that helped move the Committee on the Records of Government six years later to proclaim that "the United States is in danger of losing its memory."

In 1964, the first electronic mail message was sent from either the Massachusetts Institute of Technology, the Carnegie Institute of Technology or Cambridge University. The message does not survive, however, and so there is no documentary record to determine which group sent the pathbreaking message. Satellite observations of Brazil in the 1970s, critical for establishing a time-line of changes in the Amazon basin, are also lost on the now obsolete tapes to which they were written. Similarly, in the late 1960s, the New York State Department of Commerce and Cornell University undertook the Land Use and Natural Resources Inventory Project (LUNR).

The LUNR project produced a computerized map of New York State depicting patterns of land usage and identifying natural resources. It created a primitive geographic information system by superimposing a matrix over aerial photographs of the entire state and coding each cell according to its predominant features. In the mid-1980s, the New York State Archives obtained copies of the tapes containing the data from the LUNR inventory along with the original aerial photographs and several thousand mylar transparencies.

The LUNR project had depended on customized software programs to represent and analyze the data, and these programs were not saved with the data. Even if the software had been retained, the hardware and operating system needed to run the software were no longer available. As a consequence, researchers wishing to study changes in land use patterns now have to re-digitize the data from the hard-copy base maps and transparencies at the State Archives or rekey data from printouts at Cornell's Department of Manuscripts & University Archives. Today, information technologies that are increasingly powerful and easy to use, especially like those that support the World Wide Web, have unleashed the production and distribution of digital information. Such information is penetrating and transforming nearly every aspect of our culture. If we are effectively to preserve for future generations the portion of this rapidly expanding corpus of information in digital form that represents our cultural record, we need to understand the costs of doing so and we need to commit ourselves technically, legally, economically and organizationally to the full dimensions of the task. Failure to look for trusted means and methods of digital preservation will certainly exact a stiff, long-term cultural penalty. Preserving or archiving digital information is not a new one and has been explored at a variety of levels over the last five decades. Archivists responsible for governmental and corporate records have been acutely aware of the difficulties entailed in trying to ensure that digital information survives for future generations. Far more than their library colleagues, who have continued to collect and organize published materials primarily in paper form, archivists have observed the materials for which they are responsible shift rapidly from paper objects produced on typewriters and other analog devices to include files created in word processor, spreadsheet and many other digital forms. Early attention to the difficulties in preserving digital information focused on the longevity of the physical media on which the information is stored.

Even under the best storage conditions, however, digital media can be fragile and have limited shelf life. Moreover, new devices, processes and software are replacing the products and methods used to record, store, and retrieve digital information on breathtaking cycles of 2- to 5- years. Given such rates of technological change, even the most fragile media may well outlive the continued availability of readers for those media.

Efforts to preserve physical media thus provide only a short-term, partial solution to the general problem of preserving digital information. Indeed, technological obsolescence represents a far greater threat to information in digital form than the inherent physical fragility of many digital media. In the face of rapid technological obsolescence and to overcome the problem of media fragility, archivists have adopted the technique of "refreshing" digital information by copying it onto new media. Copying from medium to medium, however, also suffers limitations as a means of digital preservation. Refreshing digital information by copying will work as an effective preservation technique only as long as the information is encoded in a format that is independent of the particular hardware and software needed to use it and as long as there exists software to manipulate the format in current use. Otherwise, copying depends either on the compatibility of present and past versions of software and generations of hardware or the ability of competing hardware and software product lines to interoperate. In respect of these factors—backward compatibility and interoperability—the rate of technological change exacts a serious toll on efforts to ensure the longevity of digital information. Digital information today is produced in highly varying degrees of dependence on particular hardware and software. Jeff Rothenberg, for example, has recently suggested that there may be sufficient demand for entrepreneurs to create and archive emulators of software and operating systems that would allow the contents of digital information to be carried forward and used in its original format.

Refreshing digital information by copying it from medium to medium and the possibility of maintaining a complex set of emulators describe two distinct points on a continuum of approaches to preserving digital information. However, neither refreshing nor emulation sufficiently describes the full range of options needed and available for digital preservation. Instead, a better and more general concept to describe these options is migration. Migration is the periodic transfer of digital materials from one hardware/software configuration to another, or from one generation of computer technology to a subsequent generation. The purpose of migration is to preserve the integrity of digital objects and to retain the ability for clients to retrieve, display, and otherwise use them in the face of constantly changing technology.

References

Gilleland-Swetland, A. (2000). "Setting the Stage." In Introduction to Metadata: Pathways to Digital Information, M. Baca (ed.) [Online]. Available: http://www.getty.edu/research/institute/standards/intrometadata/2_articles/index.html

Keller, M.A., Reich, V.A. and Herkovic, A.C. (2003), 'What is a library anymore, anyway?', *First Monday*, 8.5, May 2003, http://firstmonday.org/issues/issue8_5/keller/index.html

Lorie, R.A. (2002), *A Methodology and System for Preserving Digital Data.* Proceedings of the Second ACM/IEEE- CS joint conference on Digital Libraries, Portland, Oregon, USA.

Preservation Metadata and the OAIS Information Model. A Metadata Framework to Support the Preservation of Digital Objects.A Report by the OCLC/RLG Working Group on Preservation Metadata, June 2002, http://www.oclc.org/research/pmwg/pm_framework.pdf

3

Emerging Trends in Information Archiving

Digital libraries are organizations that provide the resources, including the specialized staff, to select, structure, offer intellectual access to, interpret, distribute, preserve the integrity of, and ensure the persistence over time of collections of digital works so that they are readily and economically available for use by a defined community or set of communities.

The mission of libraries has long been to acquire information, organize it, make it available and preserve it. This has been their significant, distinctive and successful role with print and other artifactual materials for the past several hundred years. Most libraries are now trying to provide an ever-increasing volume of scholarly electronic information to their clienteles. Research libraries have taken on the provision, organization and preservation of information with the same long-term commitment made for print materials. It is an expensive, uncharted and difficult task.

Until the long-term commitments are undertaken, many current digital proposals will have only temporary effects. Cataloguing of networked resources will necessarily remain tentative until the objects being catalogued have a permanent network presence, whether at fixed or virtual locations. Otherwise the cataloguing that points to them will itself have an ephemeral quality. Similarly, the expensive products of recent valuable digitizing demonstration projects, from microfilm to digital form and vice versa, will be at risk after only a few years if tools and commitments are not in place for the preservation of what has been achieved.

Most important, the ability of the scholarly community to give serious weight to electronic information depends upon its trust in such information being dependably available, with authenticity and integrity maintained. Changes in scholarly publishing that might alleviate the serials crisis, for example, are bound up with the prestige of electronic journals in the academic tenure process. The ability of the academy to count on long-term, secure existence of electronic scholarly work will be an important determinant of the success of academic electronic publishing. Libraries and universities have a stake in helping electronic publishing to succeed, and therefore have an interest in establishing secure, persistent and authoritative digital research libraries. Users' needs will continue to be what they long have been. Users will want information reliably locatable, so that when they go there they can expect to find what they're looking for. Users will expect information to be available that was placed in the library's care a long time ago; and they will expect that the integrity of the information they get from the library will be assured.

The requirements of digital technologies will change the way most librarians work throughout research libraries. As it happens, professional librarians are uniquely qualified to take up the technological challenge. But if they do not, they will contribute to the stagnation of their own profession as well as fail in their professional responsibility to civilization. Preservation" in libraries has until now been a matter of preserving the artifact which provides the work inherent in it, thereby preserving the work itself. Electronic documents, by contrast, force the preservation considerations to divide into two: the preservation of the objects, as before, but also the preservation of the information contained in those objects and which is now so easily separable from them.

The primary requirement for a digital research library is that from the start it be committed to organizing, storing and providing electronic information for periods of time longer than human lives. Implementation of a digital research library will require that specific tasks be accomplished and that several commitments be undertaken.

Current Trends

The progress in digital archiving was strikingly international, and it was unevenly distributed around the globe. Trends in major developed nations are described below.

United States: Activity in the United States contrasts with that of Australia and the UK in that there seem to be several loci of activity which don't seem to have much relation to each other. Nor are any of them are very explicit as to what they are about. First, it is important to note that the substantially-funded NSF Digital Libraries projects have focused primarily on large data base construction and on social implications. Emphasis is always on "innovative applications"; archiving is mentioned in passing, but so far not funded.

The Digital Libraries Federation (DLF) has now been in existence for several years, but remains opaque to external observers. A coalition of about 20 libraries, it has developed some brief broad strategic outlines of proposed activity but has been silent as to actual projects within member libraries. In early DLF statements digital archiving was listed as one of three main priorities; more recently it is an "other" priority, with pre-eminent place given to user authentication and authorization matters. Don Waters, the primary author of the important 1996 report from RLG and the Commission on Preservation and Access, has been the DLF director since 1997.

The ARCHES (Archival Server) project, begun in 1996, is specifically intended by Research Libraries Group (RLG) to address digital archiving. In its first instance it is intended both to support a specific repository and to create a software environment that will make long-term archiving possible. Details of the digital archival commitment being made by the project are unclear, and in its beginnings the project appears to have been subordinated to the specific content respository created for it on marriage and law in the 19th century.

OCLC—the largest library utility—is well placed to create and provide archiving services, for it has readily available both the financial and intellectual capital to do so. In 1997 it committed to archiving e-journals on behalf of its members subscribers and bravely included a commitment to technological migration. However it has remained silent on details of how it intends to achieve this goal, and has not yet had to come through with this commitment in any specific instance. Also, it has included the statement that it will migrate digital objects "at its discretion," presumably depending upon the degree of difficulty. Though in practice perhaps such a statement is always implied, its unqualified emphasis so early does not add to the confidence one wishes in such a project.

United Kingdom: The Follett Commission of 1993 stimulated electronic library ("eLib") activity on a broad front in the UK, supported by millions of pounds annually and managed by the Joint Information Systems Committee (JISC) of the Higher Education Funding Councils. After several national workshops on digital archiving, in 1997 JISC inaugurated a specific program through CEDARS (CURL Exemplars in Digital Archives, where CURL is the Council of University Research Libraries of the UK). The present author is a member of this project's advisory board. The CEDARS participants comprise Cambridge, Leeds and Oxford Universities.

The main deliverables of the project will be recommendations and guidelines as well as practical, robust and scalable models for establishing distributed digital archives. It is expected that the outcomes of CEDARS will influence the development of legislation for legal deposit of electronic materials and feed directly into the emerging national strategy for digital preservation currently being developed through the National Preservation Office of the British Library.

Another JISC-funded eLib project is the Arts and Humanities Data Service, which has responded to specific requests of JISC's Digital Archiving Working Party by developing strategic policy framework statements for creating and preserving digital collections.

Canada: The Canadian Initiative on Digital Libraries began work in 1997, but to date has shown little emphasis on digital archiving. On the other hand, many Canadian libraries are members of USA consortia (e.g. OCLC and RLG) whom they may count upon to act in their behalf.

The commonwealth tradition of national planning and initiative appears in strong contrast to the fragmented, non-governmental activities in North America. It remains to be seen which approach will generate the optimal and broadly exploited archiving technologies that are needed. However one can wish from the outset that the USA groups were more communicative about what they are doing, and in particular that they would coordinate their efforts with one another; to date there is little evidence that they do so. But it is notable that regardless of where digital archiving investigation is going on, it is in consortial activity. There is uniform recognition that digital archiving is not a matter soluble by individual institutions, whether for collection reasons or for technological reasons.

Australia: Work in Australia originated in 1993 on an explicitly national basis, with funding both from the government and from the national library. It can be described as a top-down approach, aiming first at principles and goals before proceeding to implementation. PADI (Preserving Access to Digital Information) is headed by an officer of the National Library of Australia, has an office and a budget and has developed statements of vision, goals and objectives. PADI maintains strong links between the library and archive communities. Its Statement of Principles on Preservation of Australian Digital Objects reflects an early achievement of national consensus. It has been followed by reports attempting to deal with location of responsibilities, definitions of how digital information is to be preserved, and the likely costs over time of digital archiving.

Scholarly Journal Archiving

Archives serve a variety of different functions in the larger society and even within the smaller scholarly community. Research libraries in particular serve to support education, continuous learning and research for their designated constituents. The focal points of this type of collection are intellectual artifacts generally in textual and graphic formats. An increasingly significant amount of the intellectual content is published and distributed in electronic journals. Archive's specific mission is to:

> Preserve the significant intellectual content of a defined set of electronic journals independent of the form in which that content was originally delivered in order to assure that this content will be accessible to the scholarly community for the indefinite future in a readable format.

Functionally, the archive is designed to render text and still images and other formats as practically possible with no significant loss in intellectual content. The archive reserves the right to freely manipulate the internal format of the manifestation over time as long as the plain meaning of the intellectual content is preserved. In general, archiving takes place at a semantic level, not a syntactic one. This allows the archive to be constructed around the principle of data format migration, rather than access system emulation.

Based on analysis of the e-journal sample and the user survey, Harvard has defined a preliminary list of materials deemed to be in the scope of archival collection and those currently out of scope of the archival collection, and will work with selected publishers to identify which components are available. Deposits will include not only journal articles, but also associated materials (e.g., references, external links, abstracts), author-created supplementary digital files (e.g., datasets, sound files, simulations), other editorial journal content (e.g., editorials, reviews, communications, letters, threaded discussions), and selected masthead information (e.g., editor, editorial board, copyright statement). Materials currently defined as in scope should be deposited, while those defined as out of scope are not expected but may be deposited if available, with the exception of advertising which will not be accepted.

The following components should be deposited in the Archive:

- *Articles*: This includes the text and auxiliary files such as graphics, figures, tables, and/or photographs that constitute the "article proper."
- *Supplementary material/enhanced contents*: When the author has deposited to the publishers digital objects related to the article such as datasets, sound or video files, and/or computer programs — as opposed to pointing to such resources at alternate sites — those materials will be included in the Archive deposit.
- Author supplied references
- Links to external resources
- Abstracts
- Tables of contents
- Placeholder files for non-deposited object
- *Other editorial content:* This includes research, reports, columns, editorials, communications, correspondence, reviews, letters to the editor, and commentaries.
- *Bibliographic descriptions*: This includes formatted metadata describing articles and other editorial content.
- Editorial boards
- Editors
- Threaded discussions
- Copyright statements and information
- Editorial policies
- Reviewer lists
- Journal descriptions
- Cover images from the corresponding print issues

The following types of components are not expected or required for deposit in the archive:

— Information for authors: This includes copyright transfer agreements and guidelines for manuscript preparation and submission.
— Subscription information
— Advertisements
— *Other business information*: This includes reprint ordering information, information for posting advertisements, contact information, and customer service information.
— *Additional information:* This includes career/job information, etc.

Access Issues

One of the criteria to be met by this archive design is to make preserved information available to libraries under conditions negotiated with the publisher. Policies governing access to the Archive must address three questions: who can access the Archive, under what circumstances, and how will access be obtained. Fromearliest discussions about access, it was determined that publishers should deposit materials into an initially dark archive as these materials become available. A dark archive is one that allows no access for routine scholarly use. As a result of some event — a "trigger" event — material in the Archive would be made available to some set of scholarly users resulting in a light archive.

Once the archive has accepted preservation responsibility for deposited material, that content is then subject to periodic auditing to insure the efficacy of the Archive's preservation regimen and of the working of the repository system. Auditing is particularly important for the Archive since it represents the only use of archived content while that content is in its initial dark period prior to the occurrence of a trigger event. The composition of the auditors could be drawn from domain experts, subject area librarians, faculty, and scholarly societies. It remains an open question whether domain expertise is required or practical. However, initial quality control and internal and external auditing are not sufficient to insure the viability of files over time. During the grant year, Harvard had informal discussions with several organizations that gather content from various sources and store that content. Although initial quality control procedures varied, each organization maintains that actual usage is one of the best mechanisms for insuring content viability. The issue an archive must face is whether dark content not used regularly by expert users is an adequate and reliable preservation model.

Authorized Users

Harvard originally proposed that the Archive should initially be semi-dark, permitting access only to Harvard University Library's authorized users through an online process and to any user legitimately authorized by the publisher through a batch export process. Such access would allow for maintenance, auditing, and minimal exercising of the data. The publishing partners had some concerns about this position including:

— the preference for having "real" users access their own embellished systems rather than Harvard's more basic Archive interface;
— the need for monitoring to guard against unauthorized use;
— the reluctance to allow Harvard users to access material that Harvard has archived but not subscribed to or licensed.

During the resulting discussions, Harvard agreed that throughout the dark period the Archive would be accessible only by its operators and by a designated outside auditing authority. Under certain circumstances, archived material might be made available to authorized users who can present proof of their legitimate right to specific materials.

The Harvard University Library Access Management Service (AMS) allows fine granularity of access control, down to the level of permitting access to a particular object by a particular user through the use of a particular application. This level of control is appropriate and practical to support auditing, but expensive to extend to large-scale external use. An archive intending to restrict access to only those who have had a past subscription to the archived content would bear considerable expense to gather the required licensee information and to build and operate the appropriate access management system. Rather than pursue this option, Harvard believed that the increasingly wide-spread adoption of the "moving wall" concept in the scholarly journal environment suggested a more practical approach. After deposit, archived materials would enter an initial "dark" period chronologically bounded by the trigger events defined in the submission agreement. When any one of the trigger events has occurred, material would be accessible without restriction.

Trigger Events

At various times over the planning period, the following possible trigger events were discussed:

1. When material is no longer accessible online from the publisher. This trigger was intended to support the essential "failsafe" function of the Archive, insuring continued access to the scholarly record. After much discussion the provision was modified in several ways. "Material" was replaced with the more specific "volume or time-based unit of the title," recognizing that portions of the electronic run of a journal might have different availability over time. The new wording allows for part of a run to become accessible from an archive when it is no longer available elsewhere. "Accessible online" was modified to "accessible online either from the publisher or from another source as a discrete title." This allowed titles that were transferred from one publisher to another to remain "dark" if other triggers had not occurred. It also protected access to the content through title and issue units, as opposed to having the content buried in an undifferentiated aggregate database. The final form of this trigger was thus: "when a volume or time-based unit of the title is no longer available online either from the publisher or from another source as a discrete title."
2. When the publisher sells or otherwise transfers the rights to publish a given title to another body. Publishers rightfully objected that this meant that titles could not be sold, as the "lightened" content in an archive would greatly reduce the value of the retrospective content. This trigger was dropped in later discussions.
3. When the material has been in the Archive for "n" years. This trigger occasioned the greatest amount of discussion and was not fully resolved during the planning period. It was refined in later discussions slightly to "after a defined amount of time of the publisher's choosing has passed, to be determined by title and volume or time-based unit."
4. When the title ceases to be published. Some publishers objected that a ceased title may still have residual economic value. The provision was dropped from later discussions.
5. When the content enters the public domain.

Trigger events are one of the key provisions of an archiving plan. They define when the preserved content, which someone has made a considerable investment to archive, is useable. Because they touch on areas that affect the commercial value of the content and thus on the publisher's income, publishers are legitimately quite concerned that they be carefully constructed.

All parties to archiving — authors, publishers, archives, subscribing libraries — have an interest in the details of trigger definition.

Economic Issues

Economic issues are paramount in planning for archiving. In the paper environment, many of the costs of archiving are buried in library budgets. Much of what is done to preserve print journals is the same activity needed to provide day to day access to the literature. In the e-journal environment libraries are moving to an architecture which separates archiving from daily service, making archiving costs painfully apparent. Further, it is unlikely the libraries will have or need the same large-scale redundancy in e-journal archiving that they have had for paper journals. It is more likely that the operating costs of archiving will be centered in only a few places, raising obvious issues of how to spread costs fairly. Understandably, economic issues were discussed extensively during the planning year: within Harvard, with its publisher partners, and with other institutions thinking about archiving.

Beginning to understand real costs will be one of the key objectives of any implementation project. It is clear, however, that keeping costs low is enormously important; the magnitude of costs will greatly influence the outcome of the question of who is willing to share in the cost of archiving. Harvard identified some strategies for controlling costs. First, by building an archiving program over a larger digital library environment, activities (preservation monitoring), organization (computer operations), and technical infrastructure (a digital repository) already in place can be used to support the archiving activity. Second, applying smart automation to the process of adding content to the Archive can be used to reduce labor, and thus the cost, of ongoing Archive operation. Third, limiting the functionality of the Archive allows Harvard to eliminate costly development components such as subscription management systems.

Even if an archive is successful in controlling costs, the ultimate question remains "who pays." Some options for support of archiving are inappropriate for Harvard's Archive. The institution will not simply bear the cost of archiving on its own as a national library might. Certainly Harvard would expect to contribute to the cost of archiving, but it will be difficult to convince university administrators that the institution should simply dedicate resources at this level for the common good.

Some have suggested an archive should support itself, at least in part, by providing services others would pay to use based on the archived content.

Harvard has proposed that funding for a sustainable archive accompany the deposit of content from the outset. The model initially proposed was that there be an explicit "archiving surcharge" publishers would charge all institutional subscribers to archived titles that would be passed on to the Archive. The intent of the proposal was that the community that benefits from the Archive also assumes some share of the cost of archiving. Harvard's publisher partners did not want the Archive to dictate pricing policy to them, so this model was modified as follows. The publishers would pay the Archive an annual fee for archiving. They in turn could collect the required funds from any one of a number of sources including authors, sponsoring scholarly societies, or subscribers as appropriate in individual cases. The archiving fee would be composed of two elements:

1. An "ingestion" fee to pay the operating costs of day to day receipt, quality control, and archival preparation of new content.
2. An amount to be added to the Archive endowment to cover the long-term cost of storage and preservation activity. Endowment is a very appealing model to pay for a long-term commitment such as archiving.

Harvard has suggested that if it chooses to cease archiving any given set of materials, this specific content of the Archive would be transferred to another archive selected by agreement between Harvard and a stakeholder community. In addition, an amount of the remaining archiving fund proportional to the amount deposited by each publisher for those e-journal titles would be transferred to the new archiving organization. In the case where a publisher chooses to terminate its relationship with Harvard's Archive, materials that have previously been deposited will remain in the Archive, and deposit of all titles will continue until the current volumes are complete.

Technical Infrastructure

The software and hardware environment for the Archive will rely upon existing technical infrastructure developed by the Harvard University Library over the past three years under the aegis of its Library Digital Initiative.

The core component of this infrastructure is the Digital Repository Service (DRS), an Oracle-based repository for digital objects. Within the

DRS, object content streams are stored along with their associated administrative and structural metadata. The DRS, now in its second production release, currently maintains over 240,000 objects with a total size of 120 gigabytes. The DRS is responsible only for the managed preservation of the objects deposited within it; resource discovery and delivery are handled through independent systems.

Digital objects are delivered out of the DRS through media type-specific delivery applications. Delivery applications are available for simple objects, those atomically composed of a single physical content stream, such as a raster image file; and complex objects, logical aggregations of intellectually or structurally related content streams, such as an electronic monograph structurally delivered in a page turning navigational environment. Additional applications are under development for streaming audio and video media types.

Dependent upon the access rules defined for a particular digital object, delivery applications may make use of the facilities of the Access Management System (AMS) including user authentication, profile, and authorization.

Digital objects stored in the DRS can be given persistent identifiers registered with and resolved by the Name Resolution Service (NRS). NRS identifiers and their resolution mechanism are compatible with IETF recommendations for URNs.

The NRS is composed of two subsystems: an Oracle-based administrative system that maintains the mappings between URNs and URLs, and a THTTP-based resolution server. Archived e-journal components will be named in the NRS at a level of granularity corresponding to that of discovery and delivery, that is, at the issue and item level.

Descriptive metadata useful for resource discovery is contained in catalogue systems external to the DRS. For the purposes of the Archive, title and issue-level descriptive metadata will be stored in HOLLIS, Harvard's Integrated Library System (ILS), searchable through a Web-accessible OPAC. Title-level descriptive information, such as ISSN, publisher, etc., will be captured in MARC bibliographic records, while individual issue-level information, such as chronology, enumeration, etc., will be stored in related holdings records. Issue-level catalogue metadata will also include an actionable link in the form of an NRS persistent identifier to a dynamically generated, issue-specific Web page, providing table-of-contents-like access to individual e-journal issue items. Item-level metadata will be managed in a new item-level catalogue, implemented either as a separate database in the ILS, or as a stand-alone XML database. It will provide a mechanism for search and browsing and will include actionable links to dynamically generated Web pages displaying individual journal items.

Archive Architecture

The design of the Archive was conceived in relation to the OAIS reference model, with its six main archival functions: ingest, data management, archival storage, preservation, access, and administration.

Large portions of the operational aspects of the Archive are amenable to automation, including areas such as publisher registration and profiling, Submission Information Package (SIP) submission, ingest validation at a syntactic level, SIP-to-AIP (Archival Information Package) transformation, archival storage deposit, preservation migration, routine reporting, and handling and responding to access requests. This degree of automation is achievable through a strict requirement of publisher compliance to formal standards for SIPs and the definition of a small set of normative data formats. The resulting uniformity of the Archive input stream and the canonical nature of internal archive storage practices provides the opportunity to rely upon automated systems to perform routine ingest, archival storage, data management, and access functions. Through the collaborative development of community standards, there is good potential for the sharing of common infrastructure components between archiving projects and institutions.

Dependent upon the implementation details of a new ILS currently undergoing installation, serial check-in and claiming operations may also be amenable to automation. The primary remaining tasks that will require manual intervention include ingest validation at a semantic level (the degree to which this is feasible is subject to further investigation); preservation planning, primarily the monitoring of the technical obsolescence of data formats; and ongoing periodic auditing of archived materials.

Ingest

The Ingest function is responsible for accepting and acting upon submissions of material for deposit into the Archive. The technical infrastructure necessary to support the following subtasks within this function are for the most part not currently extant, and their implementation would occupy the majority of the first year of an implementation project.

SIP

From the point of view of a content provider the Archive is opaque with a single defined input interface, the SIP. The structural envelope of the SIP in the Archive is provided by METS (Metadata Encoding & Transmission Standard), a comprehensive XML framework for encapsulating digital objects.

The unit of submission to the Archive is the e-journal issue. Physically, the SIP will take the form of a three-level file system hierarchy corresponding to the e-journal title, issue, and items. The title-level directory is empty and is present only to provide a common structural parent. The issue-level directory contains a METS file encapsulating all issue-level metadata and pointers to issue-level content files and to the item-level directories, each of which in turn has a METS file containing all item-level metadata and pointers to item-level content. Content object technical metadata stored in the METS files provides the necessary representation information to facilitate archival preservation activities and content delivery. A preliminary draft specification of the SIP is undergoing public review and comment

One of the core concepts of the Archive is the use of a common archival item-level schema for articles and "article-like" content. The implications of and many design principles for such a schema are defined in a preliminary feasibility study on the subject, commissioned by Harvard and authored by Inera.

The design of this schema will begin with an investigation of existing common schemas, such as the ISO 12083 and the PubMedCentral Document Type Definitions (DTDs), for possible use as is or as the basis for additional development. If a new schema should be necessary, in whole or in part, the design and documentation of it may be contracted out to an appropriate consultant and developed with coordinated input from the larger community. As will be set out in the Archive submission agreement, when practical it will be the responsibility of content providers to transform their journal content from its internal native form into compliance with the Archive's schema when the publisher has content marked up in SGML or XML. In order to transform content to this schema, participating publishers will need a significant level of internal technical expertise or access to external technical expertise and the resources to implement the transformation workflow. It is clear that not all publishers of scholarly content will have these assets.

Since digital preservation activities are performed on a type-specific basis, minimizing the number of acceptable data formats can reduce the complexity and cost of archive operations. To place this on a formal basis, the Archive will define a small set of preferred normative formats. In general, a single normative format will be defined for each functional category of content: for example, XML for metadata, XML for full-text, TIFF for raster still images, XML/SVG for vector still images, etc. Data submitted in non-normative formats will be transformed upon ingest into an analogous normative format whenever possible without significant loss of intellectual meaning. For example, submitted JPEG files will be transformed into their analogous TIFF representations. Content objects submitted to the Archive in non-normative formats that are not susceptible to transformation into a normative analogue will be accepted, but only under the proviso that they may be preserved only at the bit level — i.e., in the form of the initially deposited bit stream — and that their usefulness over time may become problematic.

Long-term archival preservation requires the initial capture of intellectual content at the highest possible resolution, finest possible granularity, and most abstract representation. Additional criteria for the selection of normative formats include open standards, mature and robust technology, long-term viability, prevalence of commercial grade tools, and the potential for instantiated data objects to be created as far upstream as possible in publishers' production processes. The composition of the set of normative formats will undergo periodic review to insure they remain appropriate for archival purposes with regard to continual technological advances.

During Harvard's initial evaluation of the PDF format with regard to its inclusion in the set of archival normative formats, several undesirable characteristics of PDF were discovered. Foremost, perhaps, is the fact that PDF is a proprietary rather than an open standard. Although Adobe has published the specifications, this is a matter of company policy and subject to unpredictable change. The built-in extensibility of PDF allows it to provide a structural envelope into which content can be placed in a variety of base formats. For example, PDF files can be composed partially or entirely of raster page images rather than the actual text. Internal PDF content streams can be formatted or compressed using completely private schemas, some or all of which may be resistant to archival preservation. Also, PDF is most generally encoded in a binary rather than an ASCII form which tends to increase the complexity if not the difficulty of processing.

QUALITY ASSURANCE

Validation and auditing represent two independent phases of quality assurance for material deposited within the Archive. Ingest validation is performed to insure that content submitted for deposit is syntactically correct with respect to the published standards of the Archive. Additionally, validation will attempt to determine the correctness of submitted metadata (e.g., does the ISSN match the journal title and do data files actually conform to their specified formats) and the internal consistency of individual content objects (e.g., are all article bibliographic references correctly associated with the citations in the body of the text). No SIP will be accepted into the Archive until it has successfully passed ingest validation. The responsibility for correcting errors uncovered during ingest validation will rest with the submitting publisher as will be specified in the Archive submission agreement. To lower operating costs and to facilitate the effective scaling of Archive operations, ingest validation will be automated to the fullest extent possible.

Since materials deposited within the Archive will generally be dark with respect to access for some initial period of time, it is important to allocate substantial effort to the validation of the quality of submitted material upon ingest. The difficulty, and thus cost, of the identification and correction of errors in archived journal content will only increase over time.

Harvard will develope tools to perform automated quality assurance (QA) testing at a syntactic level, and as far as practicable, on a semantic level. In addition to the internal use of these tools by the Archive, they will also be made available to content providers for client-side validation prior to submission. Thus, these systems will be implemented with regard to platform independence, and keeping in mind the wide range of technical resources available to potential content providers, ease of installation and use.

Due to the wide variety of publisher production workflows and content management systems, and the fact that item-level content is submitted to the Archive in a common schema, produced by transformation from its native form, it is important for ingest QA testing also to include semantic level validation. All online content providers rely to a greater or lesser extent upon the high degree of domain expertise of their users in detecting semantic errors.

Harvard's approach to this problem is to move semantic validation to the level of copy-editing. Within the SIP, content providers are asked to provide a rendered version of all item-level content in a standard page description format, derived from the provider's internal native form of the content which is presumed to be authoritative. After SIP ingest, a rendered version of the item-level content is derived from the Archive's common schema version of that content. Proofreading between these two versions will suffice to detect semantic errors. The scope and selection of material that is validated in this manner will be adjusted over time with regard to the detected error rate, perhaps on a publisher and title basis.

Descriptive Information

After SIP validity has been confirmed, issue and item-level descriptive metadata is extracted from the issue and item-level METS files of the SIP, and transmitted to the Data Management function for storage and later use in archive administration and resource discovery.

Transformation of SIP to AIP

Following validation and descriptive cataloguing, the individual components of the SIP are transformed into the AIP format for deposit into the DRS in its capacity as the Archival Storage entity. For the most part, SIP components are deposited as is. The METS files are rewritten to include additional internal archive-specific administrative metadata, and to change the references to content files from file references valid within the SIP file system hierarchy to DRS inter-object references. Some of the technical metadata existing in the METS files may be duplicated in internal DRS storage structures in order to facilitate ongoing archive administration and preservation activities.

Data Management

The Data Management function is responsible for maintaining descriptive information about archival holdings and administrative data necessary to the internal management of the Archive. Issue and item-level descriptive metadata is received from the Ingest function. Issue-level metadata is stored in the existing HOLLIS ILS, which includes serial check-in and claiming mechanisms useful to detect and request submission of missing issues. Item-level metadata is stored in a new catalogue, implemented either in the HOLLIS ILS or as a stand-alone XML database application.

Bibliographic control

E-journal content is modeled within the Archive at both an issue level and an item level. Issues are defined loosely as primarily publisher-specified aggregations of individual items, with some additional issue-level, and generally non-citable, content such as masthead, editorial board, cover image, etc. Items are defined as indivisible pieces of citable content such as articles, editorials, reviews, letters, errata, etc. For purposes of internal administration of the Archive as well as for end-user content discovery and delivery, bibliographic control of journal content is necessary at both issue and item levels.

This two level modeling scheme is explicitly issue-centric. While Harvard's publishing partners are interested in exploring the modality of issue-less publishing in the future, none of them have indicated that this will occur during the scope of this project.

Naming

Naming is the process of assigning unique, persistent identifiers to resources. Uniqueness insures an unambiguous mapping between an identifier for a resource as described in a discovery service and the instantiation of that resource as delivered to the user. Persistence is required when identifiers for archived content are publicly visible and thus, susceptible to being captured and used in external systems outside the control of the Archive. A "bookmarked" name should always resolve to the correct named content object regardless of the passage of time or changes to the underlying architecture or implementation of the Archive. Within the Archive, naming needs to occur at the level of granularity of the discovery and delivery services, that is, at the issue and item levels.

The Digital Object Identifier (DOI) mechanism is the most widely used naming scheme for electronic journal articles. However, DOIs resolve to resource instantiations defined by the registering body for those DOIs, in this case, by the publishers. Therefore, an article DOI will resolve to that article in the publisher's content delivery service. There is no widely implemented mechanism to interrupt the DOI resolution process and substitute resolution to a local "appropriate copy" such as the Archive. Thus, it is necessary for an Archive-specific identifier to be given to named issue and item-level content components.

The Harvard University Library operates its own Name Resolution Service (NRS), composed of an administrative registry of name-to-URL mappings and a resolution server compliant with established Internet Engineering Task Force (IETF) protocols for Uniform Resource Names (URNs). Syntactically, URNs are always generated with an internal namespace designation to avoid collisions between names assigned by different naming systems. The Harvard namespace, "urn-3," is registered with the Internet Assigned Numbers Authority (IANA). Although NRS names will be used in the Archive discovery and delivery services, Archive metadata for e-journal content objects will also include other public and private identifiers associated with those objects, including DOIs and publisher-specific internal identifiers.

Archival Storage Strategy

Harvard's three publishing partners currently offer 1,137 electronic journals, annually comprising over 210,000 articles with a total size of approximately 400 gigabytes per year. They project relatively modest growth in their electronic offerings over the next five years, with an anticipated increase in titles of three percent per year.

The current storage architecture underlying Harvard's operational Digital Repository Service (DRS) uses NFS-mounted, RAID-based devices as its primary online storage mechanism, with automatic replication over a dedicated T1 network to an off-site tape library which can be mounted as a file system for remote recovery access. The operational policy for the tape library enforces automatic periodic tape refreshment on a five year schedule. The total growth capacity of the current implementation of this system is 50 terabytes. The recovery cost for storage under this system is $20/gigabyte/year.

The current practice of Harvard's publishing partners is to present journal content in the form of static text and visual images. As advanced dynamic media types, such as streaming audio and video, become more prevalent in electronic publishing, the per-issue size requirements of the Archive will increase commensurately.

The Archival Storage function of the Archive is provided by the extant DRS. The DRS batch loading process requires that each physical data stream be available as a separate file, along with an additional XML-encoded control file specifying loading and storage options. This proscribes the form of the AIP within the DRS as the complete set of SIP components with each issue and item-level METS metadata and content file deposited as individual digital objects. The Ingest function is responsible for transforming the SIP into the AIP prior to DRS deposit. After successful deposit of an AIP into the DRS, the Archive will generate and transmit an e-mail message of confirmation to the submitting content provider. The issuance of this confirmation constitutes the formal notice of the archive's assumption of archival responsibility for the deposited material.

Issue and item-level METS metadata files contain internal pointers to their component content files. In addition, the DRS has its own explicit mechanism to maintain typed relationships between individual digital objects stored within it. Thus, issue and item-level METS files will be stored within the DRS with an inter-level parent/child structural relationship. Similarly, METS metadata files and their component content files will be stored with an intra-level parent/child relationship.

Preservation Strategy

Because the purpose of this Archive is to preserve the significant intellectual content of journals — not the original form in which the content was authored or delivered — the Archive will most likely rely upon transformation to prevent obsolescence. As defined by OAIS, transformation refers to "a [type of] digital migration where there is some change in the Content Information or PDI bits while attempting to preserve the full information content."

Files that are proprietary and therefore not amenable to transformation will also be accepted into the Archive, provided they are not essential to the meaning of the journal article. The Archive will accept, store, locate, and deliver these files; the Designated Community would assume responsibility for transformation.

The Archive's preservation policies and management functions are format-specific, envisioned to meet the following objectives:

— to provide a range of preservation services according to what is viable for a given format at a given time
— to monitor and document levels of technology support for file formats in a file format registry that would:
— minimize the amount of technical metadata collected for each object
— promote collaboration among the Archive, industry, and standards bodies with domain expertise to define the "trigger" events to initiate transformation
— to minimize costs with batch processing operations for file validation, monitoring, and transformation
— to promote best practices for authors to create and submit journal articles to publishers

Preservation Planning

The central premise of the Archive's preservation policy is that viable preservation services vary according to the shifting, contemporaneous level of support that data formats enjoy with regard to standards and applications.

Levels of Preservation Service

Preservation planning is an area of active development. Although much more analysis is needed, some key distinctions have emerged in considering the technical and operational implications of assuming responsibilities to monitor obsolescence and to migrate data. Harvard's expectation is that the Archive will offer multiple levels of service in which the highest level represents the Archive's commitment to monitor formats and associated technologies, to develop and execute migration strategies that attempt to preserve all of the format's native functions and semantic integrity, and to disseminate files (e-journal components) in formats that can be rendered by contemporary applications.

The Archive will provide the highest level of preservation service for a limited set of preferred normative formats as discussed previously. Objects submitted in non-normative formats are expected to fall into two categories: those that can be transformed upon ingest into an analogous normative format and those that cannot. Objects in this latter category will receive fewer services. At a minimum, objects will receive "bitstore service" in which they are refreshed and can be disseminated from the Archive to members of the designated community or to "digital archaeologists" committed to investing the resources needed to re-render the objects with contemporary applications.

Challenges remain to define the terms and conditions in which objects will receive middle levels of preservation service — those that offer more than bitstore, but less than Level One — such as "lossy migration." The Archive's preservation policy will include statements that address how objects are classified upon ingest to receive specified levels of preservation service and what circumstances could lead to the service level being promoted or demoted over time.

Policy Implications

The implication of instituting a preservation policy with multiple service levels is that all objects associated with an e-journal item can be deposited to, and accepted by, the Archive, but those integral to the item's semantic meaning should when at all possible be deposited in normalized, repository-compliant formats for full preservation service.

Access

The Access function encompasses both e-journal resource discovery and delivery. Discovery takes place at the title and issue level through the existing Web-accessible HOLLIS OPAC. Actionable issue-level links provide users with a table-of-contents-like view of all individual issue items. Actionable item-level links from the table-of-contents-like issue display and from search result records in the item-level catalogue provide users with access to individual issue items. XML-encoded full-text content items are dynamically transformed into HTML using XSLT. Other item content media types are delivered via the appropriate DRS delivery applications.

Rather than browsing or searching these Archive catalogues for relevant content, a user may possess a priori appropriate citation information for the desired content, such as author and title, chronology and enumeration, or a DOI uniquely identifying an item. A valid access request to the Archive can be made by using this citation information in a properly formed OpenURL which encodes the citation data into an actionable URL. The Archive will implement an OpenURL service to accept such requests and respond with the appropriately displayed item.

Access authorization is a binary function. During the initial dark period following submission, e-journal content is available only to Archive staff for internal administrative and maintenance purposes, and to auditors as described in the Administration function. Once content is lit up in consequence of an appropriate trigger event, that content is available to the general public. Authorization is enforced only at the point at which the delivery of actual issue or item-level content is requested; cataloguing metadata for all content is always available to the public.

Delivery of raw e-journal issue data can be requested and returned as an OAIS Dissemination Information Package (DIP). At least one form of the DIP should be equivalent to a Submission Information Package (SIP) so that a DIP delivered from a compliant archive can be ingested directly by another archive. The Archive will consider support for additional standard DIP formats as they emerge in the future. For the wholesale batch dissemination of archived content, that content will be transformed from its internal Archival Information Package (AIP) form to a DIP. The handling of and response to requests for a DIP will be an off-line, asynchronous operation. It is highly desirable that the archiving community cooperates in the development of standard definitions of the DIP to facilitate the transformation of archival materials between participating institutions.

Administration

The Administration function is responsible for the routine operation of the Archive. A good deal of this work is manual, not automated, including the negotiation of submission agreements with content providers, supervision of the Archive staff, and the maintenance and enhancement of the Archive's technical environment and infrastructure. Nonetheless, these manual procedures will be supported by systems providing administrative database services, online registration of content provider profile information, and hardware and software monitoring tools.

The major automated task of this function is the performance of required format migrations as instigated by the Preservation Planning function. The Archive's adherence to the internal use of a limited set of normative Level One data formats constrains what would otherwise be a potentially intractable undertaking into a feasible task.

Although extensive content quality assurance occurs upon Ingest, subsequent periodic auditing of archived material will also be carried out to validate the lossless nature of migration transformations as well as the general stability of the Archive's storage environment. This auditing will occur under the purview of the Administration function by domain experts drawn from publishers, scholarly societies, and librarians. Statistical sampling of the Archive's holdings categorized by publisher, subject area, and title will be employed in the selection of material to ensure appropriate representative coverage in the auditing process.

Schedule

A fair number of issues remain to be resolved. In order to fully test the model for the Archive and to get a better understanding of the real costs involved in operating the Archive, Harvard believes it is necessary to build and run the Archive long enough to gather experience.

Responsibilities of the Archive Staff

The primary responsibilities of the Archive staff with regard to technical issues are the initial development, ongoing maintenance, and future enhancement of Archive systems. Additionally, the expertise of the staff will be helpful in monitoring technical innovation and obsolescence with regard to normative data formats and potential preservation migration transformations. This activity would be performed in cooperation with the Archive preservation manager and collection curators. All technical work will be performed using accepted industry standards and processes for technical management, design, implementation and testing methodologies, configuration management, and documentation.

The Archive architecture relies heavily on efficiencies achieved by compliance to common standards, e.g., SIP structure and the archival schema. Widespread compliance is best achieved by insuring that these standards are developed in an open collaborative process. Archive staff will be responsible for the coordination of these processes and the resultant timely publication of appropriate specifications.

Archive Content Development

Harvard's initial approach to archiving has been "publisher based," that is, oriented towards archiving all of the e-journal output of a publisher. This approach was chosen for two reasons. First, it simplifies the task of creating a large base of archival activity to test systems and operations, and to provide enough scale on which to base long-term cost projections. Second, the marginal cost of archiving another title from a publisher with whom the issues of interoperation have already been worked out would be less than taking a new title from a new publisher. The cost of archiving a title could thus be lowered.

Curatorial Responsibilities

In traditional preservation, curators are responsible for ensuring that collections remain usable. While they may store collections in centralized, environmentally-controlled storage facilities, or partner with conservators and preservation technologists to repair or copy materials, curators are ultimately fully responsible to account for the extent, condition, and usability of their collections.

The inherent fragility and complexity of digital collections require a shift in preservation responsibilities. To ensure that items do not become obsolete, curators and other owners need to delegate preservation responsibilities to technical staff with the expertise and the tools. In this new model, preservation technologists assume perpetual rather than temporary custody of the physical objects in their care. They must monitor the items as well as the environment.

Because obsolescence is inevitable for all digital formats, they must be able to develop and present migration strategies to the curators and owners, then implement the strategy the owner prefers. In traditional preservation, curators have ongoing custodial responsibility and preservation technologists intervene infrequently. In the preservation model for digital archiving, repository managers assume the ongoing custodial responsibility and curators are consulted as necessary to make decisions about migration and other issues.

Role of Stakeholders

Discussion among Harvard and its publishing partners has centered on who "owns" the Archive and who governs it. While the Archive is intended to be maintained and administered by Harvard and built on Harvard's existing digital library infrastructure, the publishing partners have suggested that a broader group with a vested interest should be involved. Who are the stakeholders and what is their role in helping the Archive do its job? This community could comprise authors, scholarly societies, publishers, and institutional subscribers as representatives of researchers. These delegated stakeholder groups should have a role in reviewing the policies and practices of the Archive as a mechanism for vetting the Archive and establishing a level of trust; however, some publishing partners have suggested that actual governance of the Archive is tied to the brightness of the Archive and the additional services that might be offered by the Archive. The brighter the Archive, the more governance a publisher should have; the more services offered, the more governance a publisher should have. Harvard, however, maintains that final governing authority is intrinsically tied to the ability to use its existing infrastructure as a starting point for the Archive, while a variety of policies and procedures related to the development, administration, ongoing maintenance, and financing of the Archive should be developed in consultation with and open for review and comment by representatives of this stakeholder community.

The Archival Community

In addition to the stakeholder community with its representative input, there is the necessity for an external auditing service. Such a service might be part of a broader confederation of archival organizations and stakeholders. Such a confederacy might be charged with establishing registries for content and format types; certifying policies, practices and procedures; and supporting the ongoing development of digital archiving.

Sharable Infrastructure

During the development of the Archive several pieces of sharable infrastructure will be produced:

- Format registry to provide a centralized store for relevant information about data formats supported by the Archive.
- SIP/DIP specifications. Community-wide agreement on these specifications will allow the free interchange of archived materials between archiving institutions and projects.
- Issue-level content schema to capture issue-level information such as masthead, editorial board, etc.
- Canonical item-level schema designed to accommodate the Archive's need for homogeneous content and allow a clean transformation path from publishers' native content formats.
- METS Java toolkit for API-level support for the procedural construction, validation, and serialization/deserialization of syntactically valid METS files.

— SIP Quality Control tool.

— XLST stylesheets for issue and item-level display, based on the specifications for the issue and item-level XML schema.

Since the conclusion of Harvard's Mellon-funded planning project, additional work on e-journal archiving has continued. Through the investigation of potential e-journal XML schemas they learned that the National Library of Medicine (NLM) was in the process of revising the document type definition (DTD) used for PubMedCentral (PMC). Since PMC receives content from various publishers, their DTD has to support heterogeneity of document structure, although all the content is within the biomedical discipline. NLM was receptive to their suggestion that the DTD be expanded to support content across academic disciplines.

The main benefits of the DTD suite are:

— It was not created by, not reflects the bias of, any specific publisher, society, typesetter, or aggregator

— The document analysis covered a wide range of academic disciplines to insure that the DTD is not biased towards any specific intellectual domain

— It is based on public standards, such as the CALS and XHTML table models, MathML, and Unicode

— It is modular and can be modified easily to meet specific needs without undermining either the code structure of the DTD or the interchange of files created according to the DTD

— It was designed so that publishers can easily transform existing content to be compliant with the DTD

Although just recently released, the DTD suite is undergoing serious evaluation and prototypical use by many content providers and suppliers. If the DTD suite fulfills its promise, it will provide for the foreseeable future a common scholarly publishing DTD for purposes of article interchange and archiving. Within archival repositories, significant economies of scale can be achieved only through large-scale automation, which in turn requires maximum homogeneity of content.

Digital and network technologies are rapidly changing the nature of scholarly communication. Scholars increasingly use the electronic medium to publish their research results. In this medium, new knowledge can be disseminated extremely quickly by anyone with access to the Internet, and accessed at any time from anywhere with a network connection.

Costs to reproduce and disseminate information — though not necessarily the costs to produce, review, and edit it — can be greatly reduced online, thus enabling organizations that could not afford to publish scholarly information to do so. The nature of the electronic medium also supports new modes of publishing. Freed from the constraints of print, scientists can publish long, complex data sets along with their articles. Sound, video, and interactive programs can be published along with text and still images. Search and linking facilities can be added to electronic versions of journals and monographs making it substantially easier for researchers to locate and use relevant research.

The interconnectedness of the Internet also allows the nature of journals to change from a set of issues with a static set of articles, to more dynamic collections and databases of published research.

While electronic journals offer new benefits, they also bring new risks. Researchers depend not only on current journals, but on the centuries-old back files of journals that they can use for scholarship. However, electronic journals are not easily preserved. Unlike print journals they live on fragile media, rely on rapidly changing technology and computing environments for their presentation, and depend on the policies and fortunes of their copyright holders for their disposition. The new types of content supported by electronic journals, the advanced search and linking facilities, and the rapid access that electronic journal readers are accustomed to, further complicate the preservation problem.

Despite the complexities of the preservation problem, though, libraries cannot afford to ignore it. Electronic versions of scholarly journals are in many cases becoming the versions of record, with important scholarly communication not included in print publications. This includes not only multimedia content, but the interactive feedback that appears in journals intended for rapid dissemination of new results, such as BMJ, the online version of the British Medical Journal.

Understanding the progress of scholarship will require continued access to this record. At the same time, as other types of work of scholarly interest also move into the electronic realm — everything from email to researchers' notes to experimental prototypes to interactive Web sites — libraries and archives will have to find ways to preserve relevant materials in those areas as well. In some respects journals, which tend to have more predictable formats and publication cycles as well as more careful editing than other types of electronic works, are a useful starting point for understanding the general problem of electronic preservation.

Preservation Strategies

When considering strategies for preserving electronic journals it is worth asking whether special archives are needed at all. After all, in the print era libraries have preserved many scholarly journals through their normal operations without having to set up special archival units or to take on formal responsibilities for preservation beyond their own local communities.

Libraries simply retained and bound copies of the journals they originally received from the publishers and kept them on their shelves. While these bound volumes can deteriorate physically over time or be subject to loss or damage, bound volumes that are over one hundred years old and still perfectly usable are not uncommon in research libraries. No copyright restrictions prevented libraries from binding and retaining old issues; no technological changes made these print journals unreadable. Moreover, libraries could exploit redundancy to fill gaps in their own holdings.

Since copies of scholarly journals were sent to multiple universities, many of which attempted to retain them, a library lacking an issue a scholar sought could simply borrow the issue or obtain a photocopy of a needed article from another institution that retained a usable copy. Similarly, when journals and other materials were copied to microform, these microforms also were distributed to many libraries.

Through these means, libraries could build up a robust preservation mechanism where the only costs beyond initial acquisition of materials were keeping them on the shelves, maintaining interlibrary loan systems, and sometimes acquiring "migrated" forms such as microfilms. Since the libraries owned the journals and the first-sale doctrine of copyright law let them dispose of these journals as they saw fit, their preservation was also largely unconstrained by the journals' copyright holders.

The same approach is not unthinkable for electronic journals, but at present few libraries retain electronic journals and provide them to their readers. As long as this is the case, an equivalent informal substitute for archiving will not suffice. Most libraries, after all, can provide access to electronic journals simply by pointing to copies on publisher or aggregator sites, without the expense involved in acquiring and storing them locally. Therefore, unless libraries see definite benefits in keeping local copies that outweigh the costs, redundant local storage networks are unlikely to arise on their own, especially if they lack the durability and freedom to copy of the print journal environment. Therefore, libraries will either need to organize or support archival organizations, or develop viable local storage networks that can reliably and cost-effectively preserve electronic journals.

An analysis of the informal print journal "archiving" network needs to consider its limitations as well as its advantages. Access to back issues of print journals is much slower than access to electronic journals, especially as libraries increasingly move older journal volumes out of primary stacks and into high-density storage. When researchers seek journal issues their institutions don't have, they may have to wait weeks for interlibrary loan. Cumulative storage costs for a journal volume redundantly stored in dozens or hundreds of locations is also significant, taken as a whole, even if the costs per institution are low. Furthermore, there is no guarantee that issues will remain obtainable.

Consider the experience of JSTOR which has digitized back issues of important scholarly print journals in the arts and sciences, with back issues provided by publishers and participating libraries. With over 1,300 participants in June 2002, JSTOR still lacked complete runs of 33 of its 218 online journals, with approximately 300 missing volumes and about 70 missing individual issues. About half of the missing volumes, and most of the missing individual issues, were not from the start of a run: that is, they represent gaps in holdings made available for digitization after libraries had started subscribing to the journals. If an average volume has six issues, these figures suggest a loss of about one-and-one-half percent of back issues for journals of interest to the JSTOR consortium, counting from the earliest available volume of journals, or a little over three percent counting from the first published issue. Many of these missing issues may well be in libraries and simply have not been made available to JSTOR. However, such issues are also likely to be relatively difficult to obtain by a scholar who might need them.

Requirements

The alternative to having libraries depend on their own and their neighbors' stored copies of electronic journals is to have them use trusted digital journal repositories. Several types of organizations could run such repositories, including the publishers of the content, particular academic or national libraries that state a commitment to preserve content, dedicated archival organizations, scholarly societies, or organized consortia of any of the preceding organizations. Whatever the nature of a repository's maintainer, however, users will have to trust that the repository will preserve content and provide access to it when needed.

Several papers have been published outlining the requirements for a trusted digital repository. In 2000, a Digital Library Federation working group that included both librarians and nonprofit publishers released a set of minimum criteria for a journal archival repository.Here is a condensed paraphrase of these criteria:

— A repository will be a trusted party that conforms to minimum requirements agreed to by both scholarly publishers and libraries.
— It will define its mission in regard to the needs of scholarly publishers and research libraries, and be explicit about what it is willing to archive and for whom.
— It will negotiate and accept appropriate deposits from scholarly publishers.
— It will have sufficient control of deposits to ensure their long-term preservation.
— It will follow documented policies and procedures to ensure preservation in all reasonable contingencies.
— It will make preserved information available to libraries under conditions negotiated with publishers.
— It will work as part of a network.

What does a repository need to do to be considered a "trusted party"? A more recent paper issued by the Research Libraries Group specified these key attributes of a trusted repository:

— Administrative responsibility
— Organization viability
— Financial sustainability
— Technological and procedural suitability
— System security

— Procedural accountability
— Compliance with the Reference Model for an Open Archival Information System (OAIS)

The first three of these attributes deal almost entirely with the persistence of the organization, rather than any technical criteria. To be trusted, the organization must commit to being responsible for the archived material and be able to sustain this commitment over the long term, including any necessary financial commitments. Implicitly, this commitment is being made to all of the people who "trust" it: in this case, the scholarly community at large, including the publishers of scholarly material. Libraries contemplating creating and maintaining a trusted digital archive, then, must consider such a commitment carefully. For many academic libraries, it represents a subtle but significant augmentation of a library's mission.

OAIS Model

One of the most important aspects of the OAIS model is its modularity. Archived materials in OAIS, and their metadata, come in Archival Information Packages (AIPs) and are likewise acquired and disseminated in similar packages. The functions of the archive are also divided into modules operating on the AIPs in various ways. This model allows us to look at an archival scheme not just as a large, monolithic unit, but as a system whose functions and responsibilities can be disseminated and replicated through a community of archival stakeholders.

Content can be replicated reliably at multiple sites by replicating its AIPs, which contain all of the information needed to access and use the content. Archival functions such as ingestion and migration, because of their modularity, can also be delegated to multiple service providers with appropriate expertise, certification, and trust. The model, in short, can apply to an archival system as a whole, not just to a single repository. In some cases, the entire system can have properties that make it trustworthy, even if no individual repository in the system is particularly trustworthy.

Archives need to decide which of the thousands of electronic journals they will preserve. Two methods of narrowing down the field occurred to us, each with its own advantages:

— It limits the number of publisher agreements that need to be made, each of which may require substantial negotiation. It is likely to reduce the number of input formats to the archive, and the diversity of procedures required to ingest journal content, thus lowering overall costs of ingesting material. Furthermore, in a networked environment, with multiple, independently run archives, responsibilities can be more cleanly partitioned by publisher than by less definite criteria like subjects.

— It allows to focus on disciplines that are of special interest to the university, and ignore those that are of little or no interest. It makes it easier for us to find experts in the disciplines that can advise us on which journals are most important to preserve, and on how they should be preserved. If the archive is sufficiently comprehensive, the archive can also serve as a self-contained research resource in its own right for its specialized disciplines. Such a resource can be "marketed" as a resource for the community engaged in that discipline, which may then fund the archive through subscriptions or grants.

— In online journals, which may have external hyperlinks, auxiliary searching and browsing scripts, dynamically updated and targeted advertisements (which may be out of the control of the actual journal publisher), comment boards, and ephemeral description files, the distinction between journal content that should be preserved and external content can blur. Since the purpose of the archive is to preserve the record of scholarship, though, the archive should at minimum preserve all refereed editorial matter published by the journals we archive. This includes not only research articles, but also reviews, letters to the editor, and other edited content.

Exceptions may need to be made to the rules above for certain journals. For example, unrefereed submissions are an important part of some journals that focus on the latest progress reports of research. For example, the BMJ, the online version of the British Medical Journal, allows appropriately credentialed readers to make "rapid responses" to articles, which are usually posted within twenty-four hours of receipt. While these responses are moderated for relevance, they are not refereed, and editing is minimal. But they represent an important part of the scholarly communication provided by this online journal. An archive of this journal, then, should attempt to preserve these responses, even if archiving an unpredictably-growing set of responses to an article is more difficult to manage than a static set of articles originally published in a journal issue.

Archives also need to decide on the form in which they will preserve journal content. Will they preserve content as readers see it ("presentation" forms), or as their publishers prepare and structure it ("source" forms), or both? Each has its advantages and disadvantages, but a comprehensive archival system should ideally preserve both.

Presentation forms. In the case of print journals, libraries save the journals in the form in which they are presented: bound, printed pages. Electronic journal archives can also save such "presentation" forms. For many electronic journals these presentation forms consist of PDF or HTML and image files that are delivered to readers when they access journals over the Web. These files faithfully reproduce the appearance of journal articles and their text. They are also in many cases automatically harvestable from publisher sites — unlike source files which may not come in as consistent formats as presentation forms — and are therefore relatively inexpensive to ingest.

However, presentation files usually lack the structural markup available in the publisher's source forms. They also do not include any server-side scripts or other functionality that would be provided on the original publisher's Web site. Hence, they might not support functions that readers of electronic journals increasingly expect, such as automatic bibliographic linking, cross-article text searching, and data analysis. Migration to other formats may also be problematic, at least for anything beyond image capture and simple text streams, particularly if a nonstandard format is used

Source Forms

Electronic journals typically produce "source" files which are the edited documents on which the presentation forms are based. For many electronic journals these are SGML files — or more recently XML files — following a structure known as a document type defintion (DTD) specified by the publisher.

The structure and markup of source files often provides information that cannot practically be extracted from presentation files, such as the structure of equations and formulas, bibliographic records, and tabular data. If the source files use a well-documented DTD for this information, programs can easily analyze journal articles to support value-added services. On the other hand, archiving only the "source" forms means that viewers of archived journals might not see exactly what readers of the original journals saw.

It may be difficult to verify whether the source materials can generate the same content and functionality of the original presentation forms, in part because source forms may not conform exactly to a standardized DTD, and also because publishers may make last-minute edits in presentation files that do not appear in the source files. There is currently no common standard used for various publisher DTDs, although many of them descend from a common ISO standard. A Harvard-sponsored study prepared by Inera recommends a common DTD that incorporates many of the elements of major publisher DTDs. If such a standard were widely adopted it would substantially reduce the costs and uncertainties of maintaining source files.

Auxiliary Forms

One of the appeals of electronic journals is that they can include digital content such as multimedia, programs, or machine-readable data sets that augment the text and illustrations of a traditional scholarly article. These supplements should be preserved in journal archives as well. However, because they often appear in complex formats that may have limited long-term support, an archive may not be able to guarantee that the supplementary content will continue to be usable by future researchers indefinitely. It may be useful, though, to support some basic supplementary data types, such as character and numeric data stored in relational tables.

For other formats, if the supplementary material can be packaged as a bit-stream, archives should at least be able to preserve this bit-stream. They should also include some metadata concerning the format of the bit-stream so that new programs can interpret that format, if researchers are sufficiently motivated. A journal archive itself need not record detailed information about the format specification, so long as it can refer to a reliably preserved copy of the format specification stored elsewhere.

Open Archival Information System (OAIS)

An Open Archival Information System (OAIS) is an archive, consisting of an organization of people and systems, that has accepted the responsibility to preserve information and make it available for a Designated Community. It meets a set of such responsibilities as defined in this document, and this allows an OAIS archive to be distinguished from other uses of the term, archive'. The term, Open' in OAIS is used to imply that this Recommendation, as well as future related Recommendations and standards, are developed in open forums, and it does not imply that access to the archive is unrestricted.

The information being maintained has been deemed to need Long Term Preservation, even if the OAIS itself is not permanent. Long Term is long enough to be concerned with the impacts of changing technologies, including support for new media and data formats, or with a changing user community.

Long Term may extend indefinitely. In this reference model there is a particular focus on digital information, both as the primary forms of information held and as supporting information for both digitally and physically archived materials. This international reference model:

— provides a framework for the understanding and increased awareness of archival concepts needed for Long Term digital information preservation and access;

— provides the concepts needed by non-archival organizations to be effective participants in the preservation process;

— provides a framework, including terminology and concepts, for describing and comparing architectures and operations of existing and future archives;

— provides a framework for describing and comparing different long term preservation strategies and techniques;

— provides a basis for comparing the data models of digital information preserved by archives and for discussing how data models and the underlying information may change over time;

— provides a foundation that may be expanded by other efforts to cover long-term preservation of information that is NOT in digital form (e.g., physical media and physical samples);

— expands consensus on the elements and processes for long-term digital information preservation and access, and promotes a larger market which vendors can support;

— guides the identification and production of OAIS-related standards.

The reference model addresses a full range of archival information preservation functions including ingest, archival storage, data management, access, and dissemination. It also addresses the migration of digital information to new media and forms, the data models used to represent the information, the role of software in information preservation, and the exchange of digital information among archives.

It identifies both internal and external interfaces to the archive functions, and it identifies a number of high-level services at these interfaces. It provides various illustrative examples and some ‚best practice' recommendations. It defines a minimal set of responsibilities for an archive to be called an OAIS, and it also defines a maximal archive to provide a broad set of useful terms and concepts.

A tremendous growth in computational power, and in networking bandwidth and connectivity, has resulted in an explosion in the number of organizations making digital information available. Transactions among all types of organizations are being conducted using digital forms that are taking the place of more traditional media such as paper.

Preserving information in digital forms is much more difficult than preserving information in forms such as paper and film. This is not only a problem for traditional archives, but also for many organizations that have never thought of themselves as performing an archival function. It is expected that this reference model, by establishing minimum requirements for an OAIS archive along with a set of archival concepts, will provide a common framework from which to view archival challenges, particularly as they relate to digital information.

This should enable more organizations to understand the issues and take the proper steps to ensure Long Term information preservation. It should also provide a basis for more standardization and, therefore, a larger market that vendors can support in meeting archival requirements.

The term, archive' has come to be used to refer to a wide variety of storage and preservation functions and systems. Traditional archives are understood as facilities or organizations which preserve records, originally generated by or for a government organization, institution, or corporation, for access by public or private communities. The archive accomplishes this task by taking ownership of the records, ensuring that they are understandable to the accessing community, and managing them so as to preserve their information content and authenticity.

Historically, these records have been in such forms as books, papers, maps, photographs, and film, which can be read directly by humans, or read with the aid of simple optical magnification and scanning aids. The major focus for preserving this information has been to ensure that they are on media with long-term stability and that access to this media is carefully controlled.

The explosive growth of information in digital forms has posed a severe challenge not only for traditional archives and their information providers, but also for many other organizations in the government, commercial and non-profit sectors. These organizations are finding, or will find, that they need to take on the information preservation functions typically associated with traditional archives because digital information is easily lost or corrupted.

The pace of technology evolution is causing some hardware and software systems to become obsolete in a matter of a few years, and these changes can put severe pressure on the ability of the related data structures or formats to continue effective representation of the full information desired. Because much of the supporting information necessary to preserve this information is more easily available or only available at the time when the original information is produced, these organizations need to be active participants in the long-term preservation effort, and they need to follow the principles espoused in this OAIS reference model to ensure that the information can be preserved for the Long Term. Participation in these efforts will minimize the lifecycle costs and enable effective long-term preservation of the information.

The explosion of computer processing power and digital media has resulted in many systems where the Producer role and the archive role are the responsibility of the same entity. These systems, which are sometimes known as Active Archives, should subscribe to the goals of Long Term Preservation discussed in this document. The design process must realize that some of the Long Term Preservation activities may conflict with the goals of rapid production and dissemination of products to Consumers. The designers and architects of such systems should document the solutions that have been reached.

Similarly, the information stored within a CD-ROM file is expressed by the bits (the data) it contains which, when they are combined with the Representation Information for those bits, are converted to more meaningful information as long as the Representation Information is understandable using the recipient's Knowledge Base. For example, assume the bits represent an ASCII table of numbers giving the coordinates of a location on the Earth measured in degrees latitude and East longitude. The Representation Information will typically include the definition of ASCII together with descriptions of the format of the numbers and their locations in the file, their definitions as latitude and longitude, and the definition of their units as degrees. It may also include additional meaning that is assigned to the table.

For digital information, this means the OAIS must clearly identify the bits and the Representation Information that applies to those bits. This required transparency to the bit level is a distinguishing feature of digital information preservation, and it runs counter to object-oriented concepts which try to hide these implementation issues. This presents a significant challenge to the preservation of digital information. As a further complication, the recursive nature of Representation Information, which typically is composed of its own data and other Representation Information, typically leads to a network of Representation Information objects. Since a key purpose of an OAIS is to preserve information for a Designated Community, the OAIS must understand the Knowledge Base of its Designated Community to understand the minimum Representation Information that must be maintained.

The OAIS should then make a decision between maintaining the minimum Representation Information needed for its Designated Community, or maintaining a larger amount of Representation Information that may allow understanding by a larger Consumer community with a less specialized Knowledge Base. Over time, evolution of the Designated Community's Knowledge Base may require updates to the Representation Information to ensure continued understanding. As a practical matter, software is used to access the Information Object, and it will incorporate some understanding of the network of Representation Information objects involved. However, this software should not be used as rationale for avoiding identifying and gathering readily understandable Representation Information that defines the Information Object, because it is harder to preserve working software than to preserve information in digital or hardcopy forms.

The OAIS reference model emphasizes the preservation of information content. As digital technology evolves, multimedia technology and the dependency on complex interplay between the data and presentation technologies will lead some organizations to require that the look and feel of the original presentation of the information be preserved. This type of preservation requirement may necessitate that the software programs and interfaces used to access the data be preserved. This problem may be further complicated by the proprietary nature of some of the software. Various techniques for preserving the look and feel of information access are currently the subject of research and prototyping.

These techniques, which include hardware level emulation, emulation of various common service APIs, and the development of a virtual machine, investigate the preservation of the original bit steam and software across technology. Though the OAIS reference model does not focus on these emerging techniques, it should provide architectural basis for the prototyping and comparison of these techniques. An Information Package is a conceptual container of two types of information called Content Information and Preservation Description Information (PDI). The Content Information and PDI are viewed as being encapsulated and identifiable by the Packaging Information. The resulting package is viewed as being discoverable by virtue of the Descriptive Information.

The Content Information is that information which is the original target of preservation. It consists of the Content Data Object (Physical Object or Digital Object, i.e., bits) and its associated Representation Information needed to make the Content Data Object understandable to the Designated Community. For example, the CDO may be an image that is provided as the bit content of one CD-ROM file together with other files, on the same CD-ROM, that contain Representation Information. Only after the Content Information has been clearly defined can an assessment of the Preservation Description Information be made. The Preservation Description Information applies to the Content Information and is needed to preserve the Content Information, to ensure it is clearly identified, and to understand the environment in which the Content Information was created. The Preservation Description Information is divided into four types of preserving information called Provenance, Context, Reference, and Fixity. Briefly, they are the following:

— Provenance describes the source of the Content Information, who has had custody of it since its origination, and its history.

— Context describes how the Content Information relates to other information outside the Information Package. For example, it would describe why the Content Information was produced, and it may include a description of how it relates to another Content Information object that is available.

— Reference provides one or more identifiers, or systems of identifiers, by which the Content Information may be uniquely identified.

Examples include an ISBN number for a book, or a set of attributes that distinguish one instance of Content Information from another.

— Fixity provides a wrapper, or protective shield, that protects the Content Information from undocumented alteration. For example, it may involve a check sum over the Content Information of a digital Information Package.

The Packaging Information is that information which, either actually or logically, binds, identifies and relates the Content Information and PDI. For example, if the Content Information and PDI are identified as being the content of specific files on a CD-ROM, then the Packaging Information would include the ISO 9660 volume/file structure on the CD-ROM, as well as the names and directory information of the files on CD-ROM disk.

The Descriptive Information is that information which is used to discover which package has the Content Information of interest. Depending on the setting, this may be no more than a descriptive title of the Information Package that appears in some message, or it may be a full set of attributes that are searchable in a catalogue service.

Preservation Policies and Procedures

It is essential for an OAIS to have documented policies and procedures for preserving its AIPs, and it should follow those procedures. The appropriate policies and procedures will depend, at minimum, on the nature of the AIPs and any ‚backup' relationships the archive may have with other archives.

The Producer and Consumer communities should be provided with submission and dissemination standards, policies, and procedures to support the preservation objectives of the OAIS. The Designated Community should be monitored to be sure the Content Information is still understandable to them. The Designated Community may lose its familiarity with some terminology, and the definition of the community may be broadened to include other members with different backgrounds. A long-term technology usage plan, updated as technology evolves, is essential to avoid being caught with very costly system maintenance, emergency system replacements, and costly data representation transformations.

By definition, an OAIS makes its AIPs visible and available to its Designated Communities. Multiple views of its holdings, supported by various search aids that may cut across collections of AIPs, may be provided.

Some AIPs may only exist as the output of algorithms operating on other AIPs. They appear as DIPs that, upon dissemination, should include documentation on how they were derived from other AIPs. The expectations of OAIS Consumers regarding access services will vary widely among archives and over time as technology evolves. Pressures for more effective access must be balanced with the requirements for preservation under the available resource constraints. Some AIPs may have restricted access and therefore may only be disseminated to Consumers who meet access restrictions. The OAIS should have published policies on access and restrictions so that the rights of all parties are protected.

In general, DIPs may be distributed by all varieties of communication paths, including networks and physical media.

Preservation Planning also designs IP templates and provides design assistance and review to specialize these templates into SIPs and AIPs for specific submissions.. Preservation Planning also develops detailed Migration plans, software prototypes and test plans to enable implementation of Administration migration goals. Access: This entity provides the services and functions that support Consumers in determining the existence, description, location and availability of information stored in the OAIS, and allowing Consumers to request and receive information products. Access functions include communicating with Consumers to receive requests, applying controls to limit access to specially protected information, coordinating the execution of requests to successful completion, generating responses and delivering the responses to Consumers. In addition to the entities described above, there are various Common Services assumed to be available.

Modern, distributed computing applications assume a number of supporting services such as inter-process communication, name services, temporary storage allocation, exception handling, security, backup and directory services. Much excellent work has already been done in the area of open system environment reference models.

Operating system services provide the core services needed to operate and administer the application platform, and provide an interface between application software and the platform. These services include the following:

— Kernel operations provide low-level services necessary to create and manage processes, execute programs, define and communicate signals, define and process system clock operations, manage files and directories, and control input-output processing to and from the external environment.

— Commands and utilities include mechanisms for operations at the operator level, such as comparing, printing, and displaying file contents; editing files; pattern searching; evaluating expressions; logging messages; moving files between directories; sorting data; executing command scripts; and accessing environment information.

— Real-time extension includes the application and operating system interfaces needed to support those application domains requiring deterministic execution, processing, and responsiveness. The extension defines the applications interface to basic system services for input/output, file system access, and process management.

— System management includes capabilities to define and manage user resource allocation and access (i.e., what resources are managed and the classes of access defined), configuration and performance management of devices, file systems, administrative processes (job accounting), queues, machine/platform profiles, authorization of resource usage, and system backup.

— Operating system security services specify the control of access to system data, functions, hardware, and software resources by users and user processes. Network services provide the capabilities and mechanisms to support distributed applications requiring data access and applications interoperability in heterogeneous, networked environments. These services include the following:

    — Data communication includes API and protocol specifications for reliable, transparent, end-to-end data transmission across communications networks.

    — Transparent file access to available files located anywhere in a heterogeneous network.

    — Personal/micro computer support for interoperability with systems based on other operating systems, particularly microcomputer operating systems, which may not be formally specified in a national or international standard.

    — Remote Procedure Call services include specifications for extending the local procedure call to a distributed environment.

— Network security services include access, authentication, confidentiality, integrity, and non-repudiation controls and management of communications between senders and receivers of information in a network.

Security services capabilities and mechanisms to protect sensitive information and treatments in the information system. The appropriate level of protection is determined based upon the value of the information to the application end-users and the perception of threats to it. These services include the following:

— Identification/authentication service confirms the identities of requesters for use of information system resources. In addition, authentication can apply to providers of data. Access control service prevents the unauthorized use of information system resources. This service also prevents the use of a resource in an unauthorized way. This service may be applied to various aspects of access to a resource (e.g., access to communications to the resource, the reading, writing, or deletion of an information/data resource, the execution of a processing resource) or to all accesses to a resource.

— Data integrity service ensures that data is not altered or destroyed in an unauthorized manner. This service applies to data in permanent data stores and to data in communications messages.

— Data confidentiality service ensures that data is not made available or disclosed to unauthorized individuals or computer processes. This service will be applied to devices that permit human interaction with the information system. In addition, this service will ensure that observation of usage patterns of communications resources will not be possible.

— Non-repudiation service ensures that entities engaging in an information exchange cannot deny being involved in it. This service may take one or both of two forms. First, the recipient of data is provided with proof of the origin of the data. This protects against any attempt by the sender to falsely deny sending the data or its contents. Second, the sender of data is provided with proof of delivery of data. This protects against any subsequent attempt by the recipient to falsely deny receiving the data or its contents.

Digital SIPs may be delivered via electronic transfer (e.g., FTP), loaded from media submitted to the archive, or simply mounted (e.g., CD-ROM) on the archive file system for access. Non-digital SIPs would likely be delivered by conventional shipping procedures. The Receive Submission function may represent a legal transfer of custody for the Content Information in the SIP, and may require that special access controls be placed on the contents. This function provides a confirmation of receipt of a SIP to the Producer, which may include a request to resubmit a SIP in the case of errors resulting from the SIP submission. The Quality Assurance function validates (QA results) the successful transfer of the SIP to the staging area. For digital submissions, these mechanisms might include Cyclic Redundancy Checks (CRCs) or checksums associated with each data file, or the use of system log files to record and identify any file transfer or media read/write errors.

The Generate AIP function transforms one or more SIPs into one or more AIPs that conform to the archive's data formatting and documentation standards. This may involve file format conversions, data representation conversions or reorganization of the content information in the SIPs. The Generate AIP function may issue report requests to Data Management to obtain reports of information needed by the Generate AIP function to produce the Descriptive Information that completes the AIP.

The Generate Descriptive Information function extracts Descriptive Information from the AIPs and collects Descriptive Information from other sources to provide to Coordinate Updates, and ultimately Data Management. This includes metadata to support searching and retrieving AIPs (e.g., who, what, when, where, why), and could also include special browse products (thumbnails, images) to be used by Finding Aids. The Coordinate Updates function is responsible for transferring the AIPs to Archival Storage and the Descriptive Information to Data Management. Transfer of the AIP includes a storage request and may represent an electronic, physical, or a virtual (i.e., data stays in place) transfer. After the transfer is completed and verified, Archival Storage returns a storage confirmation indicating (or verifying) the storage identification information for the AIP.

The Coordinate Updates function also incorporates the storage identification information into the Descriptive Information for the AIP and transfers it to the Data Management entity along with a database update request. In return, Data Management provides a database update response indicating the status of the update. Data Management updates may take place without a corresponding Archival Storage transfer when the SIP contains Descriptive Information for an AIP already in Archival Storage.

Archival Storage

The Receive Data function receives a storage request and an AIP from Ingest and moves the AIP to permanent storage within the archive. The transfer request may need to indicate the anticipated frequency of utilization of the data objects comprising the AIP in order to allow the appropriate storage devices or media to be selected for storing the AIP. This function will select the media type, prepare the devices or volumes, and perform the physical transfer to the Archival Storage volumes. Upon completion of the transfer, this function sends a storage confirmation message to Ingest, including the storage identification of the AIPs.

The Manage Storage Hierarchy function positions, via commands, the contents of the AIPs on the appropriate media based on storage management policies, operational statistics, or directions from Ingest via the storage request. It will also conform to any special levels of service required for the AIP, or any special security measures that are required, and ensures the appropriate level of protection for the AIP. These include on-line, off-line or near-line storage, required throughput rate, maximum allowed bit error rate, or special handling or backup procedures. It monitors error logs to ensure AIPs are not corrupted during transfers. This function also provides operational statistics to Administration summarizing the inventory of media on-hand, available storage capacity in the various tiers of the storage hierarchy, and usage statistics.

The Replace Media function provides the capability to reproduce the AIPs over time. Within the Replace Media function the Content Information and Preservation Description Information (PDI) must not be altered. However, the data constituting the Packaging Information may be changed as long as it continues to perform the same function and there is a straight forward implementation that does not cause information loss.

The migration strategy must select a storage medium, taking into consideration the expected and actual rates of errors encountered in various media types, their performance, and their costs of ownership. If media-dependent attributes (e.g., tape block sizes, CD-ROM volume information) have been included as part of the Content Information, a way must be found to preserve this information when migrating to higher capacity media with different storage architectures. The Error Checking function provides statistically acceptable assurance that no components of the AIP are corrupted during any internal Archival Storage data transfer. This function requires that all hardware and software within the archive provide notification of potential errors and that these errors are routed to standard error logs that are checked by the Archival Storage staff.

The PDI Fixity Information provides some assurance that the Content Information has not been altered as the AIP is moved and accessed. Similar information is needed to protect the PDI itself. A standard mechanism for tracking and verifying the validity of all data objects within the archive may also be used. For example, CRCs could be maintained for every individual data file.

A higher level of service, such as Reed-Solomon coding to support combined error detection and correction, could also be provided. The storage facility procedures should provide for random verification of the integrity of data objects using CRCs or some other error checking mechanism. The Disaster Recovery function provides a mechanism for duplicating the digital contents of the archive collection and storing the duplicate in a physically separate facility. This function is normally accomplished by copying the archive contents to some form of removable storage media (e.g., digital linear tape, compact disc), but may also be performed via hardware transport or network data transfers.

Planning for Preservation

The Develop Preservation Strategies and Standards function is responsible for developing and recommending strategies and standards to enable the archive to better anticipate future changes in the Designated Community service requirements or technology trends that would require migration of some current archive holdings or new submissions. This function receives reports from the Monitor Designated Communities and Monitor Technology functions, and it receives performance information, inventory reports and summarized consumer comments from Administration.

This function sends recommendations on system evolution to Administration. This function also receives external data standards from Monitor Technology and produces profiles of those standards that are sent to Administration as proposals on their potential usage. This function also receives issues from Develop Packaging Designs and Migration Plans in the case of unanticipated submission requirements, and responds with advice to handle the new requirements.

The Develop Packaging Designs and Migration Plans function develops new IP designs and detailed migration plans and prototypes, to implement Administration policies and directives. This activity also provides advice on the application of these IP designs and Migration plans to specific archive holdings and submissions. This function receives archive approved standards and migration goals from Administration. The standards include format standards, metadata standards and documentation standards. It applies these standards to preservation requirements and provides AIP and SIP template designs to Administration.

The Coordinate Access Activities function provides a single user interface to the information holdings of the archive. This interface will normally be via computer network or dial-up link to an on-line service, but might also be implemented in the form of a walk-in facility, printed catalogue ordering service, or fax-back type service. Three categories of Consumer requests are distinguished: query requests, which are executed in Data Management and return immediate result sets for presentation to the user; report requests, which may require a number of queries and produce formatted reports for delivery to the Consumer; and orders, which may access either or both Data Management and Archival Storage to prepare a formal Dissemination Information Package (DIP) for on- or off-line delivery.

An order may be an Adhoc Order that is executed only once, or an Event Based Order that will be maintained by the Activate Requests function in Administration, and initiated by a dissemination request that may result in periodic deliveries of requested items. The Archival Information Update function in Administration also submits dissemination requests to obtain DIPs needed to perform its update functions.

The Generate DIP function accepts a dissemination request, retrieves the AIP from Archival Storage, and moves a copy of the data to a staging area for further processing. This function also transmits a report request to Data Management to obtain Descriptive Information needed for the DIP. If special processing is required, the Generate DIP function accesses data objects in staging storage and applies the requested processes. The types of operations, which may be carried out, include statistical functions, sub-sampling in temporal or spatial dimensions, conversions between different data types or output formats, and other specialized processing (e.g., image processing). This function places the completed DIP response in the staging area and notifies the Coordinate Access Activities function that the DIP is ready for delivery.

The Deliver Response function handles both on-line and off-line deliveries of responses (DIPs, result sets, reports and assistance) to Consumers. For on-line delivery, it accepts a response from Coordinate Access Activities and prepares it for on-line distribution in real time via communication links. It identifies the intended recipient, determines the transmission procedure requested, places the response in the staging area to be transmitted, and supports the on-line transmission of the response. For off-line delivery it retrieves the response from the Coordinate Access Activities function, prepares packing lists and other shipping records, and then ships the response. When the response has been shipped, a notice of shipped order is returned to the Coordinate Access Activities function and billing information is submitted to Administration.

Logical Model for Archival Information

A basic concept of the OAIS Reference Model is the concept of information being a combination of data and Representation Information. The Information Object is composed of a Data Object that is either physical or digital, and the Representation Information that allows for the full interpretation of the data into meaningful information.

The Data Object may be expressed as either a physical object (e.g., a moon rock) together with some Representation Information, or it may be expressed as a digital object (i.e., a sequence of bits) together with the Representation Information giving meaning to those bits. The Representation Information accompanying a physical object like a moon rock may give additional meaning, as a result of some analysis, to the physically observable attributes of the rock. This information may have been developed over time and the results, if provided, would be part of the Information Object. The Representation Information accompanying a digital object, or sequence of bits, is used to provide additional meaning. It typically maps the bits into commonly recognized data types such as character, integer, and real and into groups of these data types. It associates these with higher-level meanings that can have complex inter-relationships that are also described.

The purpose of the Representation Information object is to convert the bit sequences into more meaningful information. It does this by describing the format, or data structure concepts, which are to be applied to the bit sequences and that in turn result in more meaningful values such as characters, numbers, pixels, arrays, tables, etc. These common computer data types, aggregations of these data types, and mapping rules which map from the underlying data types to the higher level concepts needed to understand the Digital Object are referred to as the Structure Information of the Representation Information object. These structures are commonly identified by name or by relative position within the associated bit sequences.

The Representation Information provided by the Structure Information is seldom sufficient. Even in the case where the Digital Object is interpreted as a sequence of text characters, and described as such in the Structure Information, the additional information as to which language was being expressed should be provided. This type of additional required information is referred to as the Semantic Information. When dealing with scientific data, for example, the information in the Semantic Information can be quite varied and complex. It will include special meanings associated with all the elements of the Structural Information, operations that may be performed on each data type, and their inter-relationships.

As an example, International Standard Organisation (ISO) 9660 describes text as conforming to the ASCII standard, but it does not actually describe how ASCII is to be implemented. It simply references the ASCII standard which is additional Representation Information that is needed for a full understanding. Therefore the ASCII standard is a part of the Representation Net associated with ISO 9660 and needs to be obtained by the OAIS in some form, or the OAIS needs to track the availability of this standard so that it may take appropriate steps in the future to ensure its ISO 9660 Representation Information is fully understandable.

Representation Networks

Representation Information, which is itself an Information Object, may be expressed in physical forms (e.g., a paper document) or in digital forms. When the Representation Information is in digital form, additional Representation Information is needed to understand the bits of the Representation Information. In principle, this recursion continues until physical forms are encountered. For example, Representation Information expressed in ASCII needs the additional Representation Information for ASCII, which might be a physical document giving the ASCII standard.

However it may also be obtained as a digital object that needs to be understood as a PDF object. Rather than actually obtaining the documentation of PDF and writing software to understand the ISO 9660 object, an OAIS may use available PDF display software to render the ISO 9660 documentation humanly visible and readable. In this role the PDF display software is referred to as Representation Rendering Software because it is used to render the Representation Information.

If the OAIS does not also obtain the associated description of PDF, it needs to record and track this fact because when PDF objects are no longer cost-effective for access and display, the ISO 9660 documentation expressed as a PDF object will need to be migrated to a new form. Access Software presents some or all of the information content of an Information Object in forms understandable to humans or systems. It may also provide some types of access service, such as displaying, manipulating, processing, or sub-setting, to an Information Object. For some types of Digital Objects, such software may be widely available. It is not necessary for the OAIS to maintain or provide such software.

The OAIS may want to maintain and provide this software for more specialized types of Digital Objects. Since Access software will incorporate some understanding of the Representation Information, some archives may attempt to use Access Software as a substitute for full Representation Information. Access Software source code, which embodies at least a partial understanding of the associated Representation Information, may be used as documentation expressing such Representation Information. A problem with this approach is that the desired Representation Information may not be clearly identifiable as it may be mixed with various processing and display algorithms, and may be incomplete since the code assumes an underlying operating environment. It may be difficult to tell, from the software code, what Representation Information is missing.

The use of Access Software executables, without the source code, such as may occur with proprietary formats, presents a much greater risk for loss of information because it is more difficult to maintain an operating environment for software than to migrate documentation over time. The practical use of emulation techniques, to preserve working software, has not yet been shown to be cost-effective. This is a significant issue for those desiring to preserve a look and feel to information access.

Preservation of Archival Description

In addition to Content Information, the Archival Information must include information that will allow the understanding of the Content Information over an indefinite period of time. The specific set of Information Objects, which are required for this function, is collectively called Preservation Description Information (PDI).

The PDI must include information that is necessary to adequately preserve the particular Content Information with which it is associated. It is specifically focused on describing the past and present states of the Content Information, ensuring it is uniquely identifiable, and ensuring it has not been unknowingly altered.

This information is typical for all types of archives and has been classified in the context of traditional archives. However, the class definitions must be extended for digital archives. The following definitions are preserving Digital Information:

— *Reference Information*: This information identifies, and if necessary describes, one or more mechanisms used to provide assigned identifiers for the Content Information. It also provides those identifiers that allow outside systems to refer, unambiguously, to this particular Content Information. Examples of these systems include taxonomic systems, reference systems and registration systems. In the OAIS Reference Model most if not all of this information is replicated in Package Descriptions, which enable Consumers to access Content Information of interest.

— *Context Information*: This information documents the relationships of the Content Information to its environment. This includes why the Content Information was created and how it relates to other Content Information objects existing elsewhere.

— *Provenance Information*: This information documents the history of the Content Information. This tells the origin or source of the Content Information, any changes that may have taken place since it was originated, and who has had custody of it since it was originated. This gives future users some assurance as to the likely reliability of the Content Information. Provenance can be viewed as a special type of context information.

— *Fixity Information*: This information provides the Data Integrity checks or Validation/Verification keys used to ensure that the particular Content Information object has not been altered in an undocumented manner. Fixity Information includes special encoding and error detection schemes that are specific to instances of Content Objects. Fixity Information does not include the integrity preserving mechanisms provided by the OAIS underlying services, error protection supplied by the media and device drivers used by Archival Storage.

The Fixity Information may specify minimum quality of service requirements for these mechanisms. The OAIS needs to explicitly decide what the exact definition of Content Information is in order to be able to ensure that it also has the PDI needed to preserve the Content Information. Once the Content Information has been determined, it is possible to assess the Preservation Description Information.

— *Packaging Information*: The Packaging Information is that information which, either actually or logically, binds or relates the components of the package into an identifiable entity on specific media. For example, if the Content Information and PDI are identified as being the content of specific files on a CD-ROM, then the Packaging Information may include the ISO 9660 volume/file structure on the CD-ROM.

These choices are the subject of local archive definitions or conventions. The Packaging Information does not necessarily need to be preserved by an OAIS since it does not contribute to the Content Information or the PDI. However, there are cases where the OAIS may be required to reproduce the original submission exactly. In this case the Content Information is defined to include all the bits submitted.

The OAIS should also avoid holding PDI or Content Information only in the naming conventions of directory or file name structures. These structures are most likely to be used as Packaging Information. Packaging Information is not preserved by Migration. Any information saved in file names or directory structures may be lost when the Packaging Information is altered.

— *Descriptive Information:* To preserving information, the OAIS must provide adequate features to allow Consumers to locate information of potential interest, analyze that information, and order desired information. This is accomplished through a specialization of the

Information Object called Descriptive Information, which contain the data that serves as the input to documents or applications called Access Aids.

The Descriptive Information is generally derived from the Content Information and PDI. The Descriptive Information can be viewed as an index to enable efficient access to the associated Information Package via associated Access Aids. Access Aids are documents or applications that can be used to locate, analyze, retrieve, or order information from the OAIS.

ARCHIVING: AN INFORMATION LIFE CYCLE APPROACH

The rapid growth in the creation and dissemination of digital objects by authors, publishers, corporations, governments, and even librarians, archivists and museum curators, has emphasized the speed and ease of short-term dissemination with little regard for the long-term preservation of digital information. However, digital information is fragile in ways that differ from traditional technologies, such as paper or microfilm. It is more easily corrupted or altered without recognition.

Digital storage media have shorter life spans, and digital information requires access technologies that are changing at an ever-increasing pace. Some types of information, such as multimedia, are so closely linked to the software and hardware technologies that they cannot be used outside these proprietary environments. Because of the speed of technological advances, the time frame in which we must consider archiving becomes much shorter. The time between manufacture and preservation is shrinking.

While there are traditions of stewardship and best practices that have become institutionalized in the print environment, many of these traditions are inadequate, inappropriate or not well known among the stakeholders in the digital environment. Originators are able to bypass the traditional publishing, dissemination and announcement processes that are part of the traditional path from creation to archiving and preservation. Groups and individuals who did not previously consider themselves to be archivists are now being drawn into the role, either because of the infrastructure and intellectual property issues involved or because user groups are demanding it.

Librarians and archivists who traditionally managed the life cycle of print information from creation to long-term preservation and archiving, must now look to information managers from the computer science tradition to support the development of a system of stewardship in the new digital environment. There is a need to identify new best practices that satisfy the requirements and are practical for the various stakeholder groups involved.

Archiving in the Framework of Information Life Cycle Management

The project managers from the "cutting edge" projects emphasized the importance of considering best practices for archiving at all stages of the information management life cycle. Acknowledging this important philosophy, the best practices identified by the study are presented in the framework of the information life cycle — creation, acquisition, cataloguing/identification, storage, preservation and access.

Creation

Creation is the act of producing the information product. The producer may be a human author or originator, or a piece of equipment such as a sensing device, satellite or laboratory instrument. Creation is viewed here in the broadest sense, as increasingly science is based on a variety of data types, products and originators.

All project managers acknowledged that creation is where long-term archiving and preservation must start. Even in rigorously controlled situations, the digital information may be lost without the initial awareness on the part of the originator of the importance of archiving. Practices used when a digital object is created ultimately impact the ease with which the object can be digitally archived and preserved. In addition, there are several key practices involving the creator that are evolving within the archiving projects. First, the creator may be involved in assessing the long-term value of the information. In lieu of other assessment factors, the creator's estimate of the long-term value of the information may be a good indication of the value that will be placed on it by people within the same discipline or area of research in the future.

The U.S. Department of Agriculture's Digital Publications Preservation Steering Committee has suggested that the creator provide a preservation indicator in the document. This would not take the place of formal retention schedules, but it would provide an indication of the long-term value that the creator, as a practicing researcher, attaches to the document's contents. Secondly, the preservation and archiving process is made more efficient when attention is paid to issues of consistency, format, standardization and metadata description in the very beginning of the information life cycle. The Oak Ridge National Laboratory recently announced guidelines for the creation of digital documents. Limits are placed on both the software that can be used and on the format and layout of the documents in order to make short and long-term information management easier.

Many project managers acknowledged that the best practice would be to create the metadata at the object creation stage, or to create the metadata in stages, with the metadata provided at creation augmented by additional elements during the cataloguing/identification stage. However, only in the case of data objects is the metadata routinely collected at the point of creation. Many of the datasets are created by measurement or monitoring instruments, and the metadata is supplied along with the data stream. This may include location, instrument type, and other quality indicators concerning the context of the measurement. In some cases, this instrument-generated metadata is supplemented by information provided by the original researcher. For smaller datasets and other objects such as documents and images, much of the metadata continues to be created "by hand" and after-the-fact. Metadata creation is not sufficiently incorporated into the tools for the creation of these objects to rely solely on the creation process. As standards groups and vendors move to incorporate XML (eXtensible Mark-up Language) and RDF (Resource Description Framework) architectures in their word processing and database products, the creation of metadata as part of the origination of the object will be easier.

Acquisition and Collection Development

Acquisition and collection development is the stage in which the created object is "incorporated" physically or virtually into the archive. The object must be known to the archive administration. There are two main aspects to the acquisition of digital objects — collection policies and gathering procedures.

Collection Policies: In most countries, the major difference in collection policies between formal print and electronic publications is the question of whether digital materials are included under current deposit legislation. Guidelines help to establish the boundaries in such an unregulated situation. It is also the case that there is just too much material that could be archived from the Internet, so guidelines are needed to tailor the general collection practices of the organization. The collection policies answer questions related to selecting what to archive, determining extent, archiving links, and refreshing site contents.

Selection: Both the National Library of Canada (NLC) and the National Library of Australia (NLA) acknowledge the importance of selection guidelines. The NLC's Guidelines state, "The main difficulty in extending legal deposit to network publishing is that legal deposit is a relatively indiscriminate acquisition mechanism that aims at comprehensiveness.

In the network environment, any individual with access to the Internet can be a publisher, and the network publishing process does not always provide the initial screening and selection at the manuscript stage on which libraries have traditionally relied in the print environment. While the scope of NLA's PANDORA (Preserving and Accessing Networked Documentary Resources of Australia) Project is only to preserve Australian Internet publishing, the NLA also acknowledges that it is still impossible to archive everything. Therefore, the NLA has formulated guidelines for the Selection of Online Australian Publications Intended for Preservation by the National Library of Australia.

These guidelines are key to the successful networking of the state libraries into the National Collection of Australian Electronic Publications, since they provide consistency across multiple acquisition activities. Scholarly publications of national significance and those of current and long term research value are archived comprehensively. Other items are archived on a selective basis "to provide a broad cultural snapshot of how Australians are using the Internet to disseminate information, express opinions, lobby, and publish their creative work."

Directly connected to the question of selection is the issue of extent. What is the extent or the boundary of a particular digital work? This is particularly an issue when selecting complex Web sites.

Archiving Links : The extensive use of hypertext links to other digital objects in electronic publications raises the question of whether these links and their content should be archived along with the source item. This issue has been addressed by the selected projects in a variety of ways.

Most organizations archive the links (the URLs or other identifiers) but not the content of the linked objects. The American Institute of Physics archives the links embedded in the text and references of its electronic journal articles but not the text or content of any of these links, unless the linked item happens to be in its publication archive or in the supplemental material which it also archives.

Similarly, the Office of Scientific and Technical Information of the U.S. Department of Energy (DOE OSTI) does not intentionally archive any links beyond the extent of the digital object itself. However, the document may be linked to another document if that document is another DOE document in the OSTI archive. NLA's decision about archiving the content of linked objects is based on its selection guidelines. If a linked item meets the selection guidelines, it's contents will be archived, otherwise it will not be.

Refreshing the Archived Contents : In cases where the archiving is taking place while changes or updates may still be occurring to the digital object, as in the case of on-going Web sites, there is a need to consider refreshing the archived contents. A balance must be struck between the completeness and currency of the archive and the burden on the system resources. Obviously, the burden of refreshing the content increases as the number of sources stored in the archive increases.

Gathering Approaches: There are two general approaches to the gathering of relevant Internet-based information -- hand-selected and automatic. In the case of the NLA, the sites are reviewed and hand-selected. They are monitored for their persistence before being included in the archive. Alternatively, the Royal Library, the National Library of Sweden, acquires material by periodically running a robot to capture sites for its Kulturarw project without making value judgments.

In addition, some material is obtained from foreign sites with material about Sweden, such as travel information or translations of Swedish literature. While the acquisition is automatic, the National Library gives priority to periodicals, static documents, and HTML pages. Conferences, usenet groups, ftp archives, and databases are considered lower priority.

The EVA Project at the University of Helsinki, National Library of Finland uses techniques similar to those used in Sweden. However, the guidelines from EVA address issues to be considered when using robots for harvesting. In order not to overload the servers being harvested, particularly those belonging to the public networks, the EVA guidelines establish time limits between visits to a single Web server and between capturing and recapturing a single URL. Even though this approach has allowed the EVA project to progress, developers at EVA consider this approach to be "very rough and not flexible enough for archiving purposes." The EVA developers would prefer that the time limits be more configurable at the server and, preferably, at the individual URL levels. The flexibility would require that the scheduler be a database application that can be modified by the librarian.

Intellectual Property Concerns: Intellectual property remains a key issue in the acquisition process. The approaches to intellectual property vary based on the type of organization doing the archiving. In the case of data centers or corporate archives where there is a close tie between the center and the owner or funding source, there is little question about the intellectual property rights related to acquisition. However, in the case of national libraries, the approaches to intellectual property rights differ from country to country. The differences are based on variant national information policies or legal deposit laws.

References

Research Libraries Group. (2002)."Open Archival Information System (OAIS) Resources." October 2002. [Online]. Available: http://www.rlg.org/longterm/oais.html

Rowlands, Ian, and David Bawden. (1999) "Building the Digital Library on Solid Research Foundations." *Aslib Proceedings* 51, September .

Schatz, Bruce R. (1997). "Information Retrieval in Digital Libraries: Bringing Search to the Net." *Science*, 17 January

Schwartz, Candy. (2000). "Digital Libraries: An Overview." *The Journal of Academic Librarianship* 26, November .

4

Digital Contents

During the 1990s, the program digitized materials from a wide variety of original sources, including pictorial and textual materials, audio, video, maps, atlases, and sheet music. Monographs and serials comprise a very small proportion of the textual materials converted. In US, National Digital Library Program's (NDLP) emphasis has been on enhancing access. No digitization has been conducted with the intent of replacing the original materials; indeed, great care is taken over handling fragile and unique resources and conservation steps often precede scanning.

Nevertheless, these digital resources represent a significant investment, and the Library is concerned that they continue to be usable over the long term. The practices described here should not be seen as policies of the Library of Congress; nor are they suggested as best practices in any absolute sense. NDLP regards them as appropriate practices based on real experience, the nature and content of the originals, the primary purposes of the digitization, the state of technology, the availability of resources, the scale of the American Memory digital collection, and the goals of the program.

They cover not just the storage of content and associated metadata, but also aspects of initial capture and quality review that support the long-term retention of content digitized from analog sources. The National Digital Library Program was established as a five-year program for fiscal years 1996-2000, building on the pilot American Memory project that ran from 1990 to 1995. Although managed as a special program, NDLP has worked closely with the divisions that have custodial responsibility for the materials it has digitized.

NDLP established a core "production" team, but also funded positions within custodial divisions, recognizing that when the program came to an end or entered a new phase, responsibility for the digitized materials would likely fall to those units. In some divisions, NDLP staff positions have been used to jumpstart a mainstream digitization activity steered by the division.

In others, the NDLP coordinators still largely drive the activity. Conversion of most materials has been carried out by contractors under multi-year contracts. Administrative responsibility for digital content is likely to remain aligned with custodianship of non-digital resources. The Library recognizes that digital information resources, whether born digital or converted from analog forms, should be acquired, used, and served alongside traditional resources in the same format or subject area.

Such responsibility will include ensuring that effective access is maintained to the digital content through American Memory and via the Library's main catalogue and, in coordination with the units responsible for the technical infrastructure, planning migration to new technology when needed. The computing support infrastructure at the Library of Congress is centralized. Responsibility for computer systems, disk- and tape-storage units, and all aspects of server operations lies with Information Technology Services (ITS).

The Library wishes to establish institution-wide practices that will ensure long-term retention of digital resources from all sources, whether created by the Library or acquired for its collection by purchase or through copyright deposit, whether born-digital or converted from analog originals. Challenges to developing a comprehensive supporting system include the following:

— the variety of materials (in both original and digital form, extant today and expected in the future)

— the variety of routes and workflow patterns that may lead to ingestion of digital content into the Library's collection

— the variety of modes in which access and output may be required

Following are the five preservation methods:

— *Better media:* Longevity and technology-independence for storage media. May be more important for offline storage than online storage because of rate of change in computing technology. Library community reliant on industry to develop and deploy better media.

— *Refreshing bits:* Includes any operation that simply involves copying a stream of bits from one location to another, whether the physical medium is the same or not. Any process that can be applied to any stream of bits regardless of characteristics of the information those bits represent is regarded as refreshing in this context.

— *Migration of content*: Includes any transformation operation from one data representation (digital format) to another. Migration to an enhanced format can improve functionality of a digital reproduction.

— *Emulation of technical environment:* Using the power of a new generation of technology to function as if it were the technology of a previous generation. For materials digitized by the Library from analog sources, the aim should be to reduce the need for future emulation through effective choice of digital formats and planning for migration.

— *Digital archaeology:* Conversion from one digital format for images to a future standard format that provides enhanced functionality; upgrading or transformation from one SGML Document Type Definition to another.

The five methods listed above can be seen as strategic methods. At an operational level, additional practices protect any digital resources: appropriate and secure environments for storage and computer systems; careful selection of storage system technology for reliability and data integrity; replication in all its variations (mirrors, routine incremental and full backups, duplicates); geographically separate storage areas for duplicates; procedures to validate refreshing actions and migrations; monitoring systems to validate integrity of files; and systems to support decision-making and transformation process management.

The challenge of ensuring long-term access to digital material demands a new preservation model for archival institutions. In the past, preservation practice has typically involved a one-time reformatting step taken many years after the creation of the original physical artifact. Effective preservation of resources in digital form requires (a) attention early in the life-cycle, at the moment of creation, publication, or acquisition and (b) ongoing management (with attendant costs) to ensure continuing usability.

The Library's current practice for retention of locally digitized materials is based primarily on ongoing refreshing of bits. Many choices are made or steps taken during capture in the hope of reducing the need for migration, retaining metadata that will support effective migration when necessary, and avoiding the future need for emulation or archaeology. All digital versions are stored online in a consistent logical structure on the primary storage system supporting the Library's central servers.

This includes files of the highest resolution captured; typically 20-60 Mb for photographic reproductions and segments of early movies and 200-400 Mb for maps. Files delivered by vendors on other media are uploaded as soon as feasible. CDs delivered by contractors are labelled according to strict specifications and are organized and stored in archival boxes to serve as an additional level of backup once files are uploaded. However, the online files are considered as the masters.

Files on the central servers are protected by standard backup and restore procedures, providing replication, and frequent refreshing. These operations can be performed unattended and show great economies of scale in administrative costs. ITS is establishing an Enterprise Storage Area Network, a network of storage devices independent of the Library's primary network based on TCP/IP.

The separate storage network will allow backup, restore, and tape archive functions to be performed without degrading network performance for regular use. The Storage Area Network is currently based on a combination of SCSI and Fibre Channel links; a full transition to Fibre Channel is planned. However, it was determined that the administrative load and software shortcomings were not justified, given the falling price of storage and increasing data density for disk units of the same physical size.

Full backups of the entire storage-system are made to magnetic tape cartridges in a robotic "library" on a two-week cycle; incremental backups (of any files that have been modified or created) are made each night. As the Enterprise Storage Area Network is expanded, two new capabilities are planned for further protection of digital data: snapshot archives of digital collections (on demand or on a schedule as determined by collection custodians); and an offsite location for an additional robotic backup facility that is accessible over the storage network.

ITS has also developed procedures for generating and comparing checksums for all files in a directory tree. These procedures can be used for periodic checks against data corruption (inadvertent or malicious) and to verify copy operations. This procedure was introduced after a problem with the hierarchical storage management system had the effect of corrupting files in some directories.

Those with administrative responsibility for the content decide which files to check and how often to check them. NDLP plans to introduce procedures that use checksums earlier in the production process (e.g., to verify correct transfer of files to delivery media by contractors and to verify correct uploading of files to the central storage system).

Management of Metadata

In US, the National Digital Library Program has identified several categories of metadata needed to support access and management for digital content. Descriptive metadata supports discovery through search and browse functions. Structural metadata supports presentation of complex objects by representing relationships between components, such as sequences of images.

Administrative metadata is needed to support management tasks, such as access control, archiving, and migration. Individual metadata elements may support more than one function, but the categorization of elements by function has proved useful. Since American Memory is aimed at access, the current system is designed to handle metadata that supports discovery and presentation of the resources.

To facilitate indexing and to avoid the need to maintain two sets of catalogue records, descriptive bibliographic metadata is stored separately from the digital reproductions. Structural metadata that relates page-images to parent documents or several related photographs to a single bibliographic description for the group is stored with the digital reproductions in ancillary files.

Other metadata elements are recorded in file headers or in documentation associated with the conversion of each collection. The need to build a more comprehensive system to store and manage digital collections for the long term has been recognized and several prototype activities have been undertaken by NDLP and more are planned within the Library. None has been wholly satisfactory; the process has illustrated the challenge of designing large-scale repositories that will support effective production, maintenance, access, and archival management for large-scale heterogeneous collections of digital materials. However, each exercise has improved understanding of the requirements and practical constraints.

It has been recognized that metadata representations appropriate for manipulation and long-term retention may not always be appropriate for real-time delivery. For example, it has been necessary to "compile" the ASCII page-turning datasets into a more efficient binary structure for generating presentations dynamically. It has also been realized that metadata embedded in image-file headers may be too hard (processor-intensive) to get at to be useful in generating presentations. It would be helpful to have pixel dimensions for images (particularly for thumbnails) more easily accessible to presentation software. Similarly, sequencing information and page characteristics should be explicitly recorded as metadata elements and not merely embedded in filenames. It has also been realized that some basic descriptive metadata should be associated with the structural and administrative metadata. The need to store and manipulate metadata of various types has led the Library of Congress to plan for a system that will allow the capture of metadata during production and the export of selected metadata in formats appropriate to different functions.

The choice of formats for master versions of digital reproductions takes into account suitability for long-term retention. Resources are named in consistent ways designed to support persistent identification. Quality review procedures check data integrity as well as faithfulness of reproduction. Capture practices are documented for future reference.

Master formats are well documented and widely deployed, preferably formal standards and preferably non-proprietary. Such choices should minimize the need for future migration or ensure that appropriate and affordable tools for migration will be developed by the industry. The Library has used a two-tiered naming approach for all American Memory materials. The digital object representing an item is identified by the "aggregate" to which it belongs and an item identifier that is unique within that aggregate. Aggregate names are registered centrally as part of the procedure for requesting storage space; this ensures that each two-part identifier is unique. These local identifiers can be used as the basis for identifiers that are globally unique and externally resolvable, for example using the Library's handle server.

NDLP commissioned development of a software utility to check TIFF and JPEG headers from one of its scanning contractors. NDLView is used as a first pass review on receipt of a batch of files before they are reviewed for image quality. Each file is opened and values within the headers of image files are validated against a contract specification profile.

DIGITAL CONTENT SERVICE DEVELOPMENT ACTIVITY

The digital content service development activity that has already taken place in the library, archive, museum and gallery and higher education sectors in the UK.

Public libraries are seen nationally as having an important role to play in the development of the information society. This role is typically threefold:

1 Access points

2 Trainers

3 Content providers

The main role identified for public libraries in the information society at a government policy level is as free public access points to the computer networks upon which the information society will depend. The content this infrastructure will carry, however, is generally seen as being provided by institutions other than libraries, such as museums and galleries, the education sector, government itself and commercial institutions. Public libraries are seen as suitable locations where people can be trained in how to access and interact with the digital material held on the networks. Public libraries will be a place where the public will be able to gain the skills they require to access their country's digital government, cultural and educational resources.

However, this content is not described in any detail or any information given on its type. The same report suggests that libraries should be involved in the development of software used in the process of lifelong learning. Generally, though, the role of public library as content provider is rarely mentioned.

The view of libraries as primarily access providers seems to be in conflict with the amount of digital content development taking place in public libraries both in the UK and abroad. This content development can be grouped in three main areas:

1 Digitisation of visual material

2 Creation of online information services

3 Creation of guides to resources

Images from local history and local studies collections, mainly photographs, maps, prints and engravings, are the most popular type of resource currently being converted into a digital format. This is because 'photographs make the obvious and attractive digitisation projects for public access because images are suited to and can often be improved by viewing on screen, and they are also selected because access to the originals can be difficult and prone to causing damage.'

Typically, this material is made available on a CD-Rom which may also contain small selections of other digital material (text, music, film etc). These materials will often have been edited to form the basis of an education learning resource. An increasing number of collections of digital material are being made available over the Internet. Leeds Libraries Service, for example, has made a percentage of its local history photograph collection available on its Web site. This collection can be searched by key word and geographical area. It should be noted, however, that much of this online material does not provide the educational learning experience that CD-Rom material has often been designed to provide.

At present, most UK public libraries are still in the planning stages of digitising their local history collections and making them Internet-accessible. Difficulties with funding, concerns about copyright issues and lack of suitable technical skills among staff are the main barriers preventing more services from putting these plans into action.

The kinds of citizen's information and public information held and supplied by public libraries, including contact details of local and national organisations, and information on transport and travel, tourism, arts and leisure, housing and accommodation, health, education and training, employment, information for disabled people, for ethnic communities, business, commercial and industrial information, etc. Typically, this kind of information is provided in a 'signposting' format. It points the way for the individual to an organisation which will be able to provide expert advice on the topic required. Most community information provided by a public library therefore consists of contact details of relevant organisations, charities and government agencies.

Initially, community information services were paper based but it was soon recognised that simple digital technology would allow the service to reach a greater number of users. Many libraries transferred their community information services on to a central computerised database that could be accessed by geographically-dispersed dumb terminals. With the development of more sophisticated computer networking technology, many libraries are now moving their community information services from the 'dumb terminal' model to an Internet-accessible one. Whereas it was previously only possible to access community information by using one of the dumb terminals, the Internet-based service is available to anyone with a networked computer.

There are now aspirations within the library sector to develop these local community information services so they can be searched jointly at a national level. Most of the this work is being done in a British Library Research and Innovation Centre (BLRIC)-funded research project called CIRCE <URL.

Public libraries are also working with their local communities to develop a new kind of community information service. Croydon Online is run by Croydon Libraries and is both a Web site for Croydon and the name of its community computing network. The content consists mainly of information on all aspects of living and working in Croydon; whilst the network is being developed to connect all Croydon and spread the opportunity to try it, find information and use e-mail. The service offers space on its Web server for local businesses and clubs to produce Web pages about themselves. Public libraries have also been developing digital services that are primarily about themselves. Many public library authorities in the UK now have Web pages. The information on these pages is typically 'brochureware': information about the library's services, its opening hours and its location.

These Web sites do not provide access to actual services and are generally very static - they are in reality online brochures. Public library Web sites have the potential for much more than 'brochureware'. They could be used for making available actual library services over the network. This can include providing access to the library catalogue, access to online databases and information about the local area, hosting Web pages for local businesses and clubs and giving information about new books and resources.

The creation of much of this content is firmly based in the concept of moving many of the library's services out of the library building and on to the network. It should be noted that many UK public libraries do not have direct control over their own Web pages. The library's Web site will be part of a much larger local authority site that will be controlled centrally by an

IT department. This arrangement makes it very hard for libraries to develop a dynamic Web site as they have little immediate control over their pages.

Public libraries are typically well advanced in the development of automated catalogues. Most libraries will have a computerised central catalogue that will run their central stock services. Catalogues for services slightly peripheral to the main ones, such as local history, will often not have been retro-converted into an electronic format and will still be paper based. There is a considerable amount of effort currently being made to change this situation. Typically these retro-conversion projects are in-house and internally funded. Public libraries are increasingly making their catalogues accessible on the Internet. Online access to catalogues is likely to increase if the public library community follows the same pattern as academic libraries. As well as providing easy access to their own resources through the use of a computerised catalogue, public libraries are also looking to make access to resources on the Internet easier.

Many libraries include on their Web pages a collection of links to Web resources which they consider to be useful for their readers. These links will be roughly classified into subjects and will usually be quite small in number and simply embedded into a basic Web page. Each library authority will have its own collections of links, which may often contain the same material collected by other libraries. Information North's Regional Information Service (RIS) has developed this idea of providing mediated access to Internet resources very fully. The service is run by Libraries Information and Media Sector Group of Northern Informatics and aims to provide structured access to a wide variety of Internet sites relevant to the region, alongside an enquiry service delivered by information professionals in libraries across the region.

This provides information about family history resources in public libraries in Britain and Ireland. It lists the resources, their opening hours, their research services and contact details in library authorities across the country. Whilst not itself providing access to any family history material, the service does provide a useful starting point for finding out what kinds of information an authority holds and when it is accessible. Public libraries are generally operating in a policy context that sees them simply as access points to digitised content created by other sectors. This is a limited view of the potential of public libraries when the kind of digital content service development that libraries themselves are undertaking is considered.

Libraries hold much valuable material on local history and family history. However, their potential for digital content service development is much greater than this.

Libraries have the ability to create content services through the development of access tools and resource guides. Through their Web services they could open up the their services to anyone with a networked computer at any time of the day. In a national policy context, museums and galleries are seen as mainly content providers. They are viewed as bodies that will benefit greatly from the opportunities of digitisation. Museums and galleries have been designed to be repositories for rare and important cultural artefacts. Owing to their rarity, these artefacts are not easily accessible as they need to be safeguarded in museums. In order to make the artefacts more accessible, it has been acknowledged at a government policy level that these materials should be digitised and made publicly accessible electronically. This concept is repeated in many policy documents.

A number of countries are taking this idea further and developing 'cultural networks'. These networks will provide access to digitised collections of archives, museums and libraries. Museums in Finland are building up databases and networks in their fields. Content production is promoted and the collections themselves are being digitised, the goal being a National Information Network for Culture. In this way, all citizens will have better access to the national cultural heritage. A digital project is to be carried out in which the paintings collections of more than 200 museums and about the same number of other institutions will be made accessible and available for use, exchange and transfer.

MUISTU is a project for the digitalisation and network delivery of the Finnish National Collections. It is run by libraries, museums and archives to develop the accessibility of the national heritage of knowledge and culture. The aim is to create databases for different types of materials, such as text, pictures, manuscripts and maps, build up a functional service environment for digital material and image processing, collect information on user reactions to digital material services.

This is a theme that appears in many national policy documents. Libraries, museums and galleries and archives are called upon to co-operate in developing a national digital heritage. Museum and gallery digital content service development activities as falling into five main types:

1 Brochureware
2 Dataware
3 Resourceware
4 Guideware
5 Courseware

It should be noted that much of this activity is still in the very early stages of development and may not yet be publicly available. Brochureware is the term for online material that gives basic information about a museum: for example, its address, opening times and charges. This kind of online resource is often little more than a brochure about the museum or gallery that has been developed into a simple Web page.

There is no interactivity and often no accessibility to any of the museum's resources. Brochureware is the type of online resource that most UK museums and galleries have made available. It is often the first step towards a more developed and complex online museum or gallery resource. Dataware can be characterised as an online catalogue of the museum or gallery's resources. As yet, very few museums or galleries make 'dataware' available, but 48 per cent of current projects are developing such services. Essentially one database will be accessed by different types of users for different reasons in different parts of the building. This is instead of creating individual interactive information points at specific locations within the building.

Many museums and galleries will already have a catalogue in a basic electronic format-i.e. simple textual records-but this catalogue will only be available for in-house staff use. Resourceware can be described as 'themed source material'. It will not only provide digital access to an object, but also access to information about its context, history and other material that will allow the object to be experienced and understood on many different levels. Currently, these kinds of digital resource can usually only be accessed in the museum itself and are generally CD-Rom based. Very little of this type of material is available online, as it is technically complicated and time intensive to make available in an Internet-accessible format. However, SCRAN (Scottish Cultural Resource Access Network) is producing a networked multimedia resource base of Scottish History and Material Culture.

Museums and galleries are seen by governments as one of the great benefactors from the development of national networks and the information society. Their scarce resources could be made accessible to millions via digital technology. Museums and galleries are themselves aware of this challenge and are beginning to make their content available. However, they are not just making digital images available, but are making their content more meaningful by developing it into courseware and resourceware.

Both courseware and resourceware are expensive to develop, and online access to existing examples is still scarce but increasing. Archives In the national policy context, archives are viewed in a very similar manner to museums and galleries. They too are seen primarily as digital cultural content providers. Not surprisingly, great emphasis is placed on the potential for collaboration between these three sectors:

The use of information reserves can be activated via co-operation between museums, libraries and archives. This implies join use of regional databases, reference databases and projects for making local regions and the associated cultural heritage known to the public. One role clearly defined for archives, although not strictly content creation, is as a repository for electronic material. As more and more documentation exists only in electronic formats, concern is growing that this material will not be preserved. Already, many important modern records of central and local government are only kept in digitised format.

The UK archives sector is already involved in storing and preserving these records. The ESRC data archive at Essex University already makes available data sets from a variety of sources such as opinion polls. In addition, the NADA project at the University of London Computer Centre has won a contract from the Public Record Office to convert, mount and make available data from a number of government bodies such as the Metropolitan Police and the Office of National Statistics. Information about the current digital content service development in UK archives has been drawn from two recent reports, Archives Online and Virtually New-Creating the Digital Collection: A Review of Digitisation Projects in Local Authorities, Libraries and Archives. In many respects, the development of digital content in archives is very similar to the initiatives that have been taking place in the local history services of public libraries.

This parallel activity highlights the similarities and synergy that exists between the two sectors. However, where public libraries have focused on the development of content, the archive community has placed a greater emphasis on the development of electronic finding aids. Current digital service development in archives falls into three main types:

1 Digitisation of visual material

2 Creation of electronic guides to resources

3 Digitisation of textual material.

Nearly 20 per cent of the local authority archives that responded to the Archives Online survey were involved in some kind of electronic image capture project. This work is generally experimental and is not done as a routine part of an archive's cataloguing process. Its experimental nature results from the lack of recognised technical standards or documentary standards for the inclusion of images in archival catalogues.

Photographs, old local newspapers and maps are the main focus of this digitisation activity. The aim of the experimental projects is to make material more widely available and to protect the original source material. Warwickshire Images will combine digitised photographs and other images with textual information and OS mapping of the whole county. Increasingly, archives are turning to the concept of resourceware and are utilising their resources to develop interactive electronic guides to a local area.

Hackney Online is an important project for the UK archive community as it has developed software that is particularly suitable for this kind of archival use. However, these services are typically only available in house in a CD-Rom format. Most archivists will have as a future aim making digitised archival material available over the Internet, but the barriers of limited resources, lack of technical expertise and concerns about copyright issues are preventing this from happening yet. The National Council on Archives has stated that, in view of the size of UK archival holdings, wholesale digitisation of them is impossible. On a national scale, the most effective primary aim for archives should be the development of electronic catalogues and indexes. Without such electronic guides, finding particular archival material is both time consuming and ineffective.

Another aspect of developing guides to resources is the creation of Web pages for each archive. Currently, these pages is very similar to those of public library Web sites: they typically provide 'brochureware'-type information about the archive. However, in the future it is likely that these Web sites will be the gateways to accessing the material that the archive has available in digital format. It is still necessary to look abroad for an example of a fully developed Web site of this type. Through the Web site of the National Archives and Records Administration (NARA) of the USA, it is possible to view online exhibitions, use NARA's database and download teaching materials from the online classroom.

UK-based initiatives include the Royal Commission on Historical Manuscripts service called ARCHON. This is a Web-based information gateway for UK archivists and users of manuscript sources for British history. From this gateway it is possible to access information on all repositories in the United Kingdom and on all repositories throughout the world that have collections of manuscripts noted on the British National Register of Archives.

In addition, archivists can access information on archival organisations and initiatives through the pages of archivists' links <URL. This service is similar in many ways to Familia, which provides information about public library local history collections. The work of the Public Record Office (PRO) in this area is particularly interesting. Information is being 'repurposed' to address the specific information needs of users, be they school students, hobbyists or professional researchers. Information is currently held in many different formats and cataloguing of materials is often incomplete.

At a local level, the main digital content service development taking place is the digitisation of visual material for use in house in a CD-Rom format. It is interesting to note that collaboration between the museum and gallery, library and archive sectors is again being promoted at a policy level. The recent introduction of information and communication technology systems has set a challenge for archivists to develop and implement best archival descriptive practices to facilitate data exchange within the profession while tailoring their automated catalogues and finding aids to offer cross-domain searches within their parent institution. This is also a challenge for their plans to provide access to digitised resources which may only exist in electronic format or which have been selected from their vast holdings of paper records for special treatment.

Digital Library Framework

Information technology and globalisation are likely to change the nature of libraries and their activities. For example, the emergence of digital libraries has been discussed for several years. The concept 'digital library' has many different meanings. Some assume that in a digital library everything has to be in digital form. This type of libraries changes the business of libraries radically. All information is in digital format which can propose that there is no staff maintaining the collections, or there are no buildings in which the collections are stored, read and borrowed. Everything happens in a virtual world via global computer networks.

In this sense digital library is something totally new which has not existed before. Certainly, digital libraries are taking over some tasks of traditional libraries, but they rather seem to supplement than replace traditional libraries. On the other hand some use the term 'digital library' to refer to all shorts of computerisation in traditional libraries. For example, CD-ROMs and on-line databases are seen as digitalisation of traditional library. In this sense the collections can be both physical and digital while the means of searching information about the collections are increasingly transforming into electronic. In this case the change in the business of library is not so radical than in the case of digital collections.

There still exists staff maintaining the collections, and buildings in which the collections are stored. The changes are mostly happening at micro-level, e.g. in the contents of librarians' jobs. One significant difference between the definitions is the notion of the content of a library. The first definition assumes library as a set of electronic resources and associated technical capabilities for creating, searching, and using information. The second definition is based on physical existence of fixed, permanent material in a specific place.

Research in digital libraries has focused on issues like interoperability, description of objects, collection management, human-computer interaction, economic, social and legal issues. For example, special types of digital libraries, supporting technologies, and national efforts and policies has been studied. Probably the most important driving force to digitalisation of the scientific libraries in Finland has been the introduction of computer-based library system in the early 1990's. In the case organisation the local library system has facilitated totally new forms of co-operation and communication between the departments of the library, and with other scientific libraries, too.

Earlier, the faculty libraries were treated as independent libraries with their own collections. Further, the system has allowed more effective utilisation of collections by the customers. However, the users have also faced a number of problems in the utilisation of the system in their work. The library system has been developed by an international software house. It is used in every scientific library in Finland with tens of thousands of users in the country. Further, different releases of the system are applied at least in several European countries and in the USA. The library system supports the core activities. Altogether 84% of the employees use the system, and the average use of the system was 55% of working hours.

Furthermore, the organisation applies around ten other important computer applications. The employees who use the central system in their work use also these applications around 16% of working hours. In other words, 84% of the employees spend 71% of their working hours using some computer-based information system which suggests that the organisation is highly dependent on information technology. The importance of the library system is more obvious if we look at the pool of information which is stored, updated, sorted and searched by the employees and the customers. The total amount of volumes in the library is huge, around 2.100.000 copies. In 1997, there were about 673.000 volumes in the library system, and the rest of the collections filed in manual card catalogues.

However, not only is the pool of information about the existing collections huge, but also the information concerning orders and acquisition of new items is significant. The collections increase by about 50.000 copies per year. Furthermore, the information related to the customer service process, i.e., ordering, borrowing and returning publications, is an important part of information flow from the perspective of information technology. The system has radically improved the quality of library activities. The users have also encountered a number of problems in the system. The most serious weaknesses were technical quality, especially complexity and clumsiness in the use of the system, and breakdowns in telecommunications.

The "community of scientific libraries in Finland" is making the selection of its new library system in the very near future. The decision makers should have a clear and shared vision of the future directions of scientific libraries in Finland. There is obvious need for shared information systems strategy between the libraries. Because of the co-operative efforts of scientific libraries at the European level, the strategy should take into account plans at this level as well. Especially, if the selected vendor is outside of Europe, as the situation is currently, possible cultural differences between co-operative parties should be pointed out and problems or conflicts tried to avoid. Increasing attention should be paid to ease of use of the future library system, because the importance of IT in library activities is growing both for employees and customers.

The emergence of digital libraries and different kinds of means to search for information requires smooth integration of computer systems. All these issues put pressure on information management skills of managers in libraries. In general, the activity of the library can be characterised by two different work processes. The goals of these processes are different. On the one hand, the library increases and maintains its collections. On the other hand, the library serves the customers by lending volumes from the collections. Furthermore, administrative tasks are important part of work in libraries.

Administration related tasks can be classified into general administration, finance, computer related tasks and other tasks. Administration includes human resource management, various planning tasks, statistics, reporting, secretary services, word processing, copy service, internal post and maintenance. Finance includes its own reporting and statistics, bill handling, archiving, and other finance related tasks. Computer related tasks include planning tasks, maintenance of existing systems,.programming, user support, user training, WWW-pages, and other computer related tasks. The class of 'other tasks' include all other tasks which can not be included in collection or service related tasks. Administrative tasks form a quite large portion of all costs in library's activities.

Because there is an increasing need for personnel, equipment, and other resources in service related tasks currently, and need is likely to become in grow in the future, there certainly exists pressure for diminishing the money and organisational effort spent on administration. On the other hand new IT based forms of publications and services increase the amount of different kinds of services in traditional physical libraries. It is possible that, for example, maintenance of these services also increases the amount of administrative tasks. The business of libraries is mainly based on collections. Collection related tasks can be classified into three main groups: acquisition, cataloguing and maintenance. Acquisition includes all tasks from making order proposals to delivery control of ordered material.

Cataloguing can be sub-divided into two sub-groups. Cataloguing I refers to tasks of recording publication data into the database while cataloguing II refers to creation of descriptive key words for publications. Maintenance of collections includes high variety of work tasks, e.g. tasks of evaluation, sorting, arranging, removals, making inventories, book binding, and stocking. The concept of digital library may cause some confusion in acquisition, cataloguing and maintenance tasks in traditional libraries. When thinking, for example, electronic periodicals the contents of library's collections are changing every once and while. This may be confusing for those workers who are used to traditional collection centred idea of a library.

Further, probably more effort has to be put on publicity, since finding of all relevant information becomes even harder for customers. In the case of digital library the ownership of a collection may become blurred. If a combination of the collections of several libraries is considered as a digital library whose collections are shown as an inseparable whole for customers, for example, the responsibility of collection related tasks has to defined clearly. If not defined the responsibility may be lost in common tasks between the libraries.

Service related tasks take one third of the work resources of the library. Service related tasks can be classified into six main groups: management, borrowing, information and training, distance lending, information services and other tasks. Information and training include work done in information desks as well as in customer training. The emergence of digital information services is likely to increase the amount of training. Training will be needed both in using different searching tools and in finding relevant sources of information. The consequence is that resources spent on borrowing will probably be needed on information and training, and on information services. Fortunately, one benefit of the increased amount of digital services in a traditional library could be the diminishing need for borrowing literature.

For example, digital library could radically diminish the need for distance lending. Currently, distance lending can be thought as an instance of digital library, because publications in any scientific library can be used by every customer. Distance lending just requires quite a lot of resources in sending publications back and forth between the libraries.

In a digital library the needed publications could be acquired electronically by a customer. The other side of the coin is that new services would be needed, for example machines for searching, reading, and printing. The idea of digital library as a library of libraries could also be interesting in the future. The community of scientific libraries could get significant benefits if all the libraries could use the same electronic publication. The departments which take care of distance lending could get the publication in electronic form and would pay for the use of the publication. In this way the use of a publication would be handled inside the national organisation and the control of copyrights would be easier that, for example access based on the Internet.

The library's work practices are partly defined by the nation-wide community of scientific libraries. The scientific libraries have a shared index (called 'Linda') of their collections. The cataloguing data of each publication acquired to any scientific library is stored to Linda. The first library that acquires a publication stores the cataloguing data including the descriptive key words, etc. to Linda. Then the other libraries which acquire the same publication add only their own identification to the same record. However, all the libraries copy the record from Linda to their own local database. For the customers in any scientific library it is possible to use Linda and find out in which libraries a certain publication is located, and then e.g. use distance lending possibilities to borrow the publication.

Both national and international co-operation provide significant opportunities in reducing the cataloguing work carried out by a single library. One possibility would be shared catalogues of scientific libraries. In this way the cataloguing data would be entered only once into a computer system. Of course, for effectiveness reasons the data should be replicated over several physical locations, but this work should not require human effort as it is now. Also, information about "have-nots", i.e. publications which are not in the collection, could be offered. However, currently there are some significant differences in work practices between the libraries, especially in cataloguing tasks. Repetition of tasks occurs, because there is no shared understanding between the libraries about key words and classifications, and the data fields that should be filled. This indicates that the cataloguing processes are likely to produce problems in the future, too, if national agreements about work practices cannot be created and followed.

International co-operation could provide most of the cataloguing data in electronic form directly from the publishing companies. For example, if the key words and classifications of publications were created by somebody else than the employees of libraries (e.g. the publishers or authors), somewhat 10% of collection related work time would be saved. In this particular library it would mean savings of 155 work hours per week, i.e. the work of one half time employee and four full time employees. Similar kind of saving would be global because the same work has to be done in libraries all over the world. The local saving of work is not very significant, however, the amount of saved work time at the global level is huge. Furthermore, global co-operation sets new challenges for work practices. Diverse work practices have already produced problems, e.g. in lending tasks, as the current system is transferred from USA to Finland.

Future globalisation probably increases the amount of partners in other countries, and it can be difficult to affect the work practices of, e.g. publishers and vendors. The only solution may be to adapt to their procedures.

Digital Libraries will have a major influence on the design of future information systems. They are the cradle from which future advanced information technologies will emerge to provide "transparent" services to a variety of users. Digital Libraries have already attracted many real-world agents, which participate for various economic reasons. For example, publishers of books are in the process of presenting their collections in digital formats in order to reduce production costs and increase profit margins.

Digital Libraries will house information objects in various media, such as text, audio, video and image, and provide information access services to a variety of users. One can envision a plethora of applications, such as collaborative computing and virtual class-rooms, using such services. Users of these applications, being heterogenous in their preferences, could request for different qualities of service for information access. The preferences of users could be based on the charge to access information. For example, users browsing through a Digital Library of video clips or image clips would prefer different qualities of service based on the charge and the availability of local resources. In designing service mechanisms for accessing information objects in digital libraries, several issues arise. One of them is the issue of pricing services to access information objects, and accounting and billing users for QoS. These are economic issues, however, they play an important role in allocating resources such as processing (CPU) time, network bandwidth, buffer, memory and cache for storing, searching, accessing, transporting, and presenting various information objects in a coherent way to the users. For example, users might want to know the prices for different qualities of service to access an information object, such as a video clip of a lecture based on a specific day.

Current networks and systems have limited resources. Therefore, allocation of resources, such as processing time and network bandwidth, can be crucial in providing efficient services. In the future, bandwidth and processing time will be more than sufficient, and information objects will be priced based on the demand for them rather than on the Digital Library system (DLSystem) that houses them.

The main approach in pricing and accounting for QoS is an economic model of the players in large Digital Libraries. This involves modeling and understanding the various tasks that are required to support Digital Libraries. There are several reasons why this form of modeling helps in understanding the interfaces between the various elements of Digital Libraries. The main reasons are as follows:

— *Limiting complexity:* Economic models provide several interesting contributions to resource sharing algorithms. The first is a set of tools for limiting the complexity by decentralizing the control of resources. The second is a set of mathematical models that can yield several new insights into resource sharing problems.

— *Decentralization:* In an economy, decentralization is provided by the fact that economic-agents attempt to achieve their goals in competitive fashion. There are two types of such agents, suppliers and consumers. A consumer attempts to maximize its benefit by obtaining the services or resource allocations that maximize its preferences under a wealth constraint. Suppliers compete in order to maximize revenue and minimize costs, which means attract more users and provide the best services.

— *Pricing and coordination:* Most economic models introduce money and pricing as techniques for coordinating the behavior of agents. Each consumer is endowed with money, which they use to purchase services or resources. The price a supplier charges for a resource or a service is determined by its supply and the market demand.

— *Usage accounting, billing and dimensioning:* In using economic models for service provisioning in distributed systems, usage accounting becomes a part of the economy. Suppliers have to keep track of resource usage in order to price resources effectively, and thereby charge/bill the users for access.

— *Administrative domains:* Large distributed systems and computer networks are spread over several domains. Each domain is typically managed and controlled by an administrator. An economic model of such an environment would imply that administrators advertise their services and prices. Therefore, providing a simple interface to negotiate between domains.

— *Scalability:* A key issue in designing architectures for services in large computer networks and distributed systems is scalability. Models of competition provide—in a natural fashion—mechanisms for scaling services appropriately based on the service-demand and resource-availability.

The novelty introduced by the economic approach is not only in modeling large decentralized, autonomous systems, but also in designing efficient systems that account naturally for user QoS requirements, and optimally allocate resources for the various services in Digital Libraries.

Model of Digital Libraries

There are three kinds of players in the economic model of Digital Libraries: Suppliers (storage and indexing), Agents (who search, transform and present information) and Users. The three players are described below:

— *Suppliers:* Commercial DLSystems buy works from various publishers and authors, and provide services to a variety of users for a fee. The DLSystems not only price information but also price QoS to access the information. Pricing is based on the user demand, and users represent their demands through agents. The prices remain fixed every time-interval, assuming that time is divided into intervals. For example, a time-interval could be a 6 hours in a day. The time-intervals are decided by each DLSystem independently based on the market demand. The suppliers provide storage, access and local indexing services.

— *Information agents:* These are suppliers that provide Value-Added Services, such as transparent searching and presentation of objects to the users. From now on, refer to Information Agents as agents. The agents charge users for QoS provided. Agents contract services and resources from DLSystems over a period of time, and provide stable set of services to the users. The stability is provided by a flat service fee over period of time to the users. Agents renegotiate for services from each DLSystem provided it is profitable, else they release resources. The agents compete to provide One-Stop Shopping services to the users.

— *Users:* They present complex queries to the information agents, and request for a service in viewing or obtaining the objects. Users could be grouped into query classes based on similar access patterns or just based on service required. Users within a group or class share the costs of the services. Users are free to choose among the various agents based on the QoS and charge. There are many classes of users who obtain services from one or many agents. The agents buy services from one or more of the DLSystems (Library Systems), and provide searching and presentation services to the users for a fee.

References

Logoze, Carl, and David Fielding, (1998). "Defining Collections in Distributed Digital Libraries." *D-Lib Magazine,* November.

Lund, William, (2001)."Digital Object Library Products", RLG DigiNews 5, no. 5.

Michelle Q. Wang Baldonado and Steve B. Cousins. (1996). Addressing heterogeneity in the networked information environment. *New Review of Information Networking*, 2:83-102.

Miller, Rush G., (2002)"Shaping Digital Library Content." The Journal of Academic Librarianship 28, no. 3 : 97-103.

5

Access to Information Archives

The rapid growth in the creation and dissemination of digital objects by authors, publishers, corporations, governments, and even librarians, archivists and museum curators, has emphasized the speed and ease of short-term dissemination with little regard for the long-term preservation of digital information. However, digital information is fragile in ways that differ from traditional technologies, such as paper or microfilm. It is more easily corrupted or altered without recognition.

Digital storage media have shorter life spans, and digital information requires access technologies that are changing at an ever-increasing pace. Some types of information, such as multimedia, are so closely linked to the software and hardware technologies that they cannot be used outside these proprietary environments. Because of the speed of technological advances, the time frame in which we must consider archiving becomes much shorter. The time between manufacture and preservation is shrinking.

While there are traditions of stewardship and best practices that have become institutionalized in the print environment, many of these traditions are inadequate, inappropriate or not well known among the stakeholders in the digital environment. Originators are able to bypass the traditional publishing, dissemination and announcement processes that are part of the traditional path from creation to archiving and preservation. Groups and individuals who did not previously consider themselves to be archivists are now being drawn into the role, either because of the infrastructure and intellectual property issues involved or because user groups are demanding it. Librarians and archivists who traditionally managed the life cycle of print information from creation to long-term preservation and archiving, must now look to information managers from the computer science tradition to support the development of a system of stewardship in the new digital environment. There is a need to identify new best practices that satisfy the requirements and are practical for the various stakeholder groups involved.

TASKS OF DIGITAL PRESERVATION

"Preservation" in libraries has until now been a matter of preserving the artifact which provides the work inherent in it, thereby preserving the work itself. Electronic documents, by contrast, force the preservation considerations to divide into two: the preservation of the objects, as before, but also the preservation of the information contained in those objects and which is now so easily separable from them. The primary requirement for a digital research library is that from the start it be committed to organizing, storing and providing electronic information for periods of time longer than human lives. Implementation of a digital research library will require that specific tasks be accomplished and that several commitments be undertaken.

Preservation of electronic information needs to be looked at as comprising three distinct tasks:

— medium preservation,

— technology preservation and

— intellectual preservation.

What is new about preservation in the digital environment is that digital information must now be dealt with separately from its medium. A crude analogy might be to place a book on a closet shelf and close the door for 500 years. At the end of that time, broadly speaking, one can open the door and read that book. With an electronic resource we don't have that confidence even after ten years: the device on which it is recorded may deteriorate, the technology for its use is liable to obsolescence, and the contents may easily and invisibly have been changed.

Medium Preservation

Over the years the recording medium of tapes flakes off its support, or the support itself gets brittle. CD-ROMs are still not considered to have a dependable life of over 15 years, for if air enters through the plastic cover the metal substrate quickly corrodes. Aside from proper environmental and handling controls, the solution has been to "refresh" the information, that is, to copy it from the potentially deteriorating medium to another, fresher medium of the same or a similar kind. Except for device-dependent formatting, the information itself is not changed in any way detectable by the user or its application program.

Technology Preservation

The preservation of the medium on which the bits and bytes of electronic information are recorded is an important concern. But such solutions will inevitably be short-term, and will not in themselves be the means of preserving information over long periods of time. Michael Lesk in 1994 urged that the greatest attention should instead be directed to the obsolescence of technologies rather than simply of the media. Lesk describes the rapid changes in the means of recording, in the storage formats, and in the software that allows electronic information to be of use. Urging what might be called technology preservation he asserts that for digital data, "preservation means copying, not physical preservation." That is, the preservation of electronic information into the indefinite future requires its being "migrated" from old to new technologies as they become available and as the old technologies cease being supported by vendors and the user community.

Information migration, or technological preservation, is the most problematic of the digital archiving challenges. Some of the evident technical problems are how to assure forward compatibility of information files within subsequently-developed application programs, given the short life-span of program versions and of their supporting corporate creators.

The logistical question is posed: should information be migrated forward in time as new programs supersede old, or should information only be migrated forward to a new program when it is specifically needed? Is it necessary to preserve the technology that supports all details of the target information or only its essentials—and what, of course, is the "essential" part? Jeff Rothenberg and Clifford Lynch have written intelligently about these problems. Rothenberg in 1998 discussed the strategy of "emulating" the software environment of a digital object. Lynch has used the analogy of textual editions, and film versions of books, to suggest that the goal of perfect information migration may not need fully to be achieved in order to satisfy future needs.

Intellectual Preservation

Intellectual preservation addresses the integrity and authenticity of the information as originally recorded. Preservation of the media and of the software technologies will serve only part of the need if the information content has been corrupted from its original form, whether by accident or design. The need for intellectual preservation arises because the great asset of digital information is also its great liability: the ease with which an identical copy can be quickly and flawlessly made is paralleled by the ease with which a change may undetectably be made.

It is very easy to replace an electronic dataset with an updated copy, and the replacement can have wide-reaching effects. The processes of authorship produce different versions which in an electronic environment can easily go into broad circulation; if each draft is not carefully labeled and dated it is difficult to tell which draft one is looking at, or whether one has the "final" version of a work.

It is the durability of those textual forms (books)that ultimately secures the continuing future of our past; it is the evanescence of the new ones that poses the most critical problem for bibliography and any further history dependent upon its scholarship. Society, like the individual, becomes senile in proportion as it loses its continuous memory, and electronic texts are now part of that memory, significant products of our civilisation. There is a new urgency with the arrival of computer-generated texts. The demands made by the evolution of texts in such forms, the speed with which versions are displaced one by another, and the question of their authority, are no less compelling than those we accept for printed books.

The problem may be put in the form of several questions that confront the user of any electronic document, whether it is text, hypertext, audio, graphic, numeric or multimedia information:

— How can I be sure that what I am viewing is what I want to see?

— How do I know that the document I have found is the same one that another used and made reference to in a footnote?

— How can I be sure that the document I now use has not been changed since the last time I used it?

— How can I be sure that a document is what it purports to be?

There are three possibilities for change in electronic texts that confront us with the need for intellectual preservation techniques:

— accidental change;

— intended change that is well-meant;

— intended change that is not well-meant; that is, fraud.

A document can sometimes be damaged accidentally, perhaps by data loss during transfer or through inadvertent mistakes in manipulation; for example, data may be corrupted in being sent over a network or between disks and memory on a computer. This no longer happens often, but it is possible. More frequent is the loss of sections of a document, or a whole version of a document, due to accidents in updating. There are at least two possibilities for intended change that is well-meant. New versions and drafts are familiar to us from dealing with authorial texts, for example, or from working with successive book editions, legislative bills, or revisions of working papers. It is desirable to keep track bibliographically of the distinction between one version and another.

Readers are accustomed to visual cues to indicate when a version is different. In addition to explicit numbering one may observe the page format, the typography, the producer's name, the binding, the paper itself. These cues are not available or dependable for distinguishing electronic versions. Structural updates, changes that are inherent in the document, also cause changes in information content. A dynamic data base by its nature is frequently updated: Books in Print, for example, or architectural drawings, or elements of the human genome project. How may one identify a given snapshot and authenticate it as representing a certain time?

The third kind of change that can occur is intentional change for fraudulent reasons. The change might be of one's own work, to cover one's tracks or change evidence for a variety of reasons, or it might be damage to the work of another. In an electronic future the opportunities for revision of history will be multiplied. An unscrupulous researcher could change experimental data without a trace. A financial dealer might wish to cover tracks to hide improper business, or a political figure might wish to hide or modify inconvenient earlier views.

Consider the consequences if political opponents could modify their own past correspondence without detection. Then consider the case if each of them could modify the other's correspondence without detection. Society, as well as each opponent, needs a defense against such cases. The need is to fix, or authenticate, a document so that a user can be sure of the unaltered text when it is needed. Such a technique must be easy to use so that it does not impede creation or access. It must also provide generality, flexibility, openness where possible but document security where desired, low cost, and — most of all — functionality over long periods of time on the human scale.

Digital time-stamping and various forms of digital signatures are among solutions available for the electronically novel problem of intellectual preservation. There are likely to be others, each with their own assets and liabilities. The preservation community must keep aware of potential solutions and urge implementation of ones most broadly suitable; most of all, preservationists must be aware that the problem exists and requires a solution beyond the important preservation of the media and the technologies.

Organizational Commitments

The organization of libraries is already changing as electronic information increasingly becomes part of their charge. Most research libraries have had substantial systems departments which maintain infrastructures while the librarians take on more and more digital information responsibilities. Some libraries locate the responsibility for electronic information distinctly from that for print. Most libraries are coming to see the forms as inseparable and include digital responsibilities along with artifactual responsibilities in assignments for collection development, cataloguing and public service.

As libraries move more into the electronic environment the historic tripartite division of libraries into public services, technical services and collection development continues functionally but in more fluid arrangements. In addition, the need for consortial activity has become evident both for provision and preservation of digital information. People who combine bibliographic understanding, problem-solving abilities, negotiating skills and process orientation will be needed throughout libraries; such staff will take on the demanding new technical, collection and service responsibilities for long-term support of digital collections.

Fiscal Commitment

The permanent existence of a digital research library will require assured continuity in operational funding. Almost any other library activity can survive a funding hiatus of a year or more. Acquisitions, building maintenance, and preservation can be suspended, or an entire staff can be dispersed and a library shut down for several years, and the artifactual collections will more or less survive. But digital collections, like the online catalogue, require continual maintenance if they are to survive more than a very brief interruption of power, environmental control, backup, migration and related technical care.

Online catalogue maintenance costs have reached a rough steady state, and the capital costs for new OPACs are decreasing relative to the capabilities provided. The catalogue size will continue to increase, but catalogue records are small relative to the information to which they refer. Digital collections, however, as a proportion of the library's supply of information, will grow for the foreseeable future, and the quantity of information requiring care will become considerable. Unit costs of storage are likely to continue falling for some time, which may make the financial burden manageable. Long term funding will be required to assure long term care. Libraries and their parent institutions will need to develop new fiscal tools and use familiar fiscal tools for new purposes. Public institutions, usually constrained to annual funding, will have particular difficulties, but existing procedures for capital or plant funding may provide precedents. One familiar technique is the endowment. It has been difficult to obtain private funding for endowments of concepts and services rather than books and mortar, but it is possible. Institutions might also build endowments out of operating funds over periods of time

Some revenue streams associated with digital research libraries may be practical. Consortial arrangements may allow for lease or purchase of shares in a digital collection. Shorter-term access might be provided to other institutions on a usage basis. Access could be sold to certain classes of users, e.g. businesses, non-local clienteles, or specific information projects. New relations with publishers, presently difficult to perceive through the miasmic fog rising from intellectual property, might provide income for storage of electronically published materials during the copyright lifetime in which publishers collect usage fees. With commitment and imagination long term fiscal tools will be found.

Institutional Commitment

All these are instrumental means of accomplishing the greatest requirement, that of conscious, planned institutional commitment to preserve that part of human culture which will flower in electronic form. While museums preserve artifacts, often beautiful, that embody information, libraries preserve information that — until now — has been embedded in artifacts. The advent of electronic information will accentuate the difference between these roles as libraries take the responsibility for the preservation of information in non-artifactual forms.

For the past century most research libraries have been associated with universities, and this connection seems likely to continue in the immediate future. Whatever the governance structure, an institution wishing to benefit from electronic information will have to make a conscious commitment to providing resources. Michael Buckland, of the University of California at Berkeley, has distinguished between a library's role and its mission. Where the role of a library is to facilitate access to information, its mission is to support the mission of its parent institution. One can extend this to understand that if a university wishes to continue gaining support for its mission from its library, it will have to make commitments to the library's role. In the electronic environment, this means new longstanding financial commitments which the library and university together must identify and accomplish.

The commitment will have to be clearly and publicly made if scholars and other libraries are to have confidence that a given digital collection is indeed likely to exist for the long term. It is essential that guidelines or standards be established defining what is meant by a long term commitment, and defining what electronic repositories of data can qualify to be called a digital research library. Just as donors of books, manuscripts and archives look for demonstration of long term care and commitment, so too will scholars and publishers as they create digital information which requires a home.

Progress in Digital Archiving

The progress in digital archiving was strikingly international, and it was unevenly distributed around the globe. Trends in major developed nations are described below.

United States: Activity in the United States contrasts with that of Australia and the UK in that there seem to be several loci of activity which don't seem to have much relation to each other. Nor are any of them are very explicit as to what they are about. First, it is important to note that the substantially-funded NSF Digital Libraries projects have focused primarily on large data base construction and on social implications. Emphasis is always on "innovative applications"; archiving is mentioned in passing, but so far not funded.

The Digital Libraries Federation (DLF) has now been in existence for several years, but remains opaque to external observers. A coalition of about 20 libraries, it has developed some brief broad strategic outlines of proposed activity but has been silent as to actual projects within member libraries. In early DLF statements digital archiving was listed as one of three main priorities; more recently it is an "other" priority, with pre-eminent place given to user authentication and authorization matters. Don Waters, the primary author of the important 1996 report from RLG and the Commission on Preservation and Access, has been the DLF director since 1997.

The ARCHES (Archival Server) project, begun in 1996, is specifically intended by Research Libraries Group (RLG) to address digital archiving. In its first instance it is intended both to support a specific repository and to create a software environment that will make long-term archiving possible. Details of the digital archival commitment being made by the project are unclear, and in its beginnings the project appears to have been subordinated to the specific content respository created for it on marriage and law in the 19th century.

OCLC—the largest library utility—is well placed to create and provide archiving services, for it has readily available both the financial and intellectual capital to do so. In 1997 it committed to archiving e-journals on behalf of its members subscribers and bravely included a commitment to technological migration. However it has remained silent on details of how it intends to achieve this goal, and has not yet had to come through with this commitment in any specific instance. Also, it has included the statement that it will migrate digital objects "at its discretion," presumably depending upon the degree of difficulty. Though in practice perhaps such a statement is always implied, its unqualified emphasis so early does not add to the confidence one wishes in such a project.

United Kingdom: The Follett Commission of 1993 stimulated electronic library ("eLib") activity on a broad front in the UK, supported by millions of pounds annually and managed by the Joint Information Systems Committee (JISC) of the Higher Education Funding Councils. After several national workshops on digital archiving, in 1997 JISC inaugurated a specific program through CEDARS (CURL Exemplars in Digital Archives, where

CURL is the Council of University Research Libraries of the UK). The present author is a member of this project's advisory board. The CEDARS participants comprise Cambridge, Leeds and Oxford Universities.

The main deliverables of the project will be recommendations and guidelines as well as practical, robust and scalable models for establishing distributed digital archives. It is expected that the outcomes of CEDARS will influence the development of legislation for legal deposit of electronic materials and feed directly into the emerging national strategy for digital preservation currently being developed through the National Preservation Office of the British Library.

Another JISC-funded eLib project is the Arts and Humanities Data Service, which has responded to specific requests of JISC's Digital Archiving Working Party by developing strategic policy framework statements for creating and preserving digital collections.

Canada: The Canadian Initiative on Digital Libraries began work in 1997, but to date has shown little emphasis on digital archiving. On the other hand, many Canadian libraries are members of USA consortia (e.g. OCLC and RLG) whom they may count upon to act in their behalf.

The commonwealth tradition of national planning and initiative appears in strong contrast to the fragmented, non-governmental activities in North America. It remains to be seen which approach will generate the optimal and broadly exploited archiving technologies that are needed. However one can wish from the outset that the USA groups were more communicative about what they are doing, and in particular that they would coordinate their efforts with one another; to date there is little evidence that they do so. But it is notable that regardless of where digital archiving investigation is going on, it is in consortial activity. There is uniform recognition that digital archiving is not a matter soluble by individual institutions, whether for collection reasons or for technological reasons.

Australia: Work in Australia originated in 1993 on an explicitly national basis, with funding both from the government and from the national library. It can be described as a top-down approach, aiming first at principles and goals before proceeding to implementation. PADI (Preserving Access to Digital Information) is headed by an officer of the National Library of Australia, has an office and a budget and has developed statements of vision, goals and objectives. PADI maintains strong links between the library and archive communities. Its Statement of Principles on Preservation of Australian Digital Objects reflects an early achievement of national consensus. It has been followed by reports attempting to deal with location of responsibilities, definitions of how digital information is to be preserved, and the likely costs over time of digital archiving.

Access Management

Digital technologies open a world that paradoxically is simultaneously more complex and, in some ways, simpler. It is more complex because now the same document or document format may intrinsically be represented in different media for different purposes, forcefully motivating the need to distinguish carefully between the format and the medium. Furthermore, different media may be used interchangeably for different stages of document handling, that is, for capture, storage, access, distribution, and use. To complicate the situation even more, the documents may be encoded in a myriad of ways at each of these stages. And yet, separation of the format and the medium—and treating each stage of document handling separately—may open up a more logical structure free from traditional constraints. In this sense, digital technologies may simplify certain aspects of librarianship.

Digital technologies present many new challenges, however, that must be considered. For example, although these varying formats may be decoded and translated back and forth among each other, many fear that the means of decoding may become lost as a result of technological obsolescence, conceivably making digitally stored documents inaccessible. There are also many who question the longevity of the physical media used in digital technologies. Others suggest that the appropriate way to address both of these problems—as well as to take advantage of the declining costs of computer storage and of increasing storage densities—may well be to copy stored documents periodically onto new media.

The main advantage of the world of digital technologies, namely that they represent a kind of "esperanto" of mutually comprehensible and interchangeable formats, may, if not properly managed, also represent their biggest weakness, because of the rapidity of change and obsolescence, and because of the wide range of choices available at any given time. Periodic recopying onto new media represents a whole new approach for libraries to the operation and financing of "inventory management". The implications could be quite extensive. Librarians tend to think in terms of periods of centuries rather than having to recopy every few years. Such considerations may either hinder the adoption of digital technologies for preservation or other purposes or eventually cause some rethinking of the underlying economics of librarianship. The incentive for such potential re-evaluation, however, is not limited to the preservation of older materials, nor is the influence of technology the only driving factor.

The underlying stimulus is a gradual transition over the centuries—perhaps spurred by the exponential growth of recorded knowledge and information—from documents with associated physical or conceptually useful lifetimes, times between new editions, or, more generically, times between "instances", that can be measured in decades or centuries; to documents with associated times between instances measured in much shorter units of time—even, in the case of "active documents", measured in minutes or seconds. The financial and other implications of this could undoubtedly be far-reaching for libraries, introducing into the library milieu unfamiliar concepts associated with continuous processes or processes with relatively short lifetimes, such as "depreciation" and "lifecycle costing." These are concepts that are familiar to the world of digital electronic processing and quite normal outside of universities, but that have been avoided in worlds—such as research libraries—that depend to a greater or lesser extent upon irregular gifts or grants of varying or unpredictable size, donations directed to the purchase and immediate storage of documents, but not to their maintenance. Indeed, one of the most serious questions facing librarians in the future may be how to effect a match between the changing economic demands of "continuous processes" and the traditional nature of many funding sources.

Yet the potential of digital technologies and of the flexibility they offer is boundless. Over the coming decades, these technologies may open up vistas of ever-increasing storage densities to where entire libraries can be electronically stored in the space of a single room; of blinding access and distribution speeds allowing whole documents to be moved almost instantly across the nation's (and indeed the world's) data networks, leading to the concept of the "distributed library;" of ease of replication at very modest cost (another cause for alarm, particularly to those concerned with protection of intellectual property); of "print-on-demand" where paper copies of documents are only printed "just in time" and not inventoried in advance of need; of accessibility at a distance away from where the "digital document" or preservation copy was created or is stored; and of intelligent automated document analysis. Indeed, the means of creation and production of documents have already been revolutionised by these technologies. These technologies also open up horizons for totally new document formats, such as active documents whose contents may combine different media such as text, sound, video or voice; or whose contents may change dynamically with time, what Harvey Wheeler called "the fungible book."

The preservation of these new "active" formats is not of direct interest to the subject of preservation of more traditional formats, but is of indirect interest because digitally preserved traditional documents can be incorporated into such active documents. Some view the introduction of digital technologies into the world of libraries as likely to cause a revolution as far-reaching as that caused by the printing-press: a massive paradigm shift. Others view the introduction with concern, an intimidating perturbation that disturbs an equilibrium and modalities of scholarship that have served well for many decades or even for centuries. Either way, digital technologies cannot be ignored. The next twenty years are likely to be times of extraordinary change. Our libraries—indeed our universities, colleges, and our scholarly communities—may well be remade by the consequences of this technological revolution. And yet—in spite of technology's impact and of the revolutionary consequences of that impact—it must be recognised that technology itself is not the ultimate driving force. It is the inexorable pressure caused by the exponential growth of recorded knowledge, and the ever-increasing complexity, costs, and other problems associated with the storage and distribution of, and access to, such information.

Technology can provide some solutions: it is not an end in itself. Furthermore—for many reasons too numerous to detail here—the "digital library" is not about to replace the "paper library." Both will need to coexist in a shifting environment, at least for the foreseeable future. This in itself will present librarians with many economic, organisational, social, technical, and other challenges. Between the eager apostles of technology and those who approach change with extreme caution lies the mass of professionals who are trying to understand and grapple with the potential of this shifting environment, many of them implementing prototype activities designed to elucidate greater insight, many working to close the gap between promise and reality.

The rash of new information technology has raised major problems for librarians and archivists, faced with a flood of new kinds of media such as audio and video tape or computer disks. Most of these technologies were designed and manufactured without permanence as a prime consideration. A worse problem is the short life of the reading devices; even the less than permanent tapes or disks often do not deteriorate until long after the machines to read them become unavailable. Digital preservation thus depends upon copying, not on the survival of the physical media. Librarians and archivists must prepare for reformatting as a regular step in information management. In this, they must join with computer center managers, individual computer owners, and all others who need to keep machine-readable data for more than a few years.

The fate of data will largely depend on the strategies adopted by libraries, publishers, archivists, and individual researchers. The future of the archive depends on how information storage is conceptualised. Rather than making temporary plans in the hopes of a future permanent solution, it is advantageous to visualise all information preservation as an evolving, ever-changing ecosystem. As technology continues to develop apace, those seeking to preserve and to update are faced with ever-expanding options of how best to do this. It is an exercise in futility to try to pick the technological winner, for "the latest" will be hopelessly outdated in ten years' time. What is necessary is a permanent strategy for handling perpetual change. This will involve periodic reassessment, the migration of material from one platform to the next, and the allocation of resources. The vision of creating digital libraries that will be able to preserve our heritage currently rests on technological quicksand. There is as yet no viable long-term strategy to ensure that digital information will be readable in the future. Not only are digital documents vulnerable to loss via media decay and obsolescence, but they become equally inaccessible and unreadable if the software needed to interpret them—or the hardware on which that software runs—is lost or becomes obsolete.

Documents, data, records, and informational and cultural artifacts of all kinds are rapidly being converted to digital form, if they were not created digitally to begin with. This rush to digitise is being driven by powerful incentives, including the ability to make perfect copies of digital artifacts, to publish them on a wide range of media, to distribute and disseminate them over networks, to reformat and convert them into alternate forms, to locate them, search their contents, and retrieve them, and to process them with automated and semi-automated tools. Yet the longevity of digital content is problematic for a number of complex and interrelated reasons. It is now generally recognised that the physical lifetimes of digital storage media are often surprisingly short, requiring information to be "refreshed" by copying it onto new media with disturbing frequency. The technological obsolescence of these media poses a different and equally urgent threat.

Most digital documents and artifacts exist only in encoded form, requiring specific software to bring their bit streams to life and make them truly usable; as these programmes become obsolete, the digital documents that depend on them become unreadable—held hostage to their own encoding. This problem is paradoxical, given the fact that digital documents can be copied perfectly, which is often naively taken to mean that they are eternal. In addition to the technical aspects of this problem, there are administrative, procedural, organisational, and policy issues surrounding the management of digital material. Digital documents are different from traditional paper documents in ways that have significant implications for the means by which they are generated, captured, transmitted, stored, maintained, accessed, and managed.

Paramount among these differences is the greatly reduced lifetime of digital information without some form of active preservation. This mandates new approaches to accessioning and saving digital documents to avoid their loss. These approaches raise nontechnical issues concerning jurisdiction, funding, responsibility for successive phases of the digital document life cycle, and the development of policies requiring adherence to standard techniques and practices to prevent the loss of digital information. However, few of these nontechnical issues can be meaningfully addressed in the absence of a sound, accepted technical solution to the digital longevity problem.

Preservation constitutes one leg of a tripod that supports informational institutions such as libraries, the other legs being access and the development and management of collections. Without preservation, access becomes impossible, and collections decay and disintegrate. Informational artifacts include documents, data, and records of all kinds, in all media, which can be referred to as "documents" for simplicity. The essence of preserving informational artifacts is the retention of their meaning. This requires the ability to recreate the original form and function of a document when it is accessed, for example, to establish its authenticity, validity, and evidential value and to allow the document's users to understand how its creator and original viewers saw it, what they were able to infer from it, what insights it may have conveyed to them, and what aesthetic value it may have had for them.

The preservation of digital documents involves a number of distinctive requirements. In particular, all such documents possess a unique collection of core digital attributes that must be retained. These attributes include their ability to be copied perfectly, to be accessed without geographic constraint, to be disseminated at virtually no incremental cost, and to be machine-readable so that they can be accessed, searched, and processed by automated mechanisms that can modify them, reformat them, and perform arbitrary computations on their contents in all phases of their creation and distribution. Furthermore, new inherently digital document forms, such as dynamic, distributed, interactive hypertext and hypermedia, must retain their unique functionality, including their ability to integrate information from disparate traditional sources, such as books, periodicals, newspapers, mail, phone messages, data, imagery, and video.In response to the difficulty of saving digital documents it is sometimes suggested that they be printed and saved in hard-copy form. This is a rearguard action and not a true solution. Printing any but the simplest, traditional documents results in the loss of their unique functionality, and printing any document makes it no longer truly machine-readable, which in turn destroys its core digital attributes. Beyond this loss of functionality, printing digital documents sacrifices their original form, which may be of unique historical, contextual, or evidential interest.

Proposed alternatives to printing digital documents include translating digital documents into standard forms or extracting their contents without regard to their original nature. Though these approaches have traditional analogues, they are fraught with danger. The meaning of a document may be quite fragile, since meaning is in the eye of the beholder: what may be a trivial transformation to a casual reader may be a disastrous loss to a scholar, historian, or lawyer. Examples of loss of meaning abound in our daily experience of converting digital documents from their native form into that of some other software application in order to read them. At its best, such conversion often sacrifices subtleties; at its worst, it leaves out entire segments or produces meaningless garbage.

While it is often useful to create contemporary vernacular transcriptions of historical documents, society places a high value on retaining the originals so that we may verify that content has not been lost in transcription, as well as for scholarly and aesthetic purposes. For digital documents, retaining an original may not mean retaining the original medium, but it should mean retaining the functionality, look, and feel of the original document. The preservation of digital documents is a matter of more than purely academic concern. In its short history, computer science has become inured to the fact that every new generation of software and hardware technology entails the loss of information, as documents are translated between incompatible formats. The most serious losses are caused by paradigm shifts (such as those between networked, hierarchical, and relational databases), which often require the complete redesign of documents to migrate to the new paradigm. Whenever this happens, documents that are not in continuing use may well be orphaned by the demise of their original formats, that is, they may be abandoned to save the cost of migration, while each document that does migrate may be turned into something unrecognisably different from its original, which is generally lost.

Even when migration does not involve a major paradigm shift, it can result in subtle losses of context and content. Yet aside from this ad hoc migration process, there exists no proven strategy for preserving (or translating) documents over time. The scope of this problem extends beyond the traditional library domain, affecting government records, environmental and scientific baseline data, documentation of toxic waste disposal, medical records, corporate data (such as the documentation of drug trials for pharmaceutical companies or of geologic survey data for petrochemical companies), electronic-commerce transactions, and electronic records needed to support forthcoming digital government initiatives.

The library and archives communities have identified at least some critical aspects of this problem and have recognised that preserving digital documents may require substantial new investments and commitments by institutions and government agencies. Showing admirable foresight, these communities have begun to discuss alternative economic and administrative policies for funding and managing digital preservation and have begun to develop conceptual frameworks for metadata that are not restricted to the print medium. Yet the lack of any long-term technical solution to the problem of digital preservation limits the efficacy of such explorations, since attempting to allocate responsibilities and assess costs for a nonexistent process is of questionable value.

Responsibility for Access

The responsibility for access lies with whoever manages the digital material. The manager may be a library, a publisher, a Webmaster, or the creator of the information. Parts of the responsibility may be delegated. If a library controls the materials and makes them available to users, the library sets the policies and implements them, usually guided by external restraints, such as legal restrictions, licenses from publishers, or agreements with donors. If a publisher mounts materials and licenses access, then the publisher is the manager, but may delegate key activities, such as authorisation of users, to others.

When a user accesses a computer system, a two-step process of identification usually takes place. The first is authentication which establishes the identify of the individual user. The second is to determine what a user is authorised to do. A wide variety of techniques are used to authenticate users; some are simple but easy to circumvent, while others are more secure but complex. The techniques divide into four main categories:

— What does the user know? A standard method of authentication is to provide each user with a login name and a password. This is widely used but has weaknesses. Passwords are easily stolen. Most people like to select their own password and often select words that are easy to remember and hence easy to guess, such as personal names, or everyday words.

— What does the user possess? Examples of physical devices that are used for authentication include the magnetically encoded cards used by bank teller machines, and digital smart-cards that execute an authentication program. Smart-cards are one of the best systems of authentication; they are highly secure and quite convenient to use.

— What does the user have access to? A common form of authentication is the network address of a computer. Anybody who has access to a computer with an approved intellectual property address is authenticated. Data on many personal computers is unprotected except by physical access; anybody who has access to the computer can read the data.

— What are the physical characteristics of the user? Authentication by physical attributes such as voice recognition is used in a few esoteric applications, but has had little impact in digital libraries.

Policies for access management rarely specify users by name. They are usually tied to categories of users or the role of a user. An individual user can have many roles. At different times, the same person may use a digital library for teaching, private reading, or to carry out a part-time business. The digital library may have different policies for the same individual in these various roles. Most users of digital libraries are people using personal computers, but the user can be a computer with no person associated, such as a program that is indexing Web pages or a mirroring program that replicates an entire collection. Some sites explicitly ban access by automatic programs.

For access management, digital materials must be clearly identified. Identification associates some name or identifier with each item of material. This is a major topic in both digital libraries and electronic publishing. Authentication of digital materials assures both users and managers of collections that materials are unaltered. In some contexts this is vital. In most digital libraries, the accuracy of the materials is not verified explicitly. Where the level of trust is high and the cost of mistakes are low, no formal authentication of documents is needed. Deliberate alterations are rare and mistakes are usually obvious. In some fields, however, such as medical records, errors are serious. Digital libraries in these areas should seriously consider using formal methods of authenticating materials. To ensure the accuracy of an object, a digital signature can be associated with it. A digital signature ensures that a file or other set of bits has not changed since the signature was calculated. Panel A group of methods that are related to authentication of materials are described by the term watermarking. They are defensive techniques used by publishers to deter and track unauthorised copying. The basic idea is to embed a code into the material in a subtle manner that is not obtrusive to the user, but can be retrieved to establish ownership. A simple example is for a broadcaster to add a corporate logo to a television picture, to identify the source of the picture if is copied. Digital watermarks can be completely imperceptible to a users, yet almost impossible to remove without trace.

Access management policies frequently treat different material in varying ways, depending upon properties or attributes of the material. These attributes can be encoded as administrative metadata and stored with the object, or they can be derived from some other source. Some attributes can also be computed. Thus the size of an object can be measured when required. Some examples are given below:

— *Division into sub-collections:* Collections often divide material into items for public access and items with restricted access. Publishers may separate the full text of articles from indexes, abstracts and promotional materials. Web sites have public areas, and private areas for use within an organisation.

— *Licensing and other external commitments:* A digital library may have material that is licensed from a publisher or acquired subject to terms and conditions that govern access, such as materials that the Library of Congress receives through copyright deposit.

— *Physical, temporal, and similar properties:* Digital libraries may have policies that depend upon the time since the date of publication or physical properties, such as the size of the material. Some newspapers provide open access to selected articles when they are published while requiring licenses for the same articles later.

— *Media types:* A digital library may have access policies that depend upon format or media type, for example treating digitised sound differently from textual material, or computer programs from images.

Attributes need to be assigned at varying granularity. If all the materials in a collection have the same property, then it is convenient to assign the attribute to the collection as a whole. At the other extreme, there are times when parts of objects may have specific properties. The rights associated with images are often different from those associated with the text in which they are embedded and will have to be distinguished. A donor may donate a collection of letters to a library for public access, but request that access to certain private correspondence be restricted. Digital libraries need to offer flexibility, so that attributes can be associated with entire collections, sub-collections, individual library objects, or elements of individual objects.

Access management policies often specify or restrict the operations and the various actions that a user is authorised to carry out on library materials. Some of the common categories of operation include:

— *Computing actions:* Some operations are defined in computing terms, such as to write data to a computer, execute a program, transmit data across a network, display on a computer screen, print, or copy from one computer to another.

— *Extent of use:* A user may be authorised to extract individual items from a database, but not copy the entire database.

These operations can be controlled by technical means, but many policies that an information manager might state are essentially impossible to enforce technically. They include:

— *Business or purpose:* Authorisation of a user might refer to the reason for carrying out an operation. Examples include commercial, educational, or government use.

— *Intellectual operations:* Operations may specify the intellectual use to be made of an item. The most important is the rules that govern the creation of a new work that is derived from the content of another. The criteria may need to consider both the intent and the extent of use.

Systems for access management have to consider both direct operations and subsequent use of material. Direct operations are actions initiated by a repository, or another computer system that acts as a agent for the managers of the collection. Subsequent use covers all those operations that can occur once material leaves the control of the digital library. It includes all the various ways that a copy can be made, from replicating computer files to photocopying paper documents. Intellectually, it can include everything from extracting short sections, the creation of derivative works, to outright plagiarism. When an item, or part of a item, has been transmitted to a personal computer it is technically difficult to prevent a user from copying what is received, storing it, and distributing it to others. This is comparable to photocopying a document. If the information is for sale, the potential for such subsequent use to reduce revenue is clear. Publishers naturally have concerns about readers distributing unauthorised copies of materials. At an extreme, if a publisher sells one copy of an item that is subsequently widely distributed over the Internet, the publisher might end up selling only that one copy. As a partial response to this fear, digital libraries are often designed to allow readers access to individual records, but do not provide any way to copy complete collections. While this does not prevent a small loss of revenue, it is a barrier against anybody undermining the economic interests of the publisher by wholesale copying.

Digital libraries are distributed computer systems, in which information is passed from one computer to another. If access management is only at the repository, access is effectively controlled locally, but once material leaves the repository problems multiply.The issue of subsequent use has already been introduced; once the user's computer receives information it is hard for the original manager of the digital library to retain effective control, without obstructing the legitimate user. With networks, there is a further problem. Numerous copies of the material are made in networked computers, including caches, mirrors, and other servers, beyond the control of the local repository. To date, most digital libraries have been satisfied to provide access management at the repository, while relying on social and legal pressure to control subsequent use. Usually this is adequate, but some publishers are concerned that the lack of control could damage their revenues. Therefore, there is interest in technical methods that control copying and subsequent, even after the material has left the repository. The methods fall into two categories: trusted systems and secure containers.

A repository is an example of a trusted system. The managers of a digital library have confidence that the hardware, software, and administrative procedures provide an adequate level of security to store and provide access to valuable information. There may be other systems, linked to the repository, that are equally trusted. Within such a network of trusted systems, digital libraries can use methods of enforcement that are simple extensions of those used for single repositories. Attributes and policies can be passed among systems, with confidence that they will be processed effectively. Implementing networks of trusted systems is not easy. The individual systems components must support a high level of security and so must the processes by which information is passed among the various computers.

For these reasons, trusted systems are typically used in restricted situations only or on special purpose computers. If all the computers are operated by the same team or by teams working under strict rules, many of the administrative problems diminish. An example of a large, trusted system is the network of computers that support automatic teller machines in banks. No assumptions can be made about users' personal computers and how they are managed. In fact, it is reasonable not to trust them. For this reason, early applications of trusted systems in digital libraries are likely to be restricted to special purpose hardware, such as smart cards or secure printers, or dedicated servers running rightly controlled software.

Since networks are not secure and trusted system difficult to implement, several groups are developing secure containers for transmitting information across the Internet. Digital material is delivered to the user in a package that contains data and metadata about access policies. Some or all of the information in the package is encrypted. To access the information requires a digital key, which might be received from an electronic payment system or other method of authentication. An advantage of this approach is that it provides some control over subsequent use. The package can be copied and distributed to third parties, but the contents can not be accessed without the key. Secure containers face a barrier to acceptance. They are of no value to a user unless the user can acquire the necessary cryptographic keys to unlock them and make use of the content. This requires widespread deployment of security service and methods of electronic payment. Until recently, the spread of such services has been rather slow, so that publishers have had little market for information delivered via secure containers.

Open Access Digital Library

Conventional libraries are expensive and research libraries are particularly expensive. Even in the United States, few people can afford good access to scientific, medical, legal and scholarly information. In less affluent countries the situation is worse; even the best universities cannot afford good libraries. With the growth of the web, this situation is changing. An ever-increasing amount of high quality information is available on the web with open access. Anybody connected to the Internet has access to this information at no charge. Moreover, free services, such as the web search services, are emerging that organize this information and provide access to it. Already, many people use the web as their library.

Open access is one of the marvels of the web. Vast collections of high-quality information are available for everybody to use without payment. Creating and distributing this information is expensive, yet individuals and organizations provide it freely. Sometimes, the open access service is not as good as the fee-based service, but often it is a genuine substitute. And these are just a few examples. With a web search engine and a little ingenuity, a user can find high-quality information about almost any topic, from Texan wildlife to international taxation. In some disciplines, all the primary materials needed to teach an advanced course or carry out research are available with open access.

This abundance was not anticipated. Early digital libraries assumed that restrictions on access were essential for high-quality information to be distributed over the Internet. This misunderstanding came from a mindset that the only incentive for creating information is to make money — royalties to authors and profits for publishers. A glance at the web today shows that this view was wrong. Most open-access web sites do not generate revenue. They are supported by external funding, usually by the producers of the material on them. When the web provides an efficient channel to reach the desired audiences, existing budgets have been transferred from print products to the web. Marketing and promotion are obvious examples; government information is another. In many other cases, organizations have developed new budgets to publish open access information on the web. The publication of scientific research is an important example. Ten years ago, very little scientific research was available free of charge. Today, huge volumes are online with open access.

In areas such as these, the creators of the information have strong incentives to have their materials used. Their interests are best served by eliminating barriers to use. The result is that every year additional information is provided with no restrictions on access. For the web to function as a library requires more than high-quality collections. Services must be provided to manage the collections and help people use them effectively. The term "automated digital library" can be used to describe a digital library where all tasks are carried out automatically, including tasks that were traditionally carried out by skilled professionals. These include selection, cataloguing and indexing, seeking for information, reference services, and so on. Each of these activities requires considerable mental activity, the type of activity that people are skilled at and computers find difficult.

Good services in automated digital libraries do not replicate the procedures of classical librarianship. Automated libraries provide users with equivalent services but rethink the way that they are delivered. The contrast between web search engines and conventional library catalogues is illuminating. Almost everything that is best about a library catalogue is done badly by a web search service. On the other hand, web search services are strong in ways that catalogues are weak. It is wrong to claim that conventional catalogues or indexes are superior because of their quality control and it is equally wrong to claim that the web search services are superior because of their coverage and currency. The value to users depends on what the user wants to achieve.

Consider the choice between Google and Inspec as tools to discover information about computing. In computing, almost every significant result first appears on a web site and only later reaches the printed journals, if ever. Hence, a web search service such as Google is more up to date and its coverage is broader than Inspec, which is restricted to formally published materials. In computing, substantially the same information is often available from several sources. Google provides a direct link to an open access version. Inspec references the official version, which is usually printed or online with restricted access. By conventional criteria Inspec has much higher quality, but for many people Google's broad coverage and convenient links make it the better tool.

Simple algorithms plus immense computing power can often outperform human intelligence. The rate of progress in computing power is described by Moore's Law, that the number of transistors on a semiconductor doubles every eighteen months. This is roughly equivalent to saying that computing power increases 100-fold in 10 years or 10,000-fold in 20 years. Few people can appreciate the implications of such dramatic change, but the future of automated digital libraries is likely to depend more on brute force computing than on sophisticated algorithms.

Here are some current examples of how this computing power is being used. Each example is the direct result of research in computer science or digital libraries.

- The web search services are the state-of-the-art in automated information discovery. Computers can index every word in a billion pages (roughly the size of the web) and search the indexes for simple patterns almost instantaneously.
- To decide how closely a document matches a query would seem to require human judgment, yet standard methods of information retrieval do remarkably well. They use the power of computers to match word patterns as a surrogate for the human ability to relate concepts. A basic method, developed by Salton at Cornell University, represents each document as a multi-dimensional vector and uses the angle between the vectors to measure the similarity between two documents.

— Evaluating the importance of documents would appear to be another task that requires human understanding, but Google's ranking algorithm, developed by Page and Brin at Stanford University, does very well and is entirely automatic. It ranks web pages by analyzing what other pages link to them.

— Citation analysis is a long-standing success story of applying computers to library information. Automatic systems are becoming capable of extracting a reference from a document and linking it to the digital object that it references. Currently, the most versatile system for reference linking is the SFX system, created by Van de Sompel and colleagues at the University of Ghent.

— ResearchIndex is a digital library of computer science materials, created entirely automatically by Lawrence and colleagues at NEC. It makes extensive use of citation analysis and reference linking.

— There are a number of projects that extract metadata from digital objects automatically. Perhaps the most remarkable is the Informedia project, led by Wactlar at Carnegie Mellon University. Informedia has the extremely ambitious goal of providing access to segments of video, such as television news, entirely automatically.

The development of the web as a library that is open to everybody is a powerful and welcome trend. Research in computers science and digital libraries can claim credit for much of the success. However, the web as a library presents challenges that need to be the subject of further research. Perhaps the most worrying is quality. In conventional publishing, publishers and libraries play an important role in evaluating the quality of materials. On the Internet, with most information mounted by the creators, it is hard for users to distinguish good information sources from inaccurate, sloppy, malicious or fraudulent information. With a few minor expectations, the user is forced to make private decisions on what information to respect, based on very limited clues.

Important information on web sites may be supported by transient organizations. Yet, increasingly, vital information exists only online. Information integrity is the subject of the Prism project, led by Lagoze at Cornell as part of the NSF's Digital Libraries Initiative, but this is a huge topic and much more work is needed. One success story in automatic preservation is the Internet Archive, directed by Brewster Kahle. Each month, a web crawler gathers every open access web page. The Internet Archive preserves these files for the future and mounts them on computers for scholarly research today. Without the work of the Internet Archive many of these materials would already have been lost.

Automated digital libraries built on open access information offer to provide the Model T Ford of information. The Model T Ford was the car that brought motoring to the American public. Nobody would claim that it was equal to the handcrafted cars of its generation, but few people could afford a hand-built car. Automated digital libraries cannot approach the personal service available to the faculty of a well-endowed university, but few people have easy access to a major research library. The low cost of automated digital libraries is already bringing scientific, scholarly, medical and legal information to new audiences.

Authentication

When a user accesses a computer system, a two-step process of identification usually takes place. The first is authentication which establishes the identify of the individual user. The second is to determine what a user is authorized to do. A wide variety of techniques are used to authenticate users; some are simple but easy to circumvent, while others are more secure but complex. The techniques divide into four main categories:

— What does the user know? A standard method of authentication is to provide each user with a login name and a password. This is widely used but has weaknesses. Passwords are easily stolen. Most people like to select their own password and often select words that are easy to remember and hence easy to guess, such as personal names, or everyday words.

— What does the user possess? Examples of physical devices that are used for authentication include the magnetically encoded cards used by bank teller machines, and digital smart-cards that execute an authentication program. Smart-cards are one of the best systems of authentication; they are highly secure and quite convenient to use.

— What does the user have access to? A common form of authentication is the network address of a computer. Anybody who has access to a computer with an approved IP address is authenticated. Data on many personal computers is unprotected except by physical access; anybody who has access to the computer can read the data.

— What are the physical characteristics of the user? Authentication by physical attributes such as voice recognition is used in a few esoteric applications, but has had little impact in digital libraries.

Roles

Policies for access management rarely specify users by name. They are usually tied to categories of users or the role of a user. An individual user can have many roles. At different times, the same person may use a digital library for teaching, private reading, or to carry out a part-time business. The digital library may have different policies for the same individual in these various roles. Typical roles that may be important include:

— Membership of a group. The user is a member of the Institute of Physics. The user is a student at the U.S. Naval Academy.

— Location. The user is using a computer in the Carnegie Library of Pittsburgh. The user is in the USA.

— Subscription. The user has a current subscription to Journal of the Association for Computing Machinery.

— Robotic use. The user is an automatic indexing program, such as a Web crawler.

— Payment. The user has a credit account with Lexis. The user has paid $10 to access this material.

Digital Material

Identification and Authenticity

For access management, digital materials must be clearly identified. Identification associates some name or identifier with each item of material.

Authentication of digital materials assures both users and managers of collections that materials are unaltered. In some contexts this is vital. In one project, we worked with a U.S. government agency to assemble a collection of documents relevant to foreign affairs, such as trade agreements and treaties. With such documents the exact wording is essential; if a document claims to be the text of the North America Free Trade Agreement, the reader must be confident that the text is accurate. A text with wrong wording, whether created maliciously or by error, could cause international problems.

In most digital libraries, the accuracy of the materials is not verified explicitly. Where the level of trust is high and the cost of mistakes are low, no formal authentication of documents is needed. Deliberate alterations are rare and mistakes are usually obvious. In some fields, however, such as medical records, errors are serious. Digital libraries in these areas should seriously consider using formal methods of authenticating materials. A digital signature ensures that a file or other set of bits has not changed since the signature was calculated.

Electronic registration and deposit for copyright

The U.S. Copyright Office is a separate department of the Library of Congress. Under United States law, all works published in the U.S. are subject to mandatory deposit and the library is entitled to receive two copies for its collections. While deposit of published works is mandatory, the copyright law since 1978 has not required registration of copyrighted works, though registration is encouraged by conferring significant benefits.

The method of copyright registration is straightforward. The owner of the copyright sends two copies of the work to the Copyright Office, with an application form and a fee. The copyright claim and the work are examined and, after approval, a registration certificate is produced. Published works are transferred to the Library of Congress, which decides whether to retain the works for its collections or use them in its exchange program.

In 1993, the Copyright Office and CNRI began work on a system, known as CORDS (Copyright Office Electronic Registration, Recordation and Deposit System) to register and deposit electronic works. The system mirrors the traditional procedures. The submission consists of a web form and a digital copy of the work, delivered securely over the Internet. The fee is processed separately. Digital signatures are used to identify claims that are submitted for copyright registration in CORDS. The submitter signs the claim with the work attached, using a private key. The submission includes the claim, the work, the digital signature, the public key, and associated certificates. The digital signature verifies to the Copyright Office that the submission was received correctly and confirms the identity of the submitter. If, at any future date, there is a copyright dispute over the work, the digital signature can be used to authenticate the claim and the registered work.

A group of methods that are related to authentication of materials are described by the term watermarking. They are defensive techniques used by publishers to deter and track unauthorized copying. The basic idea is to embed a code into the material in a subtle manner that is not obtrusive to the user, but can be retrieved to establish ownership. A simple example is for a broadcaster to add a corporate logo to a television picture, to identify the source of the picture if is copied. Digital watermarks can be completely imperceptible to a users, yet almost impossible to remove without trace.

Attributes of Digital Material

Access management policies frequently treat different material in varying ways, depending upon properties or attributes of the material. These attributes can be encoded as administrative metadata and stored with the object, or they can be derived from some other source. Some attributes can also be computed. Thus the size of an object can be measured when required. Here are some typical examples:

— *Division into sub-collections.* Collections often divide material into items for public access and items with restricted access. Publishers may separate the full text of articles from indexes, abstracts and promotional materials. Web sites have public areas, and private areas for use within an organization.

— *Licensing and other external commitments.* A digital library may have material that is licensed from a publisher or acquired subject to terms and conditions that govern access, such as materials that the Library of Congress receives through copyright deposit.

— *Physical, temporal, and similar properties*. Digital libraries may have policies that depend upon the time since the date of publication or physical properties, such as the size of the material. Some newspapers provide open access to selected articles when they are published while requiring licenses for the same articles later.

— *Media types.* A digital library may have access policies that depend upon format or media type, for example treating digitized sound differently from textual material, or computer programs from images.

Attributes need to be assigned at varying granularity. If all the materials in a collection have the same property, then it is convenient to assign the attribute to the collection as a whole. At the other extreme, there are times when parts of objects may have specific properties. The rights associated with images are often different from those associated with the text in which they are embedded and will have to be distinguished. A donor may donate a collection of letters to a library for public access, but request that access to certain private correspondence be restricted. Digital libraries need to offer flexibility, so that attributes can be associated with entire collections, subcollections, individual library objects, or elements of individual objects.

Operations

Access management policies often specify or restrict the operations and the various actions that a user is authorized to carry out on library materials. Some of the common categories of operation include:

— *Computing actions.* Some operations are defined in computing terms, such as to write data to a computer, execute a program, transmit data across a network, display on a computer screen, print, or copy from one computer to another.

— *Extent of use.* A user may be authorized to extract individual items from a database, but not copy the entire database. These operations can be controlled by technical means, but many policies that an information manager might state are essentially impossible to enforce technically. They include:

— *Business or purpose.* Authorization of a user might refer to the reason for carrying out an operation. Examples include commercial, educational, or government use.

— *Intellectual operations.* Operations may specify the intellectual use to be made of an item. The most important is the rules that govern the creation of a new work that is derived from the content of another. The criteria may need to consider both the intent and the extent of use.

Subsequent Use

Systems for access management have to consider both direct operations and subsequent use of material. Direct operations are actions initiated by a repository, or another computer system that acts as a agent for the managers of the collection. Subsequent use covers all those operations that can occur once material leaves the control of the digital library. It includes all the various ways that a copy can be made, from replicating computer files to photocopying paper documents. Intellectually, it can include everything from extracting short sections, the creation of derivative works, to outright plagiarism.

When an item, or part of a item, has been transmitted to a personal computer it is technically difficult to prevent a user from copying what is received, storing it, and distributing it to others. This is comparable to photocopying a document. If the information is for sale, the potential for such subsequent use to reduce revenue is clear.

Policies

An informal definition of a policy is that it is a rule, made by information managers that states who is authorized to do what to which material. Typical policies in digital libraries are:

— A publication might have the policy of open access. Anybody may read the material, but only the editorial staff may change it.

— A publisher with journals online may have the policy that only subscribers have access to all materials. Other people can read the contents pages and abstracts, but have access to the full content only if they pay a fee per use.

— A government organization might classify materials, e.g., "top secret", and have strict policies about who has access to the materials, under what conditions, and what they can do with them.

Policies are rarely as simple as in these examples. For example, while D-Lib Magazine has a policy of open access, the authors of the individual articles own the copyright. The access policy is that everybody is encouraged to read the articles and print copies for private use, but some subsequent use, such as creating a derivative work, or selling copies for profit requires permission from the copyright owner. Simple policies can sometimes be represented as a table in which each row relates a user role, attributes of digital material, and certain operations.

Because access management policies can be complex, a formal method is needed to express them, which can be used for exchange of information among computer system. Perhaps the most comprehensive work in this area has been carried out by Mark Stefik of Xerox. The Digital Property Rights Language, which he developed, is a language for expressing the rights, conditions, and fees for using digital works. The purpose of the language is to specify attributes of material and policies for access, including subsequent use. The manager of a collection can specify terms and conditions for copying, transferring, rendering, printing, and similar operations. The language allows fees to be specified for any operation, and it envisages links to electronic payment mechanisms. The notation used by the language is based on Lisp, a language used for natural language processing. Some people have suggested that, for digital libraries, a more convenient notation would use XML, which would be a straightforward transformation. The real test of this language is how effective it proves to be when used in large-scale applications.

Access Management Policies

Access management is not simply a question of developing appropriate policies. Information managers want the policies to be followed, which requires some form of enforcement.

Some policies can be enforced technically. Others are more difficult. There are straightforward technical methods to enforce a policy of who is permitted to change material in a collection, or search a repository. There are no technical means to enforce a policy against plagiarism, or invasion of privacy, or to guarantee that all use is educational. Each of these is a reasonable policy that is extremely difficult to enforce by technical means. Managing such policies is fundamentally social. There are trade-offs between strictness of enforcement and convenience to users. Technical method of enforcing policies can be annoying. Few people object to typing in a password when they begin a session, but nobody wants to be asked repeatedly for passwords, or other identification. Information managers will sometimes decide to be relaxed about enforcing policies in the interests of satisfying users. Satisfied customers will help grow the size of the market, even if some revenue is lost from unauthorized users. The publishers who are least aggressive about enforcement keep their customers happy and often generate most total revenue. This is the strategy now used for most personal computer software. Data from publishers such as HighWire Press is beginning to suggest the same result with electronic journal publishing.

If technical methods are relaxed, social and legal pressures can be effective. The social objective is to educate users about the policies that apply to the collections, and coax or persuade people to follow them. This requires policies that are simple to understand and easy for users to follow. Users must be informed of the policies and educated as to what constitutes reasonable behavior. One useful tool is to display an access statement when the material is accessed; this is text that states some policy. An example is, "For copyright reasons, this material should not be used for commercial purposes." Other non-technical methods of enforcement are more assertive. If members of an organization repeatedly violate a licensing agreement or abuse policies that they should respect, a publisher can revoke a license. In extreme cases, a single, well-publicized legal action will persuade many others to behave responsibly.

Early experience with software for personal computers provides an example of what happens when attempts to enforce policies are unpleasant for the users. Software is usually licensed for a single computer. The license fee covers use on one computer only, but software is easy to copy. Manufacturers lose revenue from unlicensed copying, particularly if there develops widespread distribution of unlicensed copies.

In the early days of personal computers, software manufacturers attempted to control unlicensed copying by technical means. One approach was to supply their products on disks that could not be copied easily. This was called copy-protection. Every time that a program was launched, the user had to insert the original disk. This had a powerful effect on the market, but not what the manufacturers had hoped. The problem was that it became awkward for legitimate customers to use the software that they had purchased. Hard disk installations were awkward and back-up difficult. Users objected to the inconvenience. Those software suppliers who were most assertive about protection lost sales to competitors who supplied software without copy-protection.

Microsoft was one of the companies that realized that technical enforcement is not the only option. The company has become extremely rich by selling products that are not technically protected against copying. Instead, Microsoft has worked hard to stimulate adherence to its policies by non-technical methods. Marketing incentives, such as customer support and low-cost upgrades, encourage customers to pay for licenses. Social pressures are used to educate people and legal methods are used to frighten the worst offenders. Unlicensed copying still costs the software manufacturers money, but, by concentrating on satisfying their responsible customers, the companies are able to thrive.

Access to Repositories

Most digital libraries implement policies at the repository or collection level. Digital libraries are distributed computer systems, in which information is passed from one computer to another. If access management is only at the repository, access is effectively controlled locally, but once material leaves the repository problems multiply.

The issue of subsequent use has already been introduced: once the user's computer receives information it is hard for the original manager of the digital library to retain effective control, without obstructing the legitimate user. With networks, there is a further problem. Numerous copies of the material are made in networked computers, including caches, mirrors, and other servers, beyond the control of the local repository. To date, most digital libraries have been satisfied to provide access management at the repository, while relying on social and legal pressure to control subsequent use. Usually this is adequate, but some publishers are concerned that the lack of control could damage their revenues. Therefore, there is interest in technical methods that control copying and subsequent, even after the material has left the repository. The methods fall into two categories: trusted systems and secure containers.

Trusted Systems

A repository is an example of a trusted system. The managers of a digital library have confidence that the hardware, software, and administrative procedures provide an adequate level of security to store and provide access to valuable information. There may be other systems, linked to the repository, that are equally trusted. Within such a network of trusted systems, digital libraries can use methods of enforcement that are simple extensions of those used for single repositories. Attributes and policies can be passed among systems, with confidence that they will be processed effectively.

Implementing networks of trusted systems is not easy. The individual systems components must support a high level of security and so must the processes by which information is passed among the various computers. For these reasons, trusted systems are typically used in restricted situations only or on special purpose computers. If all the computers are operated by the same team or by teams working under strict rules, many of the administrative problems diminish. An example of a large, trusted system is the network of computers that support automatic teller machines in banks. No assumptions can be made about users' personal computers and how they are managed. In fact, it is reasonable not to trust them. For this reason, early applications of trusted systems in digital libraries are likely to be restricted to special purpose hardware, such as smart cards or secure printers, or dedicated servers running rightly controlled software.

Since networks are not secure and trusted system difficult to implement, several groups are developing secure containers for transmitting information across the Internet. Digital material is delivered to the user in a package that contains data and metadata about access policies. Some or all of the information in the package is encrypted. To access the information requires a digital key, which might be received from an electronic payment system or other method of authentication. An advantage of this approach is that it provides some control over subsequent use. The package can be copied and distributed to third parties, but the contents can not be accessed without the key. Secure containers face a barrier to acceptance. They are of no value to a user unless the user can acquire the necessary cryptographic keys to unlock them and make use of the content. This requires widespread deployment of security service and methods of electronic payment. Until recently, the spread of such services has been rather slow, so that publishers have had little market for information delivered via secure containers.

Security of Information Archives

Security begins with the system administrators, the people who install and manage the computers and the networks that connect them. Their honesty must be above suspicion, since they have privileges that provide access to the internals of the system. Good systems administrators will organize networks and file systems so that user have access to appropriate information. They will manage passwords, install firewalls to isolate sections of the networks, and run diagnostic programs to search for problems. They will back-up information, so that the system can be rebuilt after a major incident whether it is an equipment breakdown, a fire, or a security violation.

The Internet is basically not secure. People can tap into it and observe the packets of information traveling over the network. This is often done for legitimate purposes, such as trouble-shooting, but it can also be done for less honest reasons. The general security problem can be described as how to build secure applications across this insecure network. Since the Internet is not secure, security in digital libraries begins with the individual computers that constitute the library and the data on them, paying special attention to the interfaces between computers and local networks. For many personal computers, the only method of security is physical restrictions on who uses the computer. Other computers have some form of software protection, usually a simple login name and password. When computers are shared by many users, controls are needed to determine who may read or write to each file.

The next step of protection is to control the interface between local networks and the broader Internet, and to provide some barrier to intruders from outside. The most complete barrier is isolation, having no external network connections. A more useful approach is to connect the internal network to the Internet through a special purpose computer called a firewall. The purpose of a firewall is to screen every packet that attempts to pass through and to refuse those that might cause problems. Firewalls can refuse attempts from outside to connect to computers within the organization, or reject packets that are not formatted according to a list of approved protocols. Well-managed firewalls can be quite effective in blocking intruders.

Managers of digital libraries need to have a balanced attitude to security. Absolute security is impossible, but moderate security can be built into networked computer systems, without excessive cost, though it requires thought and attention. Universities have been at the heart of networked computing for many years. Despite their polyglot communities of users, they have succeeded in establishing adequate security for campus networks with thousands of computers. Incidents of abusive, anti-social, or malicious behavior occur on every campus, yet major problems are rare.

With careful administration, computers connected to a network can be made reasonably secure, but that security is not perfect. There are many ways that an ill-natured person can attempt to violate security. In universities, most problems come from insiders: disgruntled employees or students who steal a user's login name and password. More sophisticated methods of intrusion take advantage of the complexity of computer software. Every operating system has built-in security, but design errors or programming bugs may have created gaps. Some of the most useful programs for digital libraries, such as web servers and electronic mail, are some of the most difficult to secure. For these reasons, everybody who builds a digital library must recognize that security can never be guaranteed. With diligence, troubles can be kept rare, but there is always a chance of a flaw.

Encryption

Encryption is the name given to a group of techniques that are used to store and transmit private information, encoding it in a way that the information appears completely random until the procedure is reversed. Even if the encrypted information is read by somebody who is unauthorized, no damage is done. In digital libraries, encryption is used to transmit confidential information over the Internet, and some information is so confidential that it is encrypted wherever it is stored. Passwords are an obvious example of information that should always be encrypted, whether stored on computers or transmitted over networks. In many digital libraries, passwords are the only information that needs to be encrypted.

The commonly used methods of encryption are controlled by a pair of numbers, known as keys. One key is used for encryption, the other for decryption. The methods of encryption vary in the choice of processes and in the way the keys are selected. The mathematical form of the processes are not secret. The security lies in the keys. A key is a string of bits, typically from 40 to 120 bits or more. Long keys are intrinsically much more secure than short keys, since any attempt to violate security by guessing keys is twice as difficult for every bit added to the key length.

Historically, the use of encryption has been restricted by computer power. The methods all require considerable computation to scramble and unscramble data. With today's fast computers, this is much less of a problem, but the time to encrypt and decrypt large amounts of data is still noticeable. The methods are excellent for encrypting short message, such as passwords, or occasional highly confidential messages, but the methods are less suitable for large amounts of data where response times are important.

Private Key Encryption

Private key encryption is a family of methods in which the key used to encrypt the data and the key used to decrypt the data are the same, and must be kept secret. Private key encryption is also known as single key or secret key encryption.

Data Encryption Standard (DES)

The Data Encryption Standard (DES) is a method of private key encryption originally developed by IBM. It has been a U.S. standard since 1977. The calculations used by DES are fairly slow when implemented in software, but the method is fast enough for many applications. A modern personal computer can encrypt about one million bytes per second.

DES uses keys that are 56 bits long. It divides a set of data into 64 bit blocks and encrypts each of them separately. From the 56 bit key, 16 smaller keys are generated. The heart of the DES algorithm is 16 successive transformations of the 64 bit block, using these smaller keys in succession. Decryption uses the same 16 smaller keys to carry out the reverse transactions in the opposite order. This sounds like a simple algorithm, but there are subtleties. Most importantly, the bit patterns generated by encryption appear to be totally random, with no clues about the data or the key. Fanatics argue that DES with its 56 bit keys can be broken simply by trying every conceivable key, but this is a huge task. For digital library applications it is perfectly adequate.

Private key encryption is only as secure as the procedures that are used to keep the key secret. If one computer wants to send encrypted data to a remote computer it must find a completely secure way to get the key to the remote computer. Thus private key encryption is most widely used in applications where trusted services are exchanging information.

Dual Key Encryption

When using private key encryption over a network, the sending computer and the destination must both know the key. This poses the problem of how to get started if one computer can not pass a key secretly to another. Dual key encryption permits all information to be transmitted over a network, including the public keys, which can be transmitted completely openly. For this reason, it has the alternate name of public key encryption. Even if every message is intercepted, the encrypted information is still kept secret.

The RSA method is the best known method of dual key encryption. It requires a pair of keys. The first key is made public; the second is kept secret. If an individual, A, wishes to send encrypted data to a second individual, B, then the data is encrypted using the public key of B. When B receives the data it can be decrypted, using the private key, which only B knows.This dual key system of encryption has many advantages and one major problem. The problem is to make sure that a key is genuinely the public key of a specific individual. The normal approach is to have all keys generated and authenticated by a trusted authority, called a certification authority.

Digital Signatures

Digital signatures are used to check that a computer file has not been altered. Digital signatures are based on the concept of a hash function. A hash is a mathematical function that can be applied to the bytes of a computer file to generate a fixed-length number. One commonly used hash function is called MD5. The MD5 function can be applied to any length computer file. It carries out a special transformation on the bits of the file and ends up with an apparently random 128 bits. If two files differ by as little as one bit, their MD5 hashes will be completely different. Conversely, if two files have the same hash, there is an infinitesimal probability that they are not identical. Thus a simple test for whether a file has been altered is to calculate the MD5 hash when the file is created; at a later time, to check that no changes have taken place, recalculate the hash and compare it with the original. If the two are the same then the files are almost certainly the same. The MD5 function has many strengths, including being fast to compute on large files, but, as with any security device, there is always a possibility that some bright person may discover how to reverse engineer the hash function, and find a way to create a file that has a specific hash value. A hash value gives no information about who calculated it. A digital signature goes one step further towards guaranteeing the authenticity of a library object. When the hash value is calculated it is encrypted using the private key of the owner of the material.

Public Key Encryption

Since the basic mathematics of public key encryption are now almost twenty years old, it might be expected that products based on the methods would have been widely deployed for many years. Sadly this is not the case. One reason for delay is that there are significant technical issues. Many of them concern the management of the keys, how they are generated, how private keys are stored, and what precautions can be taken if the agency that is creating the keys has a security break-in. However, the main problems are policy problems.Patents are part of the difficulty. Public key encryption is one of the few areas where most computer scientists would agree that there were real inventions. These method are not obvious and their inventors deserve the rewards that go with invention. Unfortunately, the patent holders and their agents have followed narrow licensing policies, which have restricted the creative research that typically builds on a break-through invention.

References

Branschofsky, M. and Chudnov, D., (2002), *Dspace: Durable Digital Documents long term-preservation*. Proceedings of the Second ACM/IEEE-CS joint conference on Digital Libraries, Portland, Oregon, USA.

CEDARS Project. *Metadata For Digital Preservation The Cedars Project Outline Specification Draft For Public Consultation,* http://www.leeds.ac.uk/cedars/metadata.html

Ladner, Sharyn J., and Hope N. Tillman. (1993)."Using the Internet for reference". *Online*, 17(1), 45-51. January.

Levy, David M., (2000) "Digital Libraries and the Problem of Purpose." *D-Lib Magazine* 6, January.

Liu, Ying, and Anita S. Coleman. (2004)."Communicating Digital Library Services to Scientific Communities." *LIBRES* 14, no. 1.

6

Information Archiving Programmes

In the twentieth century, traditional book repair and rebinding activities were complemented by a preservation microfilming program that is more vigorous today than ever before and continues to strengthen. Programs for collections conservation, special collections conservation, digitization, studio photography, and sound re-recording are equally vigorous; as are preservation field services, disaster preparedness activities, and efforts to upgrade environmental controls in library buildings throughout the institution.

The establishment of a preservation program for digital library resources will be a complex and expensive undertaking. Building such a program on top of the library's general digital collections infrastructure will help to control development and operating costs. The components of an infrastructure that are applicable to a digital archiving project include:

— A repository system to support reliable, sustained storage and management of very large numbers of digital objects;

— A "naming" system to support the identification and location of digital objects in a persistent and system-independent way;

— A generalized model of access management to protect intellectual property;

— Expertise in the design of metadata schemes, the information necessary to manage, display, preserve, and re-purpose digital objects;

— Scalable operations support to ensure the professional operation of an ongoing production service for the ingestion and storage of a significant number of digital objects.

E-journal Archiving Program

Digital preservation is a new and very immature field. An E-journal archiving program involves the exploration of many complex and ill-defined issues. There are indeed a great number of technical issues and developments involved in a sophisticated archiving program. Among the areas for investigation are:

— *Accession automation.* In order to control costs and make a large-scale operation possible, as much as possible of the process of adding materials to the archive will need to be handled by computers rather than people. Areas such as ingestion, quality control, format transformations, and metadata ingestion and creation lend themselves to automation.

— *Format investigation.* The cost and complexity of archiving will depend to a significant degree on the technical formats of the objects archived. Investigation of the formats available from publishers, as well as the formats preferable for archiving, will be a key planning issue. It may be necessary to develop a policy regarding what formats will be accepted into the archive.

— *On-going validation or auditing.* Archival collections will require periodic evaluation to ensure against the loss of content or viability. Some form of systems support for such auditing will be required. Auditing may also require third-party access facilities.

— *Bibliographic control.* It is not clear what level of bibliographic control over the archival collection will be needed. It is likely that some new bibliographic facility will be required for at least some objects.

— *Naming.* Analysis is needed to determine what archival objects will require formal naming, where such names should be recorded, and what the relationship is between archived objects and existing formal naming systems such as the Digital Object Identifier.

— *Access management.* Depending on the nature of archiving licenses, extensions will probably be needed to provide for appropriate external access.

— *Output facilities.* A key issue will be who has access to archived materials, and what the service expectations of such users will be.

Internal institutional roles

Traditional preservation activities are a shared responsibility between curatorial departments and preservation technologists. Archiving necessarily involves fundamental curatorial issues, such as deciding when to migrate materials and to what format, and periodically assessing the state of the archival collection.

External relationships

No institution will archive solely for its own use, nor rely solely on its own archiving program. Therefore no institution can decide on the nature of its archiving operation in isolation. Cooperation with other libraries on the following aspects will help to the efficiency of an archivinh program:

— requirements for archiving licenses, and the negotiation of such licenses,

— decisions about what specific components of journals should be included in an archive,

— the standards and "good practices" an archive must follow to be relied upon by other institutions subscribing to the archived content,

— the appropriate level of inter-institutional auditing, and

— the output formats that must be immediately available from an archive in order to respond to the access needs of other institutions.

Costs and economic issues

The most important single economic issue in archiving electronic journals will be managing costs. The level of archiving eventually undertaken, and the distribution of responsibilities and costs among the players will be very sensitive to the total cost of the enterprise. It is critical that the archiving process be designed to minimize marginal costs. The factors will have the greatest impact on costs include:

— effective automation of the archiving process to reduce labor and complexity;

— sophisticated selection of archiving hardware and software; and

— the efficiencies inherent in large-scale archiving operations.

All three factors will be a constant focus of the efforts in both the planning and implementation phases.

Manuscript librarians should have a profound knowledge of their collections and they should provide access by making bibliographical descriptions according to high standards. From of old these tasks are at the core of the work of a manuscript librarian. However, the information and communication technologies initiate methodological changes in manuscript studies.

A narrow material conception of manuscript librarianship, as hitherto had been worked out by the tradition, has proven insufficient in this new environment. The rapid changes in the field of information management do not leave the departments of the special collections unaffected. It has become an inseparable part of the work of a manuscript librarian to fill the originating electronic and digital environment with historical and manuscript material. They are expected to have knowledge of digitisation, project management and marketing in order to increase the use of their collections. This inevitably leads to re-formulating the tasks of the manuscript librarianship as a profession.

Despite the differences, all manuscript departments in Europe have one thing in common: their position at the core of the library is not self-evident anymore. The paradigm shift 'from collection to connection' has its consequences for the manuscript departments as well. Traditionally there was a strong focus on the collections. The manuscript collection, often being the most rare and precious of all, attracted a lot of permanent attention both from the management and from the public. Consequently, the curator of the manuscript department had an important position in the library management, being the head of the department that possesses all these treasures.

The manuscripts formed the heart of the collection and therefore of the library itself. Efforts were focussed on the handling of the items themselves: cataloguing and preservation. In many cases, the collections were not freely accessible: users needed to show a hand-written permit. At the present the focus has shifted from collection to connection. The accessibility of the collections is now the centre of attention and in most libraries the items in manuscript departments are not particularly well attainable. Whereas manuscript librarians have tried to protect their treasures from wastage by heavy use for centuries, now they should open the vaults and allow everybody to see these rare and vulnerable documents?!

Evidently, preserving the treasures and making high quality catalogues is not enough anymore: manuscript librarians should think of new services, start up digitisation projects and make expositions on the World Wide Web. Users consider access to the collections as their right and libraries are beginning to realise that: now is a watershed: they have to adapt otherwise they will lose their customers.

Australian university libraries contain very significant collections of material, including print and electronic resources. The scope of these collections, including the extent of unique holdings and collection overlap, has been a subject of discussion and speculation for a number of years. Australian university libraries have developed collections to support teaching, learning and research in their institutions over many years. The extent and nature of the collections required to support each university's activities could be expected to be unique to some degree, because of the specific nature of research in each institution.

There is likely, however, to be greater duplication of resources required to support teaching and learning in those subjects which are taught across a number of universities. This overlap is inevitable if students are to have timely access to required information resources. A variety of approaches to establishing collection development policies have emerged in the university sector around the world. Studies in the United States have sought to define a 'core collection' of resources to support teaching, learning and research in particular fields of study.

In Canada and the United Kingdom, considerable investment has been made to provide all universities with convenient access to a comprehensive collection of scholarly and educational materials. These programs have been co-ordinated nationally and received significant government funding. Few initiatives of this kind have occurred in Australia.

Collection development has, over the past twenty years been an area of considerable pressure for Australian universities. There is now wide acceptance that 'libraries can no longer hope to own all the materials that their readers know or want' and that financial limitations affecting all library purchasing have shaped a new perspective on library collections. The 'serials crisis', of the 1990s, for example, was experienced because significant ongoing increases in serial prices without commensurate increases in library budgets led to a reduction in the number of titles purchased by Australian libraries. The historic concept of 'ownership' of library materials has also been reshaped by the move to an access paradigm for electronic resources. The development of purchasing consortia, such as the Committee of Australian University Librarians (CAUL) Electronic Information Resources Committee (CEIRC), has assisted Australian university libraries to provide wider access to electronic resources.

Current consortia purchasing, however, operates largely within a framework of local needs and financial limitations which has inhibited the development of a comprehensive collection of scholarly and educational materials available to all universities. The need for new forms of co-operation, particularly in regard to digital publications, has emerged as a topic for discussion in the library community and is beginning to attract support throughout the higher education sector. Australians university libraries have developed a number of co-operative arrangements over time which have influenced the level of collection uniqueness and improved the range of information resources available. University library co-operative activities in every state have affected collection access and development.

At a national level, the CAUL national borrowing scheme (University Library Australia), has provided easier access to resources. These activities are supplemented by the national inter-lending scheme and by arrangements with commercial document delivery services. The national scheme has been in operation for decades and enables resources not held locally to be accessed through interlibrary lending.

Use of interlending/document delivery is an effective means of sharing resources. Studies have shown that for serials where up to ten articles are requested per year, interlibrary requesting is less costly than purchase. This is partly due to the on-costs of serial acquisition including the cataloguing, acquisition and storage components and also because the requested copies may well range across many years of any particular serial. Libraries regularly review the balance of material held on site and that requested through interlibrary lending. The Australian Interlibrary Resource Sharing (ILRS) Code, endorsed by the Australian Library and Information Association (ALIA), the Council of Australian State Libraries (CASL), the Council of Australian University Librarians (CAUL) and the National Library of Australia forms the standard for Australian resource sharing.

The level of interlibrary lending and document supply by Australian university libraries is significant. For example in 2001, university libraries received 383 555 items from other libraries and document suppliers, and supplied 304 834 copies and loans to other libraries. Academic staff and postgraduate students however, do not always perceive traditional interlibrary lending as serving them well. While electronic resources are increasingly available at the desktop, scholars continue to require access to many resources which may never be available in digital form. Improved access to print collections will continue to be important and ongoing financial and space constraints will necessitate improved collaborative approaches. Knowledge about the composition of university library collections will assist in the provision of appropriate services and facilities.

Collection 'overlap' studies have been undertaken since the 1930s as a means of assessing collections. There have generally been three purposes for these studies. Most commonly they have been undertaken by library co-operative networks or by libraries with a large number of branches to provide a basis for reduction in the number of duplicate titles.

Library co-operation has also provided a motive for overlap studies to reveal the relative strengths of library collections as a basis for collaboration in collection development and access. Finally studies have provided a basis for consideration of issues that would improve co-operative activity such as adoption of common cataloguing standards or shared catalogues. The use of national union catalogues, such as the National Bibliographic Database [NBD] has enabled a large amount of data to be utilised. But there are limitations to using a national union catalogue for such a study and some libraries will have reported only a part of their collections to the catalogue. For example, in Australia, holdings of the electronic aggregate collections, such as ScienceDirect, have not been reported by all university libraries. There are also issues in relation to duplicate records created by variation in cataloguing practices.

New Age Skills for Information Professionals

It has always been difficult for library users to understand precisely what librarians do, or why some of the people employed in libraries pointedly identify themselves as professional workers, while the work of other library employees is not considered to be professional.

Now, in a time of massive change in the ways that information is produced and distributed, located and used, the continued relevance of both librarianship and the library as an institution are increasingly called into question. As ever-greater amounts of information are directly accessible in interactive electronic environments, researchers in law and other disciplines are likely to modify their information-seeking behaviours to include more direct searching for information, leaving librarians not only with the need to justify their claims to professional status, but the added burden of explaining why they are needed at all. In the United States, the traditional defining characteristics of the legal information professional have included a graduate degree in library science, perhaps a law degree, and employment by a law library. Because nearly all legal information professionals have been librarians, credentials and place of employment were enough to define the field, differentiating the law librarian from librarians working in other types of libraries and from other law library employees.

In 1998, however, law librarians no longer meet all information needs in law schools, courts, law firms, or other organizations using legal information. In organizations of all sizes, network computing and the demand for ready access to electronic information at the desktop have created and expanded the roles of information technologists, whose backgrounds and training fall outside librarianship, and who might be based either in the library or in any of several other places within the organization. Whether employed by the library or not, information technologists do not think of themselves as librarians. Yet, like librarians, they, too, work with information and assist users in locating and accessing information. How will the relationships between these groups evolve? Will information needs in law continue to be met primarily by librarians, or will the technologists responsible for facilitating users' direct access to digital legal information take on a primary role?

Perhaps an information environment that is increasingly dependent on networked access to digital information will require a whole new breed of legal information professional. Will librarianship or another profession provide the foundation for this new profession? Because the environment in which all professionals work is continually changing as new professional groups emerge, new technologies are invented, and the political environment in the workplace shifts, competition is inherent in professional life. In the long run, competition should be healthy for any profession, because of the challenges it poses. For librarianship, the major issues involve what we need to compete and indeed to thrive as a profession in a time when information appears to be ever more readily accessible to information seekers, and when other groups may be seeking to play roles that librarians have traditionally played.

Librarians, together with information technologists and several other professional groups, make up what Andrew Abbott has called "the information professions." For Abbott, "groups that provide others with information [occupy] a general information area of the system of professions.... In general, information professionals help clients overburdened with material from which thay [sic] cannot retrieve usable information."

Writers on the professions have identified the following representative information professionals: accountants, archivists, librarians, records managers, information systems analysts, management scientists, museum curators, archivists, publishers, and information scientists. Richard O. Mason notes that, regardless of their area of specialization, all information professionals are mediators and have one purpose in mind: "to get the right information from the right source to the right client at the right time in the form most suitable for the use to which it is to be put and at a cost that is justified by its use."

What distinguishes one information profession from the others? Abbott finds that, historically, there have been two general types of information professionals: those who work with qualitative information (an area generally occupied by librarians) and those who work with quantitative information (the domain of cost accountants, management engineers, statisticians, operations researchers, systems analysts, and others). He notes that the rapid development of computer technologies after the second world war encouraged the development of "[a] sort of computer profession" involved in both the traditional qualitative and quantitative areas, but presumably with greater affinities for the quantitative area. As the development and growth of desktop and network computing technologies in the modern workplace have made nearly everyone in an organization dependent on a desktop computer to be productive, computing staffs have grown in size while becoming more active and visible as providers of user assistance and support.

In this environment, distinctions among the tasks performed by members of traditionally separate information professions are often expressed in terms of whether the work primarily involves information content (the domain of librarians) or the technologies used to communicate, access, or deliver information content (the domain of technologists). Librarians assist the user in determining where and how to search for information, while technologists provide the means through which the search takes place and ensure that they work properly. The distinction between content and access technologies may be helpful as a means for allocating support responsibilities within an organization, but it cannct be carried too far as a principle for provision of services.

In a network environment where the computer is used for information-seeking and research as well as for other purposes, technologists may find themselves providing content assistance, while librarians may be asked for help with research and access technologies. Users in need of assistance cannot be expected to make these kinds of distinctions in an environment that is increasingly dependent on networked information and in which it is increasingly difficult to establish clear boundaries between information content and the technologies (such as the world wide web) that provide access to the content and make it useable.

Information professionals in both groups may also find the distinction too limiting. A special librarian argues in terms that might well be employed by an information technologist: This distinction is false, misleading, and dangerous. It is false because content is meaningless until communicated; thus content and access technology are inextricably linked. It is misleading because it suggests that roles may be clearly confined based on this distinction. It is dangerous because it removes from our control some of the most important tools we have to do our fundamental job: connecting people with the information they need. Because of the wide diffusion in the workplace of both information technology and the skills necessary to use and develop it, the lines between content and access technologies are no longer as bright as they might have seemed in the past. As a result, the boundaries between the information professions are increasingly indistinct, and the content/access distinction can no longer provide the basis for differentiating among them.

New relationships among the information professions are developing and will evolve in their common workplace. As they do, it will become increasingly less useful for any group to justify its claims for jurisdiction on earlier understandings about allocations of responsibility. According to Abbott, professions seek recognition from society through claims for exclusive rights, or jurisdiction, over specific areas of work. Claims of jurisdiction can be made by: 1) obtaining powers of licensing and regulation controlling who may perform the work; 2) building a public image associating the profession with the area of work; and 3) competing with other groups in the workplace itself for control. Because librarianship is not a regulated or licensed profession, librarians must assert claims of jurisdiction in the arenas of public opinion and the workplace.

Client relationships are central to success in any profession. Like other information professionals, librarians must know their clients well enough to be able to anticipate their information needs and to exercise judgment on their behalf. According to Mason, judgment is enhanced by the information professional's "intellectual empathy" with the client's needs and situation. Abbott differentiates among librarians on the basis of what clientele they serve, noting that the work of academic and special librarians has generally been in workplaces shared with other professional groups, such as faculties, attorneys, and physicians.

The special librarians claimed that they knew the sources and means to find material that working professionals didn't have the time (and sometimes the ability) to find. They held further that "what you ought to know to solve a problem" could be better defined by a practical knowledge of what the sources make it possible to know than by a theoretical knowledge of what it is in principle necessary to know. But, the decision about what information is relevant to a problem's solution "is a central part of the [client's] claim of professional jurisdiction." Therefore, as Abbott notes, "Deciding what is relevant information inevitably embroils the information client and the information professional."

Because the "information professions are in some sense specialists in diagnosis [they]... represent a general threat to all professions," and "are, by definition, involved in continuously negotiated and contested professional divisions of labour. The potentially transformational impacts of the Internet and the world wide web indicate that these sorts of conflicts are likely to intensify as technology becomes more and more important in all workplaces. Some forecast potential conflict between librarians and university faculties as instructional technologies become more important in higher education. The point to be drawn from this is that, at least in academic and special libraries, the relationship between librarians and clients is not purely one of service, but bears resemblance to relationships with other groups in the workplace.

Interprofessional conflicts of various types are not a new phenomenon for librarians, nor are they likely to diminish in the future. To compete in the arena of public opinion, a profession must establish a clear identity vis a vis other groups in the workplace. Abbott notes that discourse about jurisdiction in the public arena is usually about discrete and homogeneous groups: in the public mind, the roles of doctors and nurses are clearly distinguished. The same may be observed in the relationships among attorneys, paralegals, and law librarians in the legal workplace. According to Abbott, there is a "tremendous inconsistency between the public and workplace realities of professional life." Discussions in the public arena do not usually acknowledge that on the job there might be significant overlapping in the tasks that members of individual groups perform.

This can be observed both in the extent to which separate professions share tasks and in degree to which nonprofessionals perform tasks that the public assumes are professional in nature. If a professional is incompetent, organizational function demands that his or her work be done by someone else who is probably not officially qualified to do it. In the jurisdictional system of the workplace, it is the real output of an individual, not his credentialed or noncredentialed status, that matters. These comments certainly resonate in the context of librarianship, where there is much blurring of boundaries between the work of professional and support staff, as evidenced by the difficulties that even regular library users often have in telling who is a librarian and who a clerk on the library staff, and by the comments of library support staff members that their work is no different from that of the higher paid professional staff. In larger libraries, it is probably more common for non-professionals to do specialized professional-level tasks than it is in smaller libraries, where professional librarians are often required to perform a wide range of professional and nonprofessional tasks. Some also question whether, as librarians focus increasingly on management, they will lose touch with the traditional groundings of the profession.

Mark Sandler notes that librarians have generally been able to distinguish themselves from other library workers on the basis of "their links to content and the broader principles underlying information services." Sandler points out, however, that, as libraries have grown larger and more complex, the [librarian's] relationship to content and user service has been weakened.

Librarians are increasingly unable to maintain control over the qualifications needed to perform library work, in part because information technology has challenged the traditional skill base of librarians. But, Sandler also emphasizes the effects on librarianship of the societal trend toward "business models," which place greater premium on efficiency and cost effectiveness than on traditional assumptions regarding the role of the library professional.

Abbott notes that "If the public knew the extent of workplace assimilation, it would profoundly suspect professionals' claims of comprehensive jurisdiction." He points out that "the central public argument [professionals make] against workplace assimilation holds that subordinates lack the theoretical education necessary to understand and use what they know by assimilation."

The greatest threat to any profession's claim of jurisdiction over tasks in the workplace is competition from other professions. Disputes over jurisdiction can be settled in any of several ways ranging from successful claims for full jurisdiction over an area of work (e.g., the licensing mechanisms that control the practice of law and medicine) to more limited settlement mechanisms that divide jurisdiction over segments of the area. Among the common mechanisms for resolving jurisdictional disputes are: subordination (e.g., the formal relationship of nursing to medicine) and division of labour (e.g., the relationships among architects, engineers, and others in the design of buildings). Between subordination and division of labour are two weaker and less stable forms of relationships between professions claiming jurisdiction in the same area of work: intellectual jurisdiction, in which one profession controls the cognitive knowledge of the area, but shares practice with several competitors (e.g., the relationship in psychotherapy between psychiatry and psychologists, social workers and the clergy); and advisory jurisdiction, a "weaker form of control," based on relationships between two professions already possessing independent jurisdictions of their own).

Distributed computing and access to networked information have blurred the boundaries between librarians' and technologists' established jurisdictions in the information area. Neither librarians nor information technologists have subordinated the other group, and neither group has established intellectual jurisdiction over information provision. Nor is there a formal and stable division of labour.

Most writers on the subject of the professions would agree with Talcott Parsons that "the boundaries of the group system we generally call the professions are fluid and indistinct.," as well as with his suggestion that there are several core criteria which distinguish professional work from the work of other occupations. The professional groundings of librarianship by applying the generally accepted functional characteristics of the professions under the three headings:

1) knowledge—the intellectual component of professional work
2) skills or competencies—the practical application of professional knowledge; and
3) shared values—the idea that professional work is done, not only for profit, but for socially beneficial purposes.

Knowledge

Most writers on the professions acknowledge the need for the presence of academic or abstract knowledge in order for work to be considered professional. Nathan O. Hatch defines the professions as occupations "based on a definable body of organized knowledge, an expertise that derives from extensive academic training." William Sullivan notes that the professions are typically characterized by "specialized training in a field of codified knowledge usually acquired by formal education and apprenticeship."

For Abbott, the characteristic of "abstraction" is what sets the professions apart from other occupational groups. As he points out, "control of an occupation lies in control of the abstractions that generate the practical techniques" The techniques may be delegated to others, but "only a knowledge system governed by abstractions can redefine its problems and tasks, defend them from interlopers, and seize new problems.... Abstraction enables survival in the competitive system of professions."

Larry Ostler and Therrin Dahlin note that Melvil Dewey, who is generally considered to be the dominant figure in establishing librarianship as a profession, had little interest in the theoretical issues of librarianship. In the late nineteenth century, they argue, American higher education in general responded to the industrial revolution by emphasizing practical training to increase productivity. Dewey followed suit and as a result:

Library education moved ahead with the accepted practice of its time without first getting its theoretical bearings. As long as the social and economic conditions remained the same, the profession would enjoy some degree of success and acceptance; but if conditions were to change, there was no unified body of theory to provide "conceptual lenses" to look at a completely new set of problems and suggest ways to deal with them. Of course conditions did change. As information grew in quantity and complexity, "the industrial solutions to organizing and storing information, developed by Melvil Dewey and others... did not scale well."

Today, of course, the challenges that widespread diffusion of information technology and access to information pose for users of information and for librarianship as a profession are of much greater magnitude than those posed simply by increases in the quantity of available information. Pierce notes that the library curriculum has plenty of courses on current trends, but few on reading the classic works of the field. Does librarianship have seminal thinkers? Pierce thinks so and a sidebar to her article surveys current library educators for their examples.

But, Ostler and Dahlin ask, if librarianship has important thinkers, "why are we floundering without adequate theory to direct library education successfully into the next century?" Mark Sandler found that the job qualifications distinguishing librarians from other library workers are largely knowledge-based, including: understanding the principles of bibliographic organization and having an in-depth knowledge of information tools.

To be effective, law librarians must:

1) have a solid grounding in the liberal arts;
2) understand the legal system and legal profession;
3) be well-informed about information and library science theory;
4) be knowledgeable about legal resources and legal research;
5) be well-informed about commercial, governmental, and nonprofit information providers, including Internet sources;
6) be knowledgeable about information technologies;
7) be well-versed in the culture and likely future of the organization in which they work; and
8) be well-versed in management and administration.

Library selectors will need to be knowledgeable about many more sources of information; acquisitions librarians will need to know how to choose among such alternative information formats as hard copy, microform, CD-ROM, online, video, and multimedia; reference librarians will play greater roles as information analysts, establishing profiles of individual users' information needs and providing information filters for their clients; catalogers will need to organize access to a new variety of information sources, including materials that the library may not own; and administrators will need to negotiate new kinds of contracts and licenses, maintain different kinds of accounting records, seek alternative sources of support and funding, and be prepared to market library services in the face of new kinds of competition.

These changes, all of which arguably stem from the growing role of technology in librarians' work, will expand the knowledge base required to succeed in the profession, and will perhaps alter the list of most desirable traits and characteristics of persons wishing to work as law librarians. For most professions, the university is the principle seat of training. Academic professional knowledge "legitimates professional work by clarifying its foundations and tracing them to major cultural values."

Law librarianship has itself had many distinguished practitioners and leaders who held professional degrees in law, but not in librarianship. Yet, the influence of law-trained librarians on the development of the profession led ultimately to law librarianship's emergence as a clearly identifiable specialization within librarianship, and to the early development of specialized programs in education for law librarianship, many of which continue today. In the late twentieth century, the more likely question in law libraries, as well as other libraries, is whether subject knowledge from other information fields, such as computer science or electrical engineering should be allowed to substitute for the MLS in defining a librarian. However professional knowledge is obtained by particular individuals, the existence of a body of knowledge is essential for any group wishing to be recognized as a profession.

Skills

Abstract and academic professional knowledge legitimizes a profession to outsiders and provides the basis for the training of practicing professionals. However, according to Abbott, professional knowledge in academia exists in "a peculiarly disassembled state that prevents its use," while in the workplace, "theoretical education...is often irrelevant to practice."

In practice, professionals and clients alike are more likely to be concerned with whether a practitioner has the current skills or competencies needed to serve the client's needs, than with the practitioner's academic knowledge base. What is the relationship, then, between knowledge and skills? The dean of the University of California-Berkeley's School of Information Management and Systems (SIMS) provides a simple distinction.

Knowledge is something that will be useful to students throughout their careers. Thus, in the SIMS program, knowledge is conveyed through conventional semester-length courses. Skills, on the other hand, are more ephemeral than knowledge: they are "things that everyone knows will be replaced by something different down the road."

The development of highly specialized skills is by itself not enough to establish professional status, because specialization in work is not limited to the professions. Laurence Veysey notes that the specialization of the professions is "of a kind that seems intricate and somewhat intellectually interesting, often awesomely arcane to outsiders, and which it requires a long time to acquire." He uses the automobile assembly line worker as an example of a highly specialized, but non-professional occupation. The literature of librarianship frequently focuses on skills or competencies, usually with the aim of identifying the competencies that librarians will need for success in the future. Professional competencies are most closely connected to the special librarian's knowledge base "in the areas of information resources, information access, technology, management, and research," while personal competencies "represent a set of skills, attitudes, and values that enable librarians to work effectively...."

Professional competencies include such things as expert knowledge of the content of information resources, specialized subject knowledge appropriate for the organization or client, use of appropriate technologies to acquire, organize, and disseminate information, ability to evaluate outcomes and conduct research, and participation as an effective member of the senior management team of the organization. Personal competencies include commitment to excellent service, interest in seeking out challenges and new opportunities, effective communications skills, the ability to both provide leadership and work in teams, personal business skills, flexibility, etc. Despite changes in how legal information is published, law librarians will continue to acquire, organize, retrieve, preserve, and disseminate information, and assist users in retrieving and using it.

Law librarians will need to be versatile, creative, adaptable, flexible, and comfortable with change. They will need to be skilled and articulate instructors, able to work collaboratively within both the library and their larger organization, and able to show equanimity in the face of the frustrations of a rapidly changing work environment. The reports of both professional organizations place their highest emphasis on personal competencies that can be applied in a variety of work settings. Changes in technology will transform not only the specifics of the librarian's skill set, but the library work environment. In a changing work environment, the successful and effective professionals will be those with the personal skills to adapt and deal with change. Thus, while there may be value in compiling comprehensive lists of professional skills, it is not necessary to insist that all librarians possess the full set, as long as the skills they do possess are underpinned by a shared set of values. A perspective that places greater emphasis on shared professional values than on lists of skills allows the profession to grow and develop, and to create new relationships with other groups.

Shared Values

The elements of professionalism are: fidelity to ethics and integrity; service with competence, dedication, and independence; education as a means for growth and replenishment; civility and respect for authority; and commitment to improving the justice system and advancing the rule of law. In librarianship, discussions of professional values often begin with the Five Laws of Library Science set out by the Indian librarian, S. R. Ranganathan. Ranganathan's principles are captured in five brief statements: "Books are for use"; "Every reader his (or her) book"; "Every book its reader"; "Save the time of the reader"; and "The library is a growing organism."

In a brief article deserving of wider circulation, Richard Leiter has elaborated upon Ranganathan's laws to show the practical implications of values and principles in the daily work of librarians. He notes ways in which such library practices as limited access to special collections, off-site storage, and licensing of materials in formats available only to designated classes of users violate Ranganathan's first principle: Books are for use. Cohen lists six principles for law librarianship. The first two principles state the importance of knowing and carrying out the purposes and policies of the organization a law librarian serves, as well as knowing the library's users and their work. The third states the case for the law librarian's role as teacher of legal bibliography and research methodology.

The final three principles are more concerned with values. Cohen's fourth principle focuses on access to information. Starting from Foskett's point that librarians are not the owners of knowledge, but its guardians, Cohen states the principle that law librarians must not only provide, but assure access to the information they collect and administer.

The librarian has to be conscious of both administrative and bibliographic issues of access, and (using today's terminology) must be proactive in both areas. The fifth principle highlights the librarian's responsibility for developing and organizing a law library's collections, noting that the responsibility must be exercised consciously and with critical intelligence. The final principle states the duty of law librarians to advance their art and profession through scholarship and innovation.

In his book on *librarianship as a profession*, Michael Winter notes that, as a group, the information professions have only recently developed such distinctly modern characteristics of the professions as university training, professional associations, licensing procedures, and codes of ethics. Even more than librarianship, the computing professions can be seen as what Winter and others would characterize as "emerging" professions. Abbott traces the beginnings of the computing profession to World War II. Others, too, have noted how quickly computing "emerged" as a field and as a profession: "as soon as computer technology was developed, it was recognized as marketable, useful for individuals and vital for the military. Overnight the elements of a profession were in place."

Some observers have pointed out similarities between computing professionals and librarians. Librarianship remains a female-dominated profession, at least in numbers. On the other hand, the stereotypical information technologist continues to be male. A recent survey of network managers showed found that 17 percent of respondents were women, and that women as a group expressed more dissatisfaction with their salaries and treatment than males. There is also evidence that the number of women preparing for careers in information technology is not rising in pace with the growth of employment opportunities in the area. Because of their common educational qualifications and the fact that they have traditionally worked in easily identifiable workplaces, librarians have generally had few problems maintaining professional identity, even as they became being highly specialized in terms of tasks performed or subject knowledge.

Computing professionals, who are also faced with increasing specialization within the profession, have traditionally based their identity in the disciplines of mathematics and engineering. Computing sits at the crossroads among the central processes of applied mathematics, science, and engineering. The three processes are of equal-and fundamental-importance in the discipline, which is a unique blend of interaction among theory, abstraction, and design.

Since 1989, however, networking and communications technologies have become increasingly integrated into all aspects of contemporary business and professional life, and the demand for skilled information technologists has grown exponentially. Computing has become much less a "back office" operation, and the backgrounds and experiences of those working in the field have become much more heterogeneous. In business, government, and education, many people have attained responsible computing or networking positions with little or no training in the traditional academic disciplines of computing, building new careers upon the discovery that they had the talent for working with technology.

Like other professions faced with a rapidly changing work environment, computing professionals have struggled to define the professional knowledge base of a highly specialized and developing field, and to maintain meaningful relationships between academic knowledge and the practice of the profession. The concern about competencies demonstrates that, like librarians and others, practicing professionals in computing think of the academic base of their profession as remote and divorced from the everyday practice of the field.

In librarianship, this concern is often manifested in debates over whether the MLS or an equivalent degree should be required of those working in librarian positions, or whether on-the-job training and appropriate experience, perhaps combined with a subject degree (e.g., in law), can substitute for the professional degree. In computing, however, the issues are less abstract than they might be in librarianship. For computing professionals and those who hire them, the need to be able to identify, measure, and demonstrate competencies and skills is a matter of immediate practical concern. More than librarians, computing professionals have been forced to deal with rapid and continual changes in their work and in the skills needed to show competency in it.

For computing professionals, the competencies and skills need for success in the workplace are most often attained through specialized, short-term training programs, rather than entry-level or advanced degrees. As a result, the field is characterized by a variety of certification programs, many of which are specialized both by job function and by software product or vendor. Microsoft's network certification programs have risen in popularity as its competing network products have penetrated those markets. Studies show that the educational qualifications of computing professionals are increasing, and changing. A growing percentage of network managers now have advanced degrees in business, or in information systems, as well as, or in place of electrical engineering or computer science degrees. Employers are looking for technologists who are broadly educated, and who demonstrate a range of skills beyond the technological.

All of these developments show a recognition that computing support in an organization is no longer a back office operation, and that information technologists are fully conscious of their roles as active intermediaries involved both in making sure that technology is functional and in helping clients use technology effectively. Librarians and information technologists both face challenging and uncertain futures, in part because of the pace of change in the information environment, and in part because ready access to information technology has blurred the traditional distinctions among areas of jurisdiction in the workplace.

Continuing development of the access technologies that provide the means for finding information will continue to affect and change the librarian's work, and require more of the librarian's attention and understanding. At the same time, the computing professional is likely to continue to interact more frequently and directly with end users of networked computing services. As end users increasingly use computers and networks both to gain access and to use information, the lines between access technologies and content will become increasingly indistinct. In this environment, the librarian's professional grounding in content expertise will remain important, but in a new sense. There is now and will be a growing need for professionals who can sift and sort through information, not only to locate pieces of information, but to put those pieces into context, and to weigh and compare different items, identify, authenticate and validate them.

Librarians and technologists alike should be thinking more about context and point of view than about content and access as separate concepts. The ability to provide context to the client's process of information seeking will be key to the future of the information professions, but context is a product of both content and access, and can be provided only through consideration and understanding of both elements. Complexity is inherent in most information-seeking, resulting from both the abundance of content and the crude methods available to access it. It is unnecessary to say much about the problems posed by the sheer masses of potentially useful information available on any topic, the difficulties in knowing whether any search has found everything that might be useful, or the problems involved in weighing and authenticating what is found.

Historically, these all are reasons for the development and endurance of the library as an institution and librarianship as a profession. But, will the institution and the profession continue to endure when information-seeking increasingly takes place in an environment where researchers have ubiquitous access to networked information of all kinds? As we think about the future of libraries and librarianship, it is necessary to keep in mind that not only the forms of published knowledge usually held in libraries, but also less formal (and formerly less accessible) sources of information have been reduced to common digital formats.

As a result, the information content that can be brought to bear to solve a problem can often go well beyond the traditional materials of library research in either print or electronic formats. For many, the promise of the digital library lies in its capacity to provide integrated access to material that is of less permanent value and less archival in nature than the usual library holdings: Seen from this new perspective, the digital library is a seamless blend of the conventional archive of current or historically important information and knowledge, along with ephemeral material such as drafts, notes, memoranda and files of ongoing activity.

The potential for blending digitally-formatted information of various types provides the impetus for the current interest of corporations (and librarians) in "knowledge management." The idea of knowledge management, the "process of capturing a company's collective expertise wherever it resides—in databases, on paper, or in people's heads—and distributing it to wherever it can help produce the biggest payoff," is made possible because information of all sorts can be collected, stored, and distributed in a common digital format.

Of course, this also adds to the rapid growth in the amount of information potentially available for any situation, leaving "knowledge workers feeling both overwhelmed by information and fearful that they're missing important details." It is easy to argue, therefore, that ready access to personal and informal information in electronic formats, as well as improved direct access to formally published information, have only increased researchers' needs for assistance of some sort in identifying and obtaining useful content.

"The problems inherent in any information system-disorientation, navigation inefficiency, and cognitive overload-are multiplied on the Internet." But, how will this need for assistance be met? Part of librarians' concern for their future is prompted by talk of "disintermediation," the idea that, as more and more useful information is directly accessible via the Internet, researchers will do their own information-seeking, perhaps with the assistance of intelligent search agents devoted to finding and delivering information tailored to a researcher's specific needs. But such purely technological solutions to the problem rely on the proposition that access technologies can be readily separated from content. As a result, they too readily dismiss the importance of "human factors" in interface design, revealing both too much faith in the abilities of intelligent interfaces to overcome the difficulties and complexities of the information-seeking process and too little understanding of the actual needs of human information seekers, who require context to be successful in their quest.

Before relying too heavily on automated devices to navigate through masses of digitized personal and archival research information, it is worth examining the computing industry's track record for developing interface and other access software. It has become commonplace to observe that the usual effect of software upgrades and improvements is to provide additional features and options at the cost of increased complexity in the software interface.

Access technologies are indeed the "means" to the information content at the end of the search, but means of access are vital to the success of the search process. And librarians may pay too little attention to them. There was a time at the last turn of the century, when librarians were not only guardians of information, but were the primary creators of indexes and other finding tools used by readers to locate information. Somewhere along the line, however, librarians gradually gave up responsibility for that work, first to the publishing industry and now to information technologists. As we near the start of a new century, in which content and access are less easily distinguished and when successful information-seeking will require increasingly sophisticated technologies, librarians need to think hard about re-entering the tool-building arena.

Content expertise alone will be increasingly less useful without the "deeper" technological proficiencies needed to provide effective access to information and help users work with it in a variety of formats. The need to develop greater proficiencies in technology does not mean that librarians should abandon the roots of their own profession. Rather, it is essential to revisit those roots and to consider what might already have been forgotten as librarians have concentrated on gaining professional recognition and dealing with the challenges of the information environment. Librarianship developed as a service-oriented, client-centered profession: one in which meeting the client's needs as the client sees them has been of more importance than the expertise of the professional.

Librarians must also consider the effects of their growing roles as managers within their organizations. Performance of the skills associated with professional work is a highly visible manifestation of professional status. Yet, as larger libraries have become more complex organizations and have placed a greater weight on managerial skills, much apparently professional library work is performed by non-librarians. Mark Sandler provides examples in cataloguing, reference, systems, and collection development to show how the larger managerial role played by librarians in research libraries has increased opportunities and visibility for non-librarian staff members in those areas of speciality.

References

Janes, Joseph. (1998). "The Internet Public Library: an intellectual history." *Library Hi Tech,* 16(2), 55-68.

OCLC/RLG Working Group on Preservation Metadata. (2002). "Preservation Metadata and the OAIS Information Model: A Metadata Framework to Support the Preservation of digital Objects." [Online]. Available: http://www.oclc.org/research/projects/pmwg/pm_framework.pdf

Thibodeau, K. (2002), *Overview of Technological Approaches to Digital Preservation and Challenges in Coming Years.* In: The State of Digital Preservation: An International Perspective.Conference Papers and Documentary Abstracts, http://www.clir.org/pubs/reports/pub107/thibodeau.html

Trusted Digital Repositories: Attributes and Responsibilities. An RLG-OCLC Report, May 2002, http://www.rlg.org/longterm/repositiories.pdf

7

Management of Digital Collections

Since the web explosion of the 1990s, a wide variety of digital collections have emerged on the Internet. While digital collections may differ in content or structure, they all share one commonality—the need for metadata. Frequently described as "data about data," metadata is a critical component of all digital collections. Metadata facilitates the discovery and retrieval of information, it provides for resource presentation and navigation, and it contains the information needed to preserve digital data files. While several digital collections of books have been created for the Internet, it is only recently that libraries and archives have begun to digitize archival collections for Web delivery.

The Barren Lands project is a full-text online collection of archival material related to two exploratory surveys conducted by the Canadian explorer, geologist, and mining engineer, Joseph Burr Tyrrell. The collection is centred on Tyrrell's 1893 and 1894 explorations of Canada's Barren Lands region west of Hudson Bay, in the area now known as Nunavut. Drawing on materials from the J.B. Tyrrell collection and related collections at the Thomas Fisher Rare Book Library, University of Toronto, the digital collection includes over 5,000 images from original field notebooks, correspondence, photographs, maps, newspaper articles, and published reports.

The first major challenge associated with the Barren Lands project centred on how to represent archival material within an online environment. A search of the Internet for similar archival projects revealed that online archival collections were most often presented in one of two ways: as an online exhibition or as a simple database of independent archival documents.

Following the "exhibition" method, institutions presented archival collections online in much the same way as they would present an exhibition of physical materials; narrative descriptions or transcriptions of items were presented with links to digital representations of those items. These Web sites tended to be small in size and highlighted materials that were considered important. The second approach followed by many institutions was to create a database-driven Web site with basic search and browse techniques. In these digital repositories, each archival document was treated as a separate entity and basic descriptive metadata elements such as title, author, and date were given for each item.

Although the Barren Lands project team found aspects of both methods of delivery appealing, they decided that neither approach was fully compatible with their vision of the project. While the "exhibition" approach provided an abundance of narrative contextual information, this method was deemed impracticable for the size of the digital collection. Similarly, a strict database approach was also not favoured, as it did not retain the contextual linkages between the documents. Instead, the Barren Lands project team decided to create two levels of descriptive metadata to provide the necessary contextual information for the archival materials and to allow for comprehensive searching.

Descriptive Metadata

In most digital collections, each book, article, map, etc. is considered to be an independent digital object. The Barren Lands project was different in that the archival collection consisted of many documents that were inter-related with each other. For example, in the case of J.B. Tyrrell's correspondence, the meaning and significance of an individual letter can only be understood if it is read within the context of a series of letters. It was essential that these natural connections be retained within the digital environment. At the same time, it was necessary that each document remain an independent digital object for the purpose of resource discovery and retrieval. The solution to this problem was to adopt a two-tiered approach to the creation of descriptive metadata—one tier to describe the archival materials as a collective unit and another to describe each digital object.

Tier 1—Describing Archival Collections

Although paper-based finding aids and item listings for some of the materials did exist for the J.B. Tyrrell and James W. Tyrrell collections, the project team was unable to use this information in the construction of the online collection. Problems with the pre-existing descriptive metadata were three-fold: first, the metadata was not in electronic format; second, the metadata did not contain all of the necessary descriptive information; and third, the archival materials were not described consistently according to archival descriptive standards. Because of these problems, the project team decided to re-describe both collections according to the Canadian descriptive standard, the Rules for Archival Description (RAD).

Once the descriptive metadata was complete, it was necessary to encode this information in a standard data structure. In order to retain the relationships between archival materials, the project team adopted the Encoded Archival Description (EAD) data structure standard, which is jointly administered by the Society of American Archivists and the Library of Congress. EAD is a non-proprietary standard in the form of a Standard Generalized Markup Language (SGML) and Extensible Markup Language (XML) Document Type Definition (DTD). Developed specifically for archival finding aids, the EAD standard has the ability to accurately represent the multilevel nature of archives in a machine-readable format. Consequently, the EAD standard facilitates access by allowing users to "drill down" into an archival finding aid, beginning at the fonds or collection level description down to the descriptions of individual items.

In the Barren Lands project, the descriptions of the J.B. Tyrrell and James W. Tyrrell fonds were encoded using the XML version of the EAD DTD. In these multi-level records, users are provided with descriptions of the entire fonds, the various series of documents that make up the fonds, and file level descriptions (e.g. descriptions of photo albums and letterbooks) if they exist. Within the description of each series or file containing digitized objects, a link is made from the title of the object to a separate item level description.

While EAD does provide the capability to describe archival materials down to the item level of description, the project team decided that within the context of the project, the standard was unsuitable for that purpose. Item level descriptions could not be included in the EAD description for three reasons. First, the EAD standard did not provide for the inclusion of all the required descriptive metadata elements for item level records. Second, EAD did not have the capability to embed the OCR or rekeyed text within the item level description. And third, the standard did not allow for the incorporation of the structural metadata needed for the project. Because the EAD standard could not adequately handle these specific needs, the project team opted to create a second tier of metadata for each individual digitized item.

Tier 2—Item Level Description

Since no existing data structure standard contained all of the features needed for the item level descriptions, the decision was made to create a customized XML DTD based on the Text Encoding Initiative (TEI). Not all features of the TEI DTD were needed for the project; in fact, only the elements contained within the TEI Header and the paragraph <p> and page break <pb> elements were included in the DTD. Furthermore, as the structure and features of the online collection became more defined, it was clear that many of the descriptive metadata elements in the DTD would need to be customized for the Barren Lands project.

The customized DTD contains many of the standard fields found in descriptive metadata schema such as title, author, extent, subject, and others that facilitate in the discovery and retrieval of information. Features that make the metadata schema unique are attributes to determine whether records are published or not, as well as attributes to identify the various types of notes and subject heading standards that are used in the item level record. The DTD also enables linking between documents—users can link from an item level record to the EAD encoded finding aid—as well as between item-level records, if a relationship has been defined.

File Naming Systems

Another significant metadata challenge with archival materials is how to incorporate different document types into an online collection. The problems associated with multiple media collections do not generally lie in the presentation of various media, but rather in their preparation for online delivery. The Barren Lands project consists of a variety of documentary forms, all of which needed to be handled in a slightly different manner. For example, published reports required OCR, manuscript letters and newspaper clippings needed to be manually re-keyed, and no additional work was required for maps and photographs. To simplify the development of the digital collection, it was necessary to create a method for quickly identifying the document type for each digital object.

As a form of structural metadata, the file naming structure was used to distinguish between documentary forms. Directories were created for each type of document, such as letters, diaries, published text, maps, photographs, and so on. Then, as each archival document was scanned, a unique identifier, containing a letter to identify the documentary form followed by a five-digit number, was recorded in a relational database.

The project team felt strongly that no semantic information be included in the file naming system as this type of information would likely become confusing rather than helpful in the long run. This file-naming system not only ensured that we had a simple, well-organized repository for the images, it also allowed the team to quickly identify which image files required OCR and which files needed rekeying.

Issues in Collection Management

Information overload may be the greatest challenge that scholars and librarians have faced in the twentieth century. Librarians whose careers spanned the pre- and post-1950s worlds noted a marked expansion in the scope of scholarship in America. Before World War II, academic research in America concentrated on Western culture and classical areas of science. After the war, American research horizons expanded to cover all areas of the world as well as applied and specialized fields of science.

Library collections grew rapidly to house the products of this expanded research effort. In the 1950s and 60s many university librarians found themselves in the midst of a "golden age" of collection development when acquisitions funds seemed plentiful, U.S. currency was strong, and there was still room in academic library book stacks.

Cooperative collection development, which in some sense is the ultimate activity of this new functional field of librarianship, has proved difficult to implement and to sustain. It is clear, both in theory and practice, that no single library can collect the entire—and exploding—record of knowledge; and, as use studies show, no library really needs to do so to satisfy most of its users' needs.

A reasonable approach would be to coordinate collection development locally, regionally, nationally, and internationally to maximize local use of library collections and broad coverage of all fields of knowledge. The Center for Research Libraries, however, emerged as a viable model for depositing and sharing highly specialized research material, and some carefully focused regional efforts, such as the one involving the academic libraries in North Carolina's Research Triangle, did provide some long-standing cooperative collection development opportunities for the libraries involved.

By and large, however, most cooperative collection development experiments from the 1950s through the mid-1980s were not successful. The strong political pull of local library autonomy, combined with the technical difficulty of moving print material quickly and economically over geographic distances, tended to make cooperative collection development difficult and impractical.

In the mid-1980s many universities and research libraries found themselves in a period of fiscal constraint and even decline. Economic constraints affected all aspects of research library operations. In fact, personnel reductions seem to have been steeper than acquisitions declines. Between 1982 and 1991 the typical portion of a total research library budget spent on acquisitions remained constant at 35 percent, while the portion of a total library budget spent on salaries declined from 56 to 52 percent.

Anecdotal evidence points to fewer full-time heads of collection development, bibliographers and subject specialists in research libraries as the 20th century closes. In 1989, John Howe, a history professor and interim director of libraries at the University of Minnesota, described the emerging situation as the "decentering of the library" within institutions of higher education. According to Howe, the library might still be the symbolic heart of the university, but for several reasons it was losing its central place as a funding priority on many campuses.

First, new information technology was creating "alternative paths" for access to scholarly information, and investments in technical infrastructure and computing centers were diverting funding from the traditional library. Second, the decline in arts and sciences and the rise of science and technology programs in universities were eroding the power of disciplines that most directly supported the traditional library. Third, the profession of librarianship itself seemed to be in disarray, fraught with uncertainty and anxiety over its future in the computer age. Fourth, libraries were not competitive enough in the new, aggressive environment of higher education.

Howe emphasized that new leadership was required to assert that libraries still played a central role in supporting teaching and research. The library could no longer take for granted a special status in the university. While confronting adverse economic conditions in the 1980s and 90s, collection management librarians were faced with an even more powerful force for change: the emergence of the digital information system.

The online catalogue was followed by electronic reference databases, and by the mid-1990s full-text digital articles and journals and digital collections were vying for collection management librarians' attention. Librarians now had to balance the demands of print and digital materials, even as they sought to understand the nature and consequences of digital, networked information and the impact a new information system would have on library operations, including the budget.

At the same time, scholarly publishing was also experiencing dramatic change. With fewer orders from libraries, university presses had to cut back the number of monograph titles they published, while commercial journal publishers, at least some of the largest science and technology publishers, were expanding and flourishing. All concerned struggled with the impact of the Internet.

A constricted library economy, the emergence of information in digital format, and the commercialization and consolidation of the publishing sector have combined to produce profound and surprising changes in collection management in research libraries at the beginning of the 21st century.

Collection management librarians—and library directors—are faced with a new and uncharted environment. Libraries have much less buying power than they had a decade ago. With fewer staff in collection management full time, many selectors and bibliographers work at collection management part time while handling a much broader range of disciplines and formats.

The technical advances in digitization are truly revolutionizing the way scholarly information is published, organized, and maintained, and both the scope and extent of this change are difficult to comprehend and manage. As difficult as it was to manage a print collection, librarians now have two equally formidable formats to consider: print and digital.

When digital resources were first introduced in research libraries, there was a good deal of conflict between the old and new format. What might be called the cultural wars between print and electronic proponents began with the demise of the card catalogue and moved to the fear of digital content taking over from print.

In fact, current practices and traditions in scholarly communication are at the base of the conflicts within collection management. The divergence among disciplines is noteworthy. Scholars in the sciences publish their research results in journals, rather than in monographs, in part to be able to report as rapidly as possible.

They are, for the most part, comfortable with digital access to journal articles and, in many cases, communicate widely electronically and share initial results of their research, e.g., electronic preprints. In some disciplines, such as mathematics, scholars regularly use back issues of journals in their fields; others, such as computer science, do not. In some areas of the humanities, however, such as history, monographs, not journal articles, are required for tenure and promotion.

Rapid dissemination of results is less important in the humanities (and hence different editing practices exist) than in the sciences, and older publications are consulted more frequently than in many scientific disciplines. There are some areas of the humanities, such as philosophy, however, where monographs play a much smaller role than do journal articles.

Blaise Cronin, Dean of the School of Library and Information Science at Indiana University, commented recently on the differences among academic disciplines within the changing world of electronic publishing: "Interestingly, cross-field variations are largely independent of the highly visible tools and technologies associated with electronic publishing. Common platforms don't breed common approaches.

Rather, publishing practices and expectations within a given research community are shaped by prevailing norms and conventions. Nothing new in that. Traditionally, a refereed conference paper has counted for something in computer science, but is likely to be given short shrift by a promotion and tenure committee in a business school. A monograph will be expected of a junior scholar in English, but not of an aspiring mathematician. This being so, our ex cathedra pronouncements about publishing really should be grounded in the multiple realities of tribal life in academe."

Within this complicated picture of needs and traditions, the rapidly increasing prices of science journals has literally eaten up limited collection budgets. In fact, despite cancellation of hundreds of thousands of dollars worth of journals since 1986, the 110 largest research libraries in the United States and Canada have spent 124% more on serials to purchase 7% fewer titles, according to the Association for Research Libraries. Although monographs are increasing in price at a slower rate than are journals, fewer monographs are purchased by libraries because of the need to fund expensive journals (both electronic and print) in the sciences.

With fewer orders from libraries, scholarly presses have reduced the number of titles and the quantity of print runs; therefore, it becomes more and more difficult for a scholar to find a publisher for a monograph. To complicate the picture further, universities and libraries have had to scramble to develop the technical infrastructure and staff expertise necessary to fully participate in the new digital information system. Some departments in the academy still lack up-to-date computer equipment and support, while others have long had a strong information technology infrastructure and continue to improve it.

Library organization and the education of many library staff were designed for work in a print information system. It is not easy to change operational procedures, organizational structures, and established work habits and outlooks—such social changes generally lag behind technological change. The amount of digital information is growing faster than most librarians would have predicted.

Despite this phenomenal growth, research libraries, for reasons stated above, are still largely dominated by print resources, both in acquisitions and collection management. It is unlikely that more than 10 to 15 percent of a research library's collection budget is used today to purchase or provide access to digital information. It is clear that research librarians need to turn more of their attention, effort, and resources to managing the new digital information system.

The fundamental structure of how scholarly information is published has yet to be altered in any significant way. Authors still submit their manuscripts, now more often than not in electronic form, to publishers. Publishers take ownership of the manuscripts, turn them into both print and electronic books and articles, and sell them to individuals and libraries.

Research librarians and faculty members are loath to give up their print collections and journal subscriptions until digital products are more stable and mature and are able to be archived successfully. In fact, many publishers still require that libraries purchase a print version along with their electronic product. One collection development expert, Robert Sewell, recently described the current electronic environment as one where a myriad of different interfaces exist; search engines crash; local loading, remote access, and operating systems have regular and recurring problems; radically different terms and conditions are found in licensing agreements; and wide fluctuations in the pricing of similar electronic products are found. He believes, however, that most research libraries have become extraordinarily adaptive in this chaotic and formative period.

At this point the digital information system is simply too immature for it to become a trusted and reliable medium for the collection and preservation of the record of scholarship. Despite its imperfections, the digital information system has and will continue to have a profound effect on scholarly communication. Several studies have appeared in this decade that demonstrate the magnitude and significance of any fundamental changes in scholarly communication as well as the great potential offered to the community of research and scholarship by developments in information technology.

Fundamental changes in scholarly communications are certainly in store. The traditional book and journal as organizing frames for scholarship will likely change as will basic production, distribution, and archiving. Odlyzko believes the new digital information system will allow scholars to become their own publishers and archivists. According to Odlyzko, "Publishers and librarians have been the middlemen between the scholars as producers of information and the scholars as consumers, and are likely to be largely squeezed out of this business."

Hidden Collections and Archives Program

As the Council on Library and Information Resources (CLIR) stated in launching its Cataloguing Hidden Special Collections and Archives Program, "Libraries, archives, and cultural institutions hold millions of items that have never been adequately described. These items are all but unknown to, and unused by, the scholars those organizations aim to serve".

According to a 1998 Association of Research Libraries (ARL) survey of special collections libraries, about 28 percent of manuscript collections are unprocessed, while 36 percent of graphic materials and 37 percent of audio materials have not been processed. As the ARL Task Force on Special Collections argues, the failure to process collections holds back research, leads to duplicates being purchased, and makes them more vulnerable to being stolen or lost because libraries and archives don't know what they have. Studies have shown that between 25 percent and 30 percent of researchers have not been able to use collections because they have not been processed. As a result, stakeholders such as researchers and donors become frustrated.

To confront the problem of unprocessed collections, Greene and Meissner promote "a new set of arrangement, preservation, and description guidelines that (1) expedites getting collection materials into the hands of users; (2) assures arrangement of materials *adequate* to user needs; (3) takes the *minimal* steps necessary to physically preserve collection materials; and (4) describes materials *sufficient* to promote use". Meeting researchers' needs for access to materials trumps achieving perfection in archival description and arrangement. Likewise, the ARL Task Force proposes minimal processing. This access can be provided through the Online Public Access Catalogue (OPAC) EAD finding aids, digital collections, or databases. Indeed, providing electronic access is crucial to making hidden collections more visible. Thus, the Library of Congress Working Group on the Future of Bibliographic Control recommends that archives "make finding aids accessible via online catalogues and available on the Internet," streamline cataloguing, and "encourage inter-institutional collaboration for sharing metadata records and authority records for rare and unique materials".

Among the criteria that archives and special collections should consider in determining how to process each collection are size, condition, significance, and, perhaps most important, the needs of researchers. Archives should keep in mind that archival descriptions may be part of distributed, federated catalogues, so they should adhere to best practices to ensure consistency of data. The ARL Task Force recognizes that some collections may require more detailed description than others and that any decision will involve trade-offs.

Institutions have devised different approaches to hidden collections based on the nature of their collections and the resources available. Through the University of Chicago's Andrew W. Mellon Foundation-funded "Uncovering New Chicago Archives Project" (UNCAP), graduate students are working with scholars and cultural heritage professionals to catalogue hidden collections housed at a local library and museum. For the museum collection, they are using item-level cataloguing, whereas they are using more standard archival practices with the library collection. In addition, a professional archivist is using minimal processing techniques to process a jazz collection and a contemporary poetry collection housed at the university. Whereas the students are producing detailed descriptions, the archivist is taking a more stripped-down approach, allowing Chicago to test the effectiveness of each model. Similarly, to reduce archival backlogs and provide research experiences for graduate students, the University of California, Los Angeles (UCLA) launched the Center for Primary Research and Training (CFPRT).

Selecting Archival Management Software

With an increasing number of options for archival management software, archivists may feel overwhelmed. Fortunately, they can adopt sound, rational processes for selecting software. The Canadian Heritage Information Network (CHIN) offers both a detailed review and an online course focused on selecting collection management software, which is closely related to archival management software. Rather than replicate that work, I will provide a few general recommendations for selecting software based on the CHIN guide and other sources.

Selecting software should be a collaborative process so that all the stakeholders can describe how they would use it and provide input into what is selected. To ensure that the selection process stays on course, the team should establish a project plan with clear milestones and areas of responsibility. As a first step, archives should conduct a needs assessment to evaluate current gaps and workflows. Do they really need new software, and is now the best time to pursue it? What are the weaknesses of their current software? How does information flow through the system? What kind of information is captured, by whom, when, and for what purposes?

Working collaboratively, team members should then prioritize requirements, generating a weighted "features checklist." In addition to features such as "support for EAD" or "support for managing locations," archivists should weigh factors such as the quality of user support, the reputation of the vendor, cost, technical requirements, and the robustness and appropriateness of the technology platform. Often the best way to evaluate the quality of the software and support is to speak with a variety of users. Through a site visit, evaluators can see the software in action and understand it in the context of archival workflows. Most vendors, and all open source projects, make available a demo version or can arrange an online demonstration of the software. Archivists should take the software through a variety of tasks to determine whether it is easy to use, does what it needs to do, and has any bugs. If a commercial application is selected, organizations should carefully spell out the terms of the contract, including support and training.

Criteria for Choosing Archival Software

No single archival management system will be appropriate for every archive, given the variation in technical support available at the institution and the need for particular features. Here are some of the criteria that archives should consider in selecting an archival management system:

Automating the processing and description of collections through the archival management system versus generating EAD by hand and managing collections through other software.

Archival management systems offer a number of advantages, particularly to archives that do not already have large quantities of EAD finding aids or are dissatisfied with current workflows. A primary advantage of archival management systems is the ability to enter data once and generate multiple outputs. Rather than being isolated in separate systems, data can be brought together through a single interface, reducing redundancy and making it easier to find and manage information.

However, archival management systems can be difficult to implement in some organizations and may not provide the flexibility that archivists require. Several archivists reported difficulty importing existing EAD data into systems such as Archon and AT, a problem due in part to the flexibility of EAD and the resulting variability of finding aids. Homegrown approaches may be more flexible and may better reflect the archive's own workflow. Furthermore, some archivists argue that putting archival description into a database structure is reductive and oversimplifies the process of producing a finding aid. In the process of encoding a finding aid, archivists better understand the texture, structure, and contents of the document.

Other archivists emphasize the importance of adhering to standards to facilitate exchange of information and consistency. Indeed, one interviewee argued that the rigor and inflexibility of archival management systems are actually strengths, since by using such software, archives will ultimately produce more consistent data and facilitate the exchange and federation of archival information. If each archive, or even each collection, took its own approach to archival description, creating a federated finding aids repository would be difficult. In that sense, the development of archival management systems such as Archon and AT is an important step toward realizing the ARL Task Force on Special Collection's recommendation.

Support for Archival Standards

To facilitate interoperability and adherence to best practices, archives will want to select software that meets archival standards such as EAD, DACS, and MARC, as well as emerging standards such as EAC. Some archival systems, such as ICA-AToM, focus more on international (ICA) standards rather than on U.S. standards. However, even many non-U.S. applications support crosswalking between standards and include EAD support.

Web-based Versus Desktop Client

Some archival management software is entirely Web based, while other such software requires a desktop client and connect to a database backend. Web-based software can be more intuitive for some users and enables distributed cataloguing, since anyone with Web access can contribute records. With systems such as Archon, information can be published to the Web as soon as it is entered. However, some archives worry about the security and reliability of an entirely Web-based system. A client-based interface may offer greater control over data, but institutions may need to pay a fee for each computer on which the software is installed. Licensing models vary, however, so this is not always the case.

Support for Publishing

Many archives face difficulty not only in creating EAD files but also in publishing them online. Some archival management systems address this problem by enabling archives to make available their finding aids on the Web. Indeed, a primary reason that Archon was developed was to facilitate publication of archival information online. Once an archivist enters information into Archon, it is automatically searchable and discoverable by

Google. Likewise, many commercial systems offer support for online access to their collections, sometimes through the purchase of an additional module. Since most browsers now provide support for XML, archives could simply upload their EAD files to a Web server, include a call-out to an XSLT stylesheet at the top of each file for the purposes of presentation, and display their finding aids without too much effort. Projects such as the EAD Cookbook have made stylesheets freely available. Although this simple approach does not offer sophisticated searching and other features, it enables archives to publish their finding aids online at minimal cost.

EAD Authoring

According to a 2006 study by Chris Prom, archivists use a variety of tools to create descriptive records, favoring "simple" tools: "Eighty-two percent use word processors; 55%, library catalogue software; 34% custom databases; 31% text or HTML editors; 22% XML editors, and 14% digital library software". Archives using XML editors typically have a larger backlog than those using word processors.

Often archives use a mix of methods to create finding aids. For instance, UC Berkeley converted legacy finding aids to EAD through a multifaceted approach, entering basic descriptive information into Web templates and employing WordPerfect to create the initial hierarchy for the collection. It then converted the WordPerfect files to EAD using macros and Perl scripts. XML editors were primarily used as "reference tool[s]." Likewise, the University of Chicago uses Web forms to create the front matter for finding aids; archivists write inventories using Word, and then a script is run to generate EAD. Post-processing is done using an XML editor such as Oxygen.

Among the particular technologies used to create EAD are the following:

XML/text Editors

XML editors enable archivists to see the entire hierarchy of a finding aid and engage in the intellectual activity of marking up an archival collection. However, relying solely on XML editors to generate finding aids can be inefficient. According to "informal studies" at the University of Illinois-Urbana Champaign, "a skilled worker took 20 hours to encode a 100-page finding aid, using standard XML markup tools, on top of the time needed to actually write the collection description and develop a general box listing of its content. XML and customizable text editors include:

1) *XMetaL*: Extensible, collaborative commercial software for authoring XML. To provide a more user-friendly interface for creating and editing finding aids, Yale University has developed a finding aids authoring tool layered over XMetaL.
2) *Oxygen:* Easy-to-use, commercial "cross platform XML editor providing the tools for XML authoring, XML conversion, XML Schema, DTD, Relax NG and Schematron development, XPath, XSLT," etc.
3) *NoteTab:* A free or inexpensive text editor. Several projects, including NC Echo, Virginia Heritage, and the EAD Cookbook, have created clipbook libraries for NoteTab that facilitate the creation of EAD.
4) *EAD Cookbook:* The EAD Cookbook aims to make it easier for archives to create finding aids by providing authoring tools for Oxygen, XMetaL, and NoteTab.
5) *MEX (Midosa-Editor in XML-Standards):* Describes itself as "a set of tools for everyday description work in archival institutions including the production of online finding aids with digitized images from the archival records."

Word Processing Templates

A number of archives use or have used word processing software such as Microsoft Word, WordPerfect, or Open Office to create preliminary finding aids. In some cases, organizations have created templates that make it easy to enter standard archival information. Often they also use macros or scripts to aid in the conversion to EAD. For example, Yale has experimented with Open Office as tool for EAD creation, the Bentley Library at the University of Michigan has developed macros to convert Word files to EAD XML, and the Utah State Archives used WordPerfect to create container lists. Similarly, the Utah State Archives produces container lists using Excel and MailMerge.

Forms

By using forms to produce finding aids, archives can speed their creation and ensure greater consistency. Forms can be Web based or desktop based:

1) *Berkeley Web Template:* CGI script is a customizable cgi-driven Web application "that generates a user-defined HTML form template and then generates markup using the values filled in by users.... Output may be in the form of METS, TEI, EAD, XML or SGML, even HTML or PDF".

2) *Online Archive of California:* Makes available Web forms "for generating collection- through series-/subseries-level finding aids that are compliant with the OAC BPG EAD and EAD Version 2002.
3) *ArchivesHub:* Provides a Web form for generating EAD 2002.
4) *EAD XForms:* Justin Banks's EAD templates allow users to enter archival information into a form.
5) *X-EAD:* The University of Utah is developing form-based desktop software for authoring and editing EAD.

EAD Validation

By validating EAD files, archives can ensure their adherence to standards and facilitate participation in union catalogues and regional repositories. Several online validation services are available, including the following:

1) *Florida Center for Library Automation's Encoded Archival Description Validator and XSL Transformer:* A Web page that was "created for museums, archives, libraries, historical societies, and similar agencies in Florida who create collection finding aids according to the Encoded Archival Description (EAD) standard, version 2002. The tools on this page permit EAD creators to a) validate (test) their EAD documents against the rules described in the EAD Document Type Definition maintained by the Library of Congress, b) generate a HTML version of their finding aid from the original EAD encoding, using a XSL stylesheet maintained for the ARCHIVES FLORIDA database, and c) derive Dublin Core metadata records from their original EAD documents."
2) *RLG EAD Report Card:* "The first automated program for checking the quality of your EAD encoding."

EAD Publishing

Publishing EAD finding aids online presents a real challenge, especially to smaller archives without much technical support. Finding aids can be converted to HTML and placed on a Web server or loaded into an XML-database/publishing system—operations that are beyond the capabilities of many archives. Alternatively, archives can upload the XML file, include a call-out to an XSLT stylesheet, and use the browser to transform XML to HTML. Some archives deposit their finding aids with a regional repository. Other archives have adopted XML publishing platforms that allow searching and presentation of finding aids, an approach that requires much more technical support but also provides greater control over data. These publishing platforms include:

1) *PLEADE:* "PLEADE is an open source search engine and browser for archival finding aids encoded in XML/EAD. Based on the SDX platform, it is a very flexible Web application."
2) *XTF:* "The CDL eXtensible Text Framework (XTF) is a flexible indexing and query tool that supports searching across collections of heterogeneous data and presents results in a highly configurable manner.
3) *Apache Cocoon:* Archives and consortia such as Five College Archives & Manuscript Collections are using the open source XML publishing framework Cocoon to publish finding aids.
4) *University of Chicago's Mark Logic XML Database*: The University of Chicago is developing an XML publishing infrastructure built on MarkLogic a native XML database.

Archival management systems may be less flexible than EAD creation tools, and getting legacy data into these systems can be challenging. However, they offer a number of features that may lead to greater efficiency and sustainability, such as support for authority control, reduced redundancy of data, easy data entry interfaces, the ability to analyze archival data through the generation of reports, and Web-publishing capabilities.

References

Faundeen, J. (2003b). "US Land Remote Sensing Archive." Presented at the ERPANET/CODATA International Archiving Workshop on the Selection, Appraisal and Retention of Digital Scientific Data held in Lisbon, Portugal, 15-17 December 2003.

Friedlander, A. (2002), 'The National Digital Information In frastructure Preservation Program,' *D-Lib Magazine*, 8.4, April 2002, http://www.dlib.org/dlib/april02/friedlander/04friedlander.html

Hunolt, G. and Booth, A. (9/2001), *ESDIS Data Center Best Practices And Bench mark Report*, Science Operations Office, Earth Science Data and Information Systems Project, Goddard Space Flight Center, NASA Contract NAS5-00154.

It's About Time: Research Challenges in Digital Archiving and Long-term Preservation. Final Report on a Workshop on Research Challenges in Digital Archiving, 12-13 April 2002. (2002), Washington, DC, Library of Congress.

8

Challenges of Archival Information

With the increasing volume of information stored in an electronic environment, library preservation strategies have evolved beyond the establishment of optimum storage conditions for books. The preservation mandate of research libraries demands a response to the concern for future access to all information objects digital resources. But to define what preservation means in a digital environment presents a challenge in itself.

Preservation is about the maintenance or recreation of the original function of information objects and their meaning to retain their authentically, validity and evidential value. This is more complex for digital materials because of the dependence of the information object on its technical environment. Fragile materials in this environment are defined less by the physical deterioration of the media, but rather at the level of software and hardware, both vulnerable to the high rate of obsolescence.

While digital technologies present more complex preservation problems than libraries have ever faced before, the fundamental principles of preservation remain unchanged, to define priorities to extend the useful life of information resources, to ensure future access.

Digital information and electronic resources have transformed academic research fundamentally. As the price of print materials, such as scholarly journals continues to rise, the accessibility and functionality of electronic versions become more attractive, and libraries invest more heavily in new technologies. A related issue in the need to preserve digital resources is a growing reliance of libraries as service providers on digital technology, which must impact on our institutional goals.

Digital technologies find their place in the preservation strategies of research libraries in the opportunities presented to one such goal - in improved public access to on-line digital surrogates. By limiting the handling of rare and fragile original materials, their rate of physical deterioration is considerably slowed.

Digitisation is now a mainstream activity of the Campbell Collections of the University of Natal, aimed at collecting, preserving and organising historical material of national and international importance in a manner that is widely accessible. The upgrading of our information management system from a text-based to a multi-media database management system is aimed primarily at making our unique range of resources widely available over the Internet. The retrieval of digital images offers a significant technological advance as a vehicle for integrated access to visual representations of historic photographs, art and ethnographic artefacts - together with traditional library resources.

Preservation digitisation has focussed on reformatting rapidly deteriorating materials, with the aim of preserving the intellectual content, as separate from the medium or carrier. Because one is able to make repeated copies of digital files without the informational loss associated with analogue copies, the impact of the technology is beguiling. No longer does the life expectancy of materials seem limited to the durability of the medium, since the digital data can be copied repeatedly without loss.

The separation of the information and the object however, takes on a new meaning in the digital environment. Complete digital conversion comprises two process, the capture by scanning of digital data, and that of the associated metadata, wrapped as a digital object and stored using containers to hold the objects and related software modules. The integrity of the digital file is threatened by alterations to the contextual data file, and the loss of the linking mechanism between the two is the same as deleting the contextual information.

Meeting the Challenge of Digital Preservation

Long term preservation of digital resources is feasible through the implementation of sound policies at the inception and in the development of digital libraries. The challenge lies in the need for libraries to move proactively in establishing digital collection development programme in an electronic environment that is conducive to preservation.

Professional collaboration: The collaboration of a wide community of information professionals was responsible for developing new strategies for data management and storage for the preservation of our own digital information resources at the Campbell Collections. The interaction between library, archive and museum professionals, together with information technology specialists, helped to clarify the myriad technical issues. The need for professional collaboration was identified in the following areas:

— to integrate the separate informational resources from library, archive and museum collections by enriching their description with digital images for Web access
— to seek cost effective descriptive models to the identification of digital collections in the use of the Dublin Core metadata element set, defined by the museum community
— to develop to archival standards, an IT development programme for scalable electronic storage environment, catering for infinite volumes of digital data
— to integrate an archival perspective into retention policies and into systems design, using the nesting principles of Encoded Archival Description.

Some of the factors noted impeding such collaboration include:

— problems of interaction within the organisation related to territoriality
— a lack of informed support and fear of change
— the anomaly presented to the IT industry in our insistence on long-term information management tools for Web access to digital information

Standards and practices: There are digital imaging projects underway at some libraries in South Africa, and a number of problems have been encountered that are difficult to overcome in isolation. The equipment is expensive, especially if it is state-of the-art, software varies in quality and local support is often lacking. Standards have not been agreed upon, and vary from one project to another.

The DISA project, a nco-operative pilot digital imaging project, based at the Campbell Collections, was designed to conform with internationally accepted standards for digital imaging, thereby setting the standard for South

Africa. The project is entitled South Africa's Struggle for Democracy: Anti-Apartheid Periodicals, 1960-1990. Encompassing the journal publications of the three key decades in the growth of opposition to apartheid rule, it represents a research resource on the period when the African National Congress (ANC), black consciousness, and other resistance movements were very active. Publications reflecting a range of subjects and different viewpoints are included. Some of the publications were short-lived and, because many were banned, of limited distribution. These factors lend a certain rarity value in that the publications are generally not well represented in research collections.

Operating within internationally accepted standards on adequate informational representation, lossless compression ratios and platform independent file formats, the project aims to be technically sustainable, the technology used able to migrate when new developments take place.

Non-proprietary models: Developing out of the distributed partnership of independent institutions in the DISA project, a number of durable project management policies have been implemented to ensure the value of the product beyond the expiration of the grant period. It was decided that non-proprietary formats should be used that were not dependent on current hardware platforms or commercial software vendors, demanding ongoing support of future upgrades. Common exchange formats and network protocols were required that could be used and understood by all participants.

For bibliographic data, the MARC format fills this role for libraries, but a wider matrix of metadata wrapped as syntactic containers for digital objects. Standard Generalized Markup Language (SGML) an international standard designed to promote text interchange, provides a definition of a document structure that can be used to encode the logical structure and content of any defined document and known by any remote system. Extensible Markup Language (XML), a simpler dialect of SGML has since been adopted, using the information community-based document type descriptions of the Text Encoding Initiative (TEI) and Encoded Archival Description (EAD), to build an infrastructure that enables interoperability between heterogeneous systems.

Persistent archive management: The most comprehensive preservation strategy currently evolving is that of a collection-based persistent archive system.A persistent archive operates in two phases, the first comprising capture of digital data wrapped as XML digital objects and ingestion to archival disk storage, using containers to hold objects along with relevant metadata and software modules for future emulation. The second is in the opposite direction, with containers brought out of storage and loaded onto new possibly new information management systems, and returned to a new, and possibly new archival storage system. The result is a product with the ability to scale its capabilities by adding resources when required. By differentiating between the storage of the bits that comprise the digital object and the related information carried by the metadata it is possible to create an infrastructure for life cycle management for digital preservation.

Searching and Advertising

This activity can include:

- an author listing their electronic documents and objects on their web page.
- browsing electronic catalogues on a network;
- an librarian or software agent searching on behalf of one or more users;
- a user specifying an electronic document or object with an electronic request.

A major problem associated with the advertising and shopping activity is the cost and time expended in developing, maintaining, and finding relevant information, products, and services, given the plenitude of available information. Obviously, this problem will become increasingly complex as more data and services become available on-line, and the choices and possibilities multiply exponentially. We need new and better ways to find electronic documents and information and to publish and update this information.

Buyers and sellers may elect to negotiate the terms of a transaction—i.e., the terms of exchange and payment. These terms may cover right to copy, copyright or license agreements, usage rights, distribution rights, refund policies, and terms of payment. These terms can be standardized for routine commodity use, or customized to suit more unique individual situations. Often, in the case of two parties with a well-established business relationship (e.g. a library membership agreement) the terms of exchange are pre-negotiated as standing contractual terms for all their future exchanges. Often, this process will also include authentication of the two parties.

The buyer eventually issues a contractual agreement of the terms of exchange, or usage, and payment. This contractual agreement is generally issued as an order, which sets forth the price and other terms of the transaction. The order may be verbal, in writing, or electronic. It usually includes an acknowledgment of agreement by the various parties in order to help prevent any future repudiation. This agreement can be confirmed electronically through cryptographic techniques such as digital signatures.

A bill can be sent to the user, either before delivery of the electronic document, with the delivery, or after the delivery. The bill generally includes remittance information—who, where and how to pay. Even when the electronic document or digital object is provided free of charge, it is desirable to provide usage data as important feedback information to the librarian and author, which can be obtained by having the user complete order or request forms.

Customer Service

Customer service entails:

- providing the buyer with timely information as to the progress of the transaction;
- handling customer requirements when transactions go awry - i.e., resolving any mistakes, disputes, or complaints concerning product quality, delivery, or payment; and
- providing expert advice and assistance in the use of the products and services.

Customer service also involves providing general cash management advice, including addressing foreign exchange imbalances and risk exposures, collection of delinquent payments and late fees.

A final key activity in electronic commerce is the collection, management, analysis, and interpretation of the various data to make more intelligent and effective transaction-related decisions. Examples include: collecting business references, coordinating and managing marketing strategies, determining new product offerings, granting/extending credit, and managing market risk. Performance of these tasks often involves the use of advanced information management techniques, including models and simulations and collaborative computing technologies to support conferencing and distributed workflow processes. These tasks will become more difficult as the sources of information grow in number and are of increasingly diverse and uncertain quality. Additionally, the use of this information may raise significant privacy concerns and issues, that will result in the imposition of significant limitations on the use of this data, and conceivably encryption of selected portions of the transaction information.

Some related issues and needs are discussed below:

— *Nature of information products:* A particularly important class of products on the Internet, and evolving NII, are products that are pure information. In the information age, a large percent of the commerce will never be embodied physically. Information products are enabled by information technology and not just distributed more efficiently by it. These products can consist not just of electronic publications, catalogues, videos and the like, but can include interactive video games, software programs, electronic keys and tokens, customized design specifications, even electronic keys that can open to hotel rooms, cars, storage compartments, and airport boarding gates. Furthermore, these information products are not just created entirely by the service provider, but can be designed or customized by the customer, adding a customer-driven activity call "design" to the purchase cycle. Indeed, information products can be continuously added to, modified, and morphed, as they pass along a chain of users. It is also likely that for these products ordering, billing, payment, and distribution would likely all happen simultaneously.

— *Advanced revenue collection methods :* The electronic commerce infrastructure will need to support advanced types of revenue collection, in addition to traditional methods. For example, an information product service provider could distribute its product widely and charge on a usage basis; i.e. charge the user only when the information is used. One innovative approach that permits usage accounting and payment is called meterware. It provides local hardware and/or software to continuously record and bill customers based on their usage. Meterware and other advanced revenue collection ideas create opportunities for reaching new customers and for distributing products and services; these make great sense in a low or zero distribution cost environment and should be supported by the electronic commerce infrastructure.

Some micro-payment schemes for use over the Internet have been proposed that are significantly weaker than those being proposed for the more traditional payment schemes. The argument is that one can safely sacrifice security for processing efficiency when the transactions are low value enough. The argument is that it is much more important to minimize the amount of computational and communications resources needed to effect payment than to ensure the integrity of the transaction—that the loss of a penny here or there will not be consequential enough to matter. But, this may not be the case when the revenue is being allocated across many parties, each getting only a small portion of the payment, and where the profit margins may be extremely thin.

The user acceptability of these new forms of payment is also questionable. Advocates point to gas meters, and telephone bills, as proof of the acceptance of bills with small payments based on usage. But, the complexity of these bills certainly pale by comparison to the sorts of bills that users might expect to see in some future "wired" world of micro-payments. Imagine sitting down to reconcile a bill comprised of thousand of penny items. Each item is small enough, but the total will probably be large enough to command attention. Also, these all these examples of usage billing are coming from businesses that have been run as a monopoly - the user has had no other alternative offered them. When given the choice, users have often opted for a more certain, fixed flat fee, even if that fee is slightly greater than their historical usage pattern.

The cost of usage billing and accounting may be unacceptably high in the future economics of the "wired" society. For example, it has been argued that a significant portion of the cost of operating the telephone and utility infrastructure today is due to the imposition of usage metering and accounting hardware and systems, and that more nimble companies offering equivalent services based on a flat fee, could operate equivalent service at much lower cost.

Electronic commerce transactions currently involve all manner of devices (e.g., phone, fax, POS - point-of-sale device) and media (e.g., electronic data, image, voice, paper), and networks (cable, wire, satellite, cellular) over which they will be delivered, so the system infrastructure must accommodate all of these devices, media and communications networks, without degrading them to the lowest common denominator. Opening up digital libraries to all these devices, at of course a greatly reduced functionality on some of the less capable devices, might still be a capability worth looking into. It would better bridge the gap between the real physical world and the future "wired" world, and it would dramatically increase the accessibility of the digital library to a much wider population faster, including the more disadvantaged citizens.

The electronic commerce domain has a large quantity of legacy systems which it needs to interface to, and ultimately phase-out, as it evolves to more modern systems, applications and processes. These legacy systems and processes will not go away overnight, and a successful electronic commerce infrastructure must allow the user to easily and transparently transfer between and switch back and forth between the new all electronic, and the older, hybrid legacy systems and processes. Digital Libraries also need to deal with similar legacy issues.

Finally, libraries of publicly available/accessible libraries and files of registered contracts, information as well as catalogues and lists of products, data and services, if made part of the NII domain-specific infrastructure being offered by various electronic commerce vendors and information providers, could be interfaced with this electronic commerce scenario to further enrich it.

A convergence of several factors has recently lifted digital libraries and electronic commerce to the promise of a new level of utility and viability. These factors include the increased availability of communications and communications bandwidth, the reduced cost and increased user-friendliness of computers and communications, the growth of the Internet and on-line services, and the drive toward global competitiveness. There are however, a number of standardized services that are needed to fully realize their complete potential. Most of these services are common to many different applications, including electronic commerce and digital libraries. Each application domain could address these issues separately, but the cost and accessibility of these services would be greatly improved if all applications utilized the same set of services, much the way they now are all utilizing the same communications networks.

Challenges of Digital Conservancies

Conservancies, which hold real property in trust for public purposes or administer easements restricting future uses of private property, are a successful means of securing public benefits within the system of private property ownership. They have been widely encouraged by governments, through tax regulations.

With the increased attention that businesses and individuals are paying to the value of knowledge assets, it should be no surprise the conservancy metaphor is now being extended to intellectual property (IP). Intellectual Property Conservancies (IPCs) are a new idea, being conceived as a means to provide public benefits by making digital content donated, or licensed to them, freely available and by ensuring its long-term preservation.

IPCs are digital libraries and therefore have all the problems associated with digital libraries. In addition, IPCs face a large number of challenges that most digital libraries do not confront. These include:

a. Obtaining content donations (persuading IP owners of the benefits of giving, possibly without any tax advantage)
b. Obtaining financial contributions (persuading philanthropists and the general public of the value of free public access)
c. Obtaining usable digital assets
d. Creating metadata to support discovery, rights management and preservation
e. Providing access to potential readers worldwide
f. Providing long-term, or even 'perpetual', access

Metadata issues

Metadata management will be critical to an IPC's success. Like any Digital Library it needs to invest in discovery (content description) metadata. An IPC must additionally invest substantially in rights management metadata and technical (migration specification) metadata. While the IPC can rely on natural partners in the library community to help provide descriptive metadata for simple resource discovery (such as Dublin Core metadata), it also needs to be able to incorporate metadata conforming to standards in the publishing community.An IPC will need to determine the requirements for rights metadata linked to delivery functionality, as discussed above. Finally, an IPC needs to manage a digital artifact over time. As such, it needs to determine what metadata will need to be acquired and kept for long-term preservation. The OAIS reference model seems a probable framework for preservation of archival originals.

Providing access to potential readers worldwide

Where the content resides is more than simply an operational consideration for an IPC. IP owners prefer that the digital data be located on their own servers; the terms of the gift would ensure that, should the IP owner fail to keep it available, the IPC can shift access to its own servers. The benefits to the IPC suggest that an architecture enabling this kind of distributed access will be necessary.

Perpetual access

The fundamental objectives of an IPC are to offer free access to its catalogue of intellectual property in perpetuity. For this, the IPC does not need to be the archival repository of the authentic, verifiable, record copy. Like a digital library, which holds a copy of a work and makes the accurate and full content available to users, the IPC doesn't claim to preserve contextual or structural authenticity. Both an IPC and a digital library focus on preservation of content as required for preservation of public access and the right-to-read.

Therefore an IPC need not preserve the initial delivery format, nor any particular subsequent delivery format. Instead, the IPC can return to its escrowed copy to generate a delivery copy in a new format, or move from one delivery format to the next, depending on cost and technology availability. Of course, an IPC still must make strategic decisions about when and how to convert data from one delivery and or long-term storage format to another, to keep the content accessible over time.

Commitments of Digital Research Library

A Digital Research Library (DRL) is a collection of electronic information organized for use in the long term. To meet user needs, the founders of a DRL must accomplish two general tasks: establishing the repository of electronic scholarly materials, and implementing the tools to use it. More important, long-term commitments are needed if scholarly information is to be available over periods longer than human life: organizational commitments, fiscal commitments and institutional commitments.

The mission of research libraries is to acquire information, organize it, make it available and preserve it. This has been their significant, distinctive and successful role with print and other artifactual materials for the past several hundred years. An implicit mission of computing science has been to make the benefits of computing technology of use to society at large. Missions, needs and capabilities now come together so that information users can have added assistance in performing research and in assuring the continuity of scholarship, today and in the future. It will take conscious, planned efforts by both librarianship and computing to make this happen.

Many libraries are now trying to provide the increasing volume of scholarly electronic information to their clienteles. Current information needs are being provided in electronic form with varying success in public, college and research libraries around the country and the world. Research libraries have only begun to take on the provision, organization and preservation of information with the same long-term commitment they have made for print materials. It is an expensive, uncharted and difficult task. But until the long-term commitments are undertaken, many currently proposed solutions will have only temporary effects. For example, discussion of cataloguing network resources will remain tentative, for until resources being catalogued have a permanent network presence, the cataloguing that points to them must also have an ephemeral quality. Similarly, the expensive products of recent valuable digitizing demonstration projects, from microfilm to digital form and vice versa, will be at risk after only a few years if tools and commitments are not in place for the preservation of what has been achieved.

The ability of the scholarly community to give serious weight to electronic information depends upon their trust in such information being dependably available, with authenticity and integrity maintained. Looked-for changes in scholarly publishing to help alleviate the serials crisis, for example, are usually thought to be bound up with the prestige of electronic journals in the academic tenure process. The ability of the academy to count on long-term, secure existence of electronic scholarly work will be an important determinant of the success of academic electronic publishing. Libraries and universities have a stake in helping electronic publishing to succeed, and therefore have an interest in establishing secure digital research libraries.

Users' needs will continue to be what they long have been. Users will want information reliably locatable, so that when they go there, they can expect to find what they're looking for. Users will want information easily accessible: the cataloguing must be clear and accurate, and the information must be promptly retrievable. In the electronic environment the need for access tools will be more evident, and users will expect appropriate and standard software to be readily available. Users will expect information to be available that was placed in the library's care a long time ago; and they will expect that the integrity of the information they get from the library will be assured.

Implementation of a Digital Research Library will require several specific tasks, broadly familiar to a computing audience, and three kinds of new commitments. In what follows the tasks are given more space, yet as technical problems they probably are the easiest to solve; they will only cost money. The institutional commitments described in the final section will be much more difficult to achieve.

All the issues are described here in cursory form. Each could be developed in great detail, but at the moment the outline and overall program are most important. Early implementations will test many of these assumptions and will add more requirements to the list.

Electronic Storage Repository

A Digital Research Library will be manifest to users as collections of information existing in various places and accessible through the use of widely available tools. The locus of information may be called the electronic storage repository; the access tools will be described below. Over time, we will learn how collection development plays out in an access environment as well as in an ownership environment. It is sometimes loosely proposed that libraries need not acquire electronic information, for it will be available somewhere on the network. Such proposals ignore the obvious truth that some institution must still, in the end, take responsibility for the information. That has always been a definition of the library responsibility.

There will be many electronic storage repositories, responding both to requirements of redundancy and to the individual needs of institutions. In contrast to print collections, it is unlikely that there will be a high degree of content duplication across many electronic repositories, since for most purposes existence in a single place allows world-wide access. Aside from their actual contents, however, repositories that are part of a DRL will have many common characteristics. Some of these are described here; in some cases, open questions are noted that need to be explored in early implementations.

Megadocument contents. Even an initial repository will comprise many gigabytes of information, growing quickly to millions of electronic documents. The medium itself is cheap and the possible resources are plentiful.

Sources and potential participants. It is easy to cite numbers of electronic scholarly resources that now exist.

Backup mechanisms. Backup/restore procedures must be in place and must be automated and economical, for libraries are never likely to have expensive labor available in quantity. Backups must be multi-generational, using remote storage, with regular disaster simulations and tests.

Staged Access. "Staging" refers to the prioritized use of different mechanical methods of storing data as it waits to be recalled. All data does not need to be immediately available on the most expensive and fastest storage media. Alternatives for providing immediate online access to the enormous potential volume of scholarly information need to be provided. What can be off line, and how can it be retrieved? Present alternatives include magnetic disks, optical disks and jukeboxes, optical disks on shelves, magnetic tapes on site, tapes in remote storage, and automated data warehouses of magnetic tapes.

Data structure standards. In a repository, does information simply exist as is or is complementary information associated with it? Widely differing examples include SGML (Standard Generalized Markup Language) headers, ICPSR codebooks, picture captions, hypertext links and early software versions for use with data files. There is an increasing need to link bit-mapped page images to ASCII text versions of the page contents.

Refreshing mechanisms. Refreshing is agreed to be necessary for long-term preservation across advances in computing technology, media and software. There will be organizational and bureaucratic issues in addition to the simply technical. If information is copied from magnetic to optical disk, copyright issues must be recognized. Automation will be necessary to reduce labor costs. Other issues include workflow and record-keeping, migration techniques, and standards and techniques that will apply independently of technology. It may be possible to link refreshment to backup techniques for expedience and economy.

Authentication and integrity. Intellectual preservation goes beyond preservation of the medium and the technology to assure the protection of the intellectual structure of information as it was recorded by its author. To meet user expectations DRL's must implement authentication and integrity techniques that combine mathematical security with ease of use, public trustworthiness and privacy protection. For example, bit patterns of texts, sound and images may be preserved through cryptographic hashing and encoding methods such as the digital time-stamping technique.

Redundancy. It will be important to establish standards for the number of repository locations necessary to assure long-term existence of specific electronic information and access to it. One location won't do for a particular major electronic document or set; will two, or three? How many? Major institutions may separately or consortially establish repositories. It is not yet clear how much redundancy of their components will be desirable among them.

Aside from assuring longevity, other issues come to bear on decisions to provide multiple permanent copies of electronic information. Informed decisions will be made about the dynamic interplay between costs of network bandwidth, response time and costs of storage. It seems likely that many library consortia will be formed on the basis of joint contracts with information vendors. Geographic location, nationalism and regionalism will likely play a role.

Tools and Policies

Usage and retrieval mechanisms. The full panoply of present access tools must be supported by a Digital Research Library with provision for the new access tools that are likely to appear regularly. The "granularity" of documents needs to be addressed: how may one retrieve only part of a document when the full document may be of substantial size.

Techniques for document update and consequent archiving and labeling need to be developed, as well as flags indicating obsolescence or supersession, e.g. for ANSI standards, monthly statistical reports or draft versions. A form of SGML may be appropriate in some cases, for example the format proposed by the TEI (Text Encoding Initiative).

Cataloguing. Providing access to voluminous information is an intellectual problem that historically has been solved in the print environment by abstracting and indexing services and by library cataloguing, with attendant rules and procedures to insure consistency and accuracy. These tools, adapted to suit new needs, will work for electronic information as well. They should be linked to the new retrieval mechanisms so that users can smoothly navigate from location of information to retrieval of it without having to shift their mode of use. Early mechanisms will probably link catalogue records to documents using tools such as the WWW, the Uniform

Resource Indicator (and Locator) or URI/URL, and the recently proposed MARC 856 field. SGML may offer other possibilities for linking of certain documents through its document description techniques. In any case, there eventually will need to be consensus both for the representation of physical electronic locations in bibliographic records and for representation of virtual locations.

If the DRL's catalogue system works well, users will be able to search for information, locate bibliographic records for desiderata, and use those records directly to draw the desired information to their workstation. Where an authentication technique is used, means for including and testing the certification must be provided. Standards for such cataloguing and remote access still need to be developed, particularly for providing catalogue access to non-owned materials.

Remote Access. A DRL should from the outset be intended for access from multiple remote locations. Internet-wide access should generally be possible. In early pilot implementations it may initially be advisable for a few libraries to plan and development catalogue and access mechanisms that integrate the individual libraries' collections with that of the DRL. Procedures for dissemination of such catalogue records will be needed; it will be not only a technical matter but a policy matter for libraries associated with the DRL to provide non-local access to their local patrons.

Fees and freedom. In practice these are often linked issues. Standards and techniques will be necessary to solve a knot of interconnected problems surrounding access and ownership, including

— Privacy preservation for users, while also protecting
— Copyright protection for intellectual property holders, while also protecting
— Fair use mechanisms, and also providing
— Fee-charging techniques, including billing, where relevant.

Commitments

Much of what has been described so far is merely technical, and the outlines of solutions are becoming clear even if the details remain to be worked out. More difficult will be the social compacts, that is, the agreements on standards, intellectual property and access modes.

Most difficult of all to achieve, if electronic preservation and access are to be accomplished on any significant scale, will be the long term commitments to these goals by institutions. Nothing makes clearer that a library is an organization, rather than a building or a collection, than the requirement for institutional commitment for electronic information to have more than a fleeting existence.

The organization of libraries is already changing as electronic information increasingly becomes part of their charge. Most research libraries now have substantial systems departments. Some libraries locate the responsibility for electronic information distinctly from that for print. Other libraries see the forms as inseparable and include electronic responsibilities along with artifactual responsibilities in assignments for collection development, cataloguing and public service.

What is new will be the permanent assignment of staff responsibility for the long term maintenance of electronic information within a library. There is no obvious artifactual parallel for this responsibility: circulation, stack maintenance, preservation and physical plant departments now share it for print. Nor are there present parallels in academic computing centers, where staffs typically focus on technological advance and availability, leaving data to the users. The electronic preservation responsibility will be focused as it will require technical expertise likely to be located in a single functional area.

As libraries move more into the electronic environment the historic tripartite division of libraries into public services, technical services and collection development will continue but in more fluid arrangements. People who combine bibliographic understanding, problem-solving abilities and process orientation have often been found in technical services as well as elsewhere in libraries. Similar librarians will take on the demanding new technical, collection and service responsibilities for long-term support of digital collections. At the same time, it is becoming clear that the traditional computing community is fertile with ideas, analysis and skills that will be important to electronic library goals.

The permanent existence of a digital research library will require assured continuity in operational funding. Almost any other library activity can survive a funding hiatus of a year or more. Acquisitions, building maintenance, and preservation can be suspended, or an entire staff can be dispersed and a library shut down for several years, and the artifactual collections will more or less survive. But digital collections, like the online catalogue, require continual maintenance if they are to survive more than a very brief interruption of power, environmental control, backup, technological advance and related technical care.

Online catalogue maintenance costs have reached a rough steady state, and the capital costs for new OPACs are decreasing relative to the capabilities provided. The catalogue size will continue to increase, but catalogue records are small relative to the information to which they refer. DRL's, however, as a proportion of the library's supply of information, will grow for the foreseeable future, and the quantity of information requiring care will become considerable. Unit costs of storage are likely to continue falling for some time, which may make the financial burden manageable.

Long term funding will be required to assure long term care. Libraries and their parent institutions will need to develop new fiscal tools and use familiar fiscal tools for new purposes. Public institutions, usually constrained to annual funding, will have particular difficulties; existing procedures for capital or plant funding may provide precedents. One familiar technique is the endowment. It has been difficult to obtain private funding for endowments of concepts and services rather than books and mortar, but it is possible. Institutions might also build endowments out of operating funds over periods of time.

Some revenue streams associated with Digital Research Libraries may be practical. Consortial arrangements may allow for lease or purchase of shares in a DRL. Shorter-term access might be provided to other institutions on a usage basis. Access could be sold to certain classes of users, e.g. businesses, non-local clienteles, or specific information projects. New relations with publishers, presently difficult to perceive through the mists rising from intellectual property, might result in fee income for storage of electronically published materials during the copyright lifetime in which publishers collect usage fees. With commitment and imagination long term fiscal tools will be found.

All these are instrumental means of accomplishing the greatest requirement, that of conscious, planned institutional commitment to preserve that part of human culture which will flower in electronic form. While museums have preserved artifacts that embody information, libraries preserved information that has been embedded in artifacts. The advent of electronic information will accentuate the difference between these roles as libraries take the responsibility for the preservation of information in non-artifactual forms.

For the past century most research libraries have been associated with universities, and this connection seems likely to continue in the immediate future. Whatever the governance structure, an institution wishing to benefit from electronic information will have to make a conscious commitment to providing resources. Michael Buckland, of the University of California at Berkeley, has distinguished between a library's role and its mission. Where the role of a library is to facilitate access to information, its mission is to support the mission of its parent institution. Thus if a university wishes to continue relying on mission support from its library, it will have to make commitments to support the library's role. In the electronic environment, this means new longstanding financial commitments which the library and university together must identify and establish.

The commitment will have to be clearly and publicly made if scholars and other libraries are to have confidence that a given DRL is indeed likely to exist for the long term. Guidelines or standards will be desirable that define what is meant by a long term commitment, and that define which electronic repositories of data can qualify to be termed part of a digital research library. Just as donors of books, manuscripts and archives look for demonstration of long term care and commitment, so too will scholars and publishers as electronic information is created and requires a home.

New Insights into Digital Archiving

In an effort to advance the state-of-the-art and practice of digital archiving, the International Council for Scientific and Technical Information (ICSTI), a community of scientific and technical information organizations that includes national libraries, research institutes, publishers, and bibliographic database producers, sponsored a study in March 1999. The topic was first raised in the joint UNESCO/International Council of Scientific Unions (ICSU) Conference on Electronic Publishing in 1996. The topic was highlighted at the technical session of the June 1997 Annual ICSTI meeting and a working group was formed. The Electronic Publications Archive Working Group presented a white paper of the major issues in December 1998. At its December 1998 meeting, the ICSTI Board approved the study on which this report is based. Based on common interest in this topic, CENDI, an interagency working group of scientific and technical information managers in the U.S. federal government, cosponsored the study. The study began with an initial survey of the ICSTI and CENDI membership, a literature review and contacts with experts in order to identify digital archiving projects. Over 30 projects were identified, from which 18 were selected as the most "cutting edge". The highlighted projects covered six countries—U.S., UK, Canada, Australia, Sweden—and Finland and four international organizations. They came from a variety of sectors including government scientific and technical programs, national archives, national libraries, publishers, and research institutes.

Project managers from the selected projects were asked a series of questions aimed at identifying emerging models and best practices for digital archiving. While technologies for storage and retrieval were discussed, technology was of secondary interest to the understanding of policy and practice.

For purposes of the study, "digital archiving" was defined as the long-term storage, preservation and access to information that is "born digital" (created and disseminated primarily in electronic form) or for which the digital version is considered to be the primary archive.

The study aimed to provide new insights into digital archiving issues elicited by many of the baseline studies and white papers on digital archiving. Primary attention was given to operational and prototype projects involving scientific and technical information at an international level. It included a variety of digital format types applicable to scientific and technical information, including data, text, images, audio, video and multimedia; and a variety of object types, such as electronic journals, monographs, satellite imagery, biological sequence data, and patents. The results, while not scientifically valid, identify emerging models and best practices for digital archives in an effort to support the development of a tradition of digital stewardship.

The project managers from the "cutting edge" projects emphasized the importance of considering best practices for archiving at all stages of the information management life cycle. Acknowledging this important philosophy, the best practices identified by the study are presented in the framework of the information life cycle — creation, acquisition, cataloguing/identification, storage, preservation and access.

Acquisition and Collection Development

Acquisition and collection development is the stage in which the created object is "incorporated" physically or virtually into the archive. The object must be known to the archive administration. There are two main aspects to the acquisition of digital objects — collection policies and gathering procedures.

Collection Policies: In most countries, the major difference in collection policies between formal print and electronic publications is the question of whether digital materials are included under current deposit legislation. Guidelines help to establish the boundaries in such an unregulated situation. It is also the case that there is just too much material that could be archived from the Internet, so guidelines are needed to tailor the general collection practices of the organization. The collection policies answer questions related to selecting what to archive, determining extent, archiving links, and refreshing site contents.

Selection: Both the National Library of Canada (NLC) and the National Library of Australia (NLA) acknowledge the importance of selection guidelines. The NLC's Guidelines state, "The main difficulty in extending legal deposit to network publishing is that legal deposit is a relatively indiscriminate acquisition mechanism that aims at comprehensiveness.

In the network environment, any individual with access to the Internet can be a publisher, and the network publishing process does not always provide the initial screening and selection at the manuscript stage on which libraries have traditionally relied in the print environment.

While the scope of NLA's PANDORA (Preserving and Accessing Networked Documentary Resources of Australia) Project is only to preserve Australian Internet publishing, the NLA also acknowledges that it is still impossible to archive everything. Therefore, the NLA has formulated guidelines for the Selection of Online Australian Publications Intended for Preservation by the National Library of Australia.

These guidelines are key to the successful networking of the state libraries into the National Collection of Australian Electronic Publications, since they provide consistency across multiple acquisition activities. Scholarly publications of national significance and those of current and long term research value are archived comprehensively. Other items are archived on a selective basis "to provide a broad cultural snapshot of how Australians are using the Internet to disseminate information, express opinions, lobby, and publish their creative work."

Directly connected to the question of selection is the issue of extent. What is the extent or the boundary of a particular digital work? This is particularly an issue when selecting complex Web sites.

Archiving Links : The extensive use of hypertext links to other digital objects in electronic publications raises the question of whether these links and their content should be archived along with the source item. This issue has been addressed by the selected projects in a variety of ways.

Most organizations archive the links (the URLs or other identifiers) but not the content of the linked objects. The American Institute of Physics archives the links embedded in the text and references of its electronic journal articles but not the text or content of any of these links, unless the linked item happens to be in its publication archive or in the supplemental material which it also archives.

Similarly, the Office of Scientific and Technical Information of the U.S. Department of Energy (DOE OSTI) does not intentionally archive any links beyond the extent of the digital object itself. However, the document may be linked to another document if that document is another DOE document in the OSTI archive. NLA's decision about archiving the content of linked objects is based on its selection guidelines. If a linked item meets the selection guidelines, it's contents will be archived, otherwise it will not be.

In a slightly different approach, the NLC has chosen to archive the text of the linked object only if it is on the same server as the object that is being archived. The NLC cites difficulties in tracking down hypertext links and acquiring the linked objects as the reason for its decision not to include the content of other links. The previous issue of the same periodical, accessed through a hypertext link, would be considered a part of the original publication. Another publication accessed through a hypertext link would not be considered part of the original publication.

Only two of the reviewed projects archive the content of all links. Internet guru Brewster Kahle's Internet Archive retains all links, because the aim of the project is to archive a snapshot of the entire Internet. Within a specific domain, the American Astronomical Society also maintains all links to both documents and supporting materials in other formats, based on extensive collaboration among the various international astronomical societies, researchers, universities, and government agencies. Each organization archives its own publications, but links are maintained not only from references in the full text and cited references of the articles, but between and among the major international astronomical databases. Within this specific domain, the contents of all linked objects are available.

Refreshing the Archived Contents : In cases where the archiving is taking place while changes or updates may still be occurring to the digital object, as in the case of on-going Web sites, there is a need to consider refreshing the archived contents. A balance must be struck between the completeness and currency of the archive and the burden on the system resources. Obviously, the burden of refreshing the content increases as the number of sources stored in the archive increases.

Gathering Approaches: There are two general approaches to the gathering of relevant Internet-based information -- hand-selected and automatic. In the case of the NLA, the sites are reviewed and hand-selected. They are monitored for their persistence before being included in the archive. Alternatively, the Royal Library, the National Library of Sweden, acquires material by periodically running a robot to capture sites for its Kulturarw project without making value judgments.

In addition, some material is obtained from foreign sites with material about Sweden, such as travel information or translations of Swedish literature. While the acquisition is automatic, the National Library gives priority to periodicals, static documents, and HTML pages. Conferences, usenet groups, ftp archives, and databases are considered lower priority.

The EVA Project at the University of Helsinki, National Library of Finland uses techniques similar to those used in Sweden. However, the guidelines from EVA address issues to be considered when using robots for harvesting. In order not to overload the servers being harvested, particularly those belonging to the public networks, the EVA guidelines establish time limits between visits to a single Web server and between capturing and recapturing a single URL. Even though this approach has allowed the EVA project to progress, developers at EVA consider this approach to be "very rough and not flexible enough for archiving purposes." The EVA developers would prefer that the time limits be more configurable at the server and, preferably, at the individual URL levels. The flexibility would require that the scheduler be a database application that can be modified by the librarian.

Intellectual Property Concerns: Intellectual property remains a key issue in the acquisition process. The approaches to intellectual property vary based on the type of organization doing the archiving. In the case of data centers or corporate archives where there is a close tie between the center and the owner or funding source, there is little question about the intellectual property rights related to acquisition. However, in the case of national libraries, the approaches to intellectual property rights differ from country to country. The differences are based on variant national information policies or legal deposit laws.

In many countries, the law has not yet caught up with the digital environment, and the libraries must make their own decisions. In the absence of digital deposit legislation, the PANDORA Project seeks permission from the copyright owner before copying the resource for the archive. In contrast, the Swedish and Finnish national library projects have an automated system and do not contact the owners.

Identification and cataloguing: Once the archive has acquired the digital object, it is necessary to identify and catalogue it. Both identification and cataloguing allow the archiving organization to manage the digital objects over time. Identification provides a unique key for finding the object and linking that object to other related objects. Cataloguing in the form of metadata supports organization, access and curation. Cataloguing and identification practices are often related to what is being archived and the resources available for managing the archive.

Metadata: All archives use some form of metadata for description, reuse, administration, and preservation of the archived object. There are issues related to how the metadata is created, the metadata standards and content rules that are used, the level at which metadata is applied and where the metadata is stored.

The majority of the projects created metadata in whole or part at the cataloguing stage. However, there is increasing interest in automatic generation of metadata, since the manual creation of metadata is considered to be a major impediment to digital archiving. A project is underway at the U.S. Environmental Protection Agency to derive metadata at the data element level from legacy databases. The Defense Information Technology Testbed (DITT) Project within the U.S. Department of Defense is also investigating automated metadata generation.

A variety of metadata formats are used by the selected projects, depending on the data type, discipline, resources available, and cataloguing approaches used. Most national libraries use traditional library cataloguing standards with some fields unable to be filled and others taking on new meaning. All titles in the NLA's PANDORA Archive receive full MARC cataloguing by the Electronic Unit Staff. However, several newer abbreviated formats developed specifically for Web-based resources are also in use. EVA uses a Dublin Core-like format. It is anticipated that an abbreviated format such as the Dublin Core may facilitate receipt of metadata directly from the publisher, eliminating the need for extensive library cataloguing.

There is even a greater variety of content standards used by the projects when entering data into the metadata fields. The national libraries tend to use traditional library cataloguing rules such as AACR2. Some communities, such as the geospatial community, have information standards, such as latitude and longitude, which are easily incorporated as metadata content standards. However, work remains to identify the specific metadata elements needed for long-term preservation as opposed to discovery, particularly for non-textual data types like images, video and multimedia.

The level at which metadata is applied depends on the type of data and the anticipated access needs. Datasets are generally catalogued at the file or collection level. Electronic journal articles may be catalogued individually, sometimes with no concern about metadata for the issue or journal title levels. Homepages provide a particularly difficult problem for determining the level at which metadata should be applied. Generally, the metadata is applied to whatever level is considered to be the full extent of the intellectual resource.

In the projects reviewed, the metadata files generally are stored separately from the archives themselves. Libraries may store the metadata in their online public access catalogues. Publishers may store the metadata in a bibliographic or citation database. However, in some instances, such as electronic journals with tagged headers for title, authors, author affiliation, etc., the information may be stored with the object itself and extracted for the catalogue. In the case of distributed archives, the metadata may be stored centrally, with the objects distributed throughout the network, or the metadata may be stored as embedded tags in the digital resource.

Discussions surrounding the interoperability of archives, both within and across disciplines, focus on the need to be able to crosswalk or translate between the various metadata formats. This is key to the development of networked, heterogeneous archives. The Open Archival Information System (OAIS) Reference Model developed by the ISO Consultative Committee for Space Data Systems addresses this issue by encapsulating specific metadata as needed for each object type in a consistent data model.

The Long Term Environmental Research (LTER) Network has developed mechanisms for "fitting" its network-specific metadata information into the broader scheme of the Federal Geographic Data Committee content standard for geographic data and other standards related to ecology.

For those archives that do not copy the digital material immediately into the archive, the movement of material from server to server or from directory to directory on the network, resulting in a change in the URL, is problematic. The use of the server as the location identifier can result in a lack of persistence over time both for the source object and any linked objects.

Despite possible problems, most archives continue to use the URL when referencing the location for the digital object. However, there are some projects that are changing this practice. The OCLC archive uses PURLs, persistent identifiers to which the changeable URL is mapped. The American Chemical Society uses the Digital Object Identifier for its journal articles and also maintains the original Manuscript Number assigned to the item at the beginning of the publication process.

A multifaceted identification system is used by the American Astronomical Society (AAS). Name resolution is used instead of URLs. In addition, the AAS uses astronomy's standard identifier, called a "Bibcode", which has been in use for fifteen years. In the spring of 1999, AAS added PubRef numbers; other identifiers can be added as needed to maintain links.

Storage

Storage is often treated as a passive stage in the life cycle, but storage media and formats have changed with legacy information perhaps lost forever. Block sizes, tape sizes, tape drive mechanisms and operating systems have changed over time. Most organizations that responded to the question about the periodicity of media migration anticipate a 3-5 year cycle.

The most common solution to this problem of changing storage media is migration to new storage systems. This is expensive, and there is always concern about the loss of data or problems with the quality when a transfer is made. Check algorithms are extremely important when this approach is used. The most rigorous media migration practices are in place at the data centers. The Atmospheric Radiation Monitoring (ARM) Center at the Oak Ridge National Laboratory plans to migrate to new technologies every 4-5 years. During each migration, the data is copied to the new technology. Each migration will require 6-12 months.

Preservation

Preservation is the aspect of archival management that preserves the content as well as the look and feel of the digital object. While the study showed that there is no common agreement on the definition of long-term preservation, the time frame can be thought of as long enough to be concerned about changes in technology and changes in the user community. Depending on the particular technologies and subject disciplines involved, the project managers interviewed estimated the cycle for hardware/software migration at 2-10 years.

New releases of databases, spreadsheets, and word processors can be expected at least every two to three years, with patches and minor updates released more often. While software vendors generally provide migration strategies or upward compatibility for some generations of their products, this may not be true beyond one or two generations. Migration is not guaranteed to work for all data types, and it becomes particularly unreliable if the information product has used sophisticated software features. There is generally no backward compatibility, and if it is possible, there is certainly loss of integrity in the result.

Plans are less rigorous for migrating to new hardware and applications software than for storage media. In order to guard against major hardware/ software migration issues, the organizations try to procure mainstream commercial technologies. For example, both the American Chemical Society and the U.S. Environmental Protection Agency purchased Oracle not only for its data management capabilities but for the company's longevity and ability to impact standards development. Unfortunately, this level of standardization and ease of migration is not as readily available among technologies used in specialized fields where niche systems are required because of the interfaces to instrumentation and the volume of data to be stored and manipulated.

Emulation, which encapsulates the behavior of the hardware/software with the object, is being considered as an alternative to migration. For example, a MS Word 2000 document would be labeled as such and then metadata information provided that indicates how to reconstruct such a document is at the engineering -- bits and bytes -- level. An alternative to encapsulating the software with every instance of the data type is to create an emulation registry that uniquely identifies the hardware and software environments and provides information on how to recreate the environment in order to preserve the use of the digital object.

At this time, there is no system in place to provide the extensive documentation and emulation information required for this approach to be operable, particularly to allow an archive to deal with the variety of older technologies. Most importantly, there is no policy that requires the manufacturers to deposit the emulation information. The best practice for the foreseeable future will be migration to new hardware and software platforms; emulation will begin to be used if and when the hardware and software industries begin to endorse it.

At the specific format level, there are several approaches used to save the "look and feel" of material. For journal articles, the majority of the projects reviewed use image files (TIFF), PDF, or HTML. TIFF is the most prevalent for those organizations that are involved in any way with the conversion of paper backfiles. For example, JSTOR, a non-profit organization that supports both storage of current journal issues in electronic format and conversion of back issues, processes everything from paper into TIFF and then scans the TIFF image. The OCR, because it cannot achieve 100% accuracy, is used only for searching; the TIFF image is the actual delivery format that the user sees. However, this does not allow the embedded references to be active hyperlinks.

HTML/SGML (Standard Generalized Mark-up Language) is used by many large publishers after years of converting publication systems from proprietary formats to SGML. The American Astronomical Society (AAS) has a richly encoded SGML format that is used as the archival format from which numerous other formats and products are made. The SGML version that is actually stored by the publisher is converted to HTML. PDF versions can also be provided by conversion routines.

For purely electronic documents, PDF is the most prevalent format. This provides a replica of the Postscript format of the document, but relies upon proprietary encoding technologies. PDF is used both for formal publications and grey literature. The National Library of Sweden transforms dissertations that are received in formats other than PDF to PDF and HTML. While PDF is increasingly accepted, concerns remain for long-term preservation and it may not be accepted as a legal depository format, because of its proprietary nature.

Preserving the "look and feel" is difficult in the text environment, but it is even more difficult in the multimedia environment, where there is a tightly coupled interplay between software, hardware and content. The U.S. Department of Defense DITT Project is developing models and software for the management of multimedia objects. Similarly, the University of California at San Diego has developed a model for object-based archiving that allows various levels and types of metadata with distributed storage of various data types. The UCSD work is funded by the U.S. National Archives and Records Administration and the U.S. Patent and Trademark Office.

A key preservation issue is the format in which the archival version should be stored. Transformation is the process of converting the native format to a standard format. On the whole, the projects reviewed favored storage in native formats. However, there are several examples of data transformation. AAS and ACS transform the incoming files into SGML-tagged ASCII format. The AAS believes that "The electronic master copy, if done well, is able to serve as the robust electronic archival copy. Such a well-tagged copy can be updated periodically, at very little cost, to take advantage of advances in both technology and standards. The content remains unchanged, but the public electronic version can be updated to remain compatible with the advances in browsers and other access technology."

The data community also provides some examples of data transformation. For example, the NASA Data Active Archive Centers (DAACs) transform incoming satellite and ground-monitoring information into standard Common Data Format. The U.K.'s National Digital Archive of Datasets (NDAD) transforms the native format into one of its own devising, since NDAD could not find an existing standard that dealt with all their metadata needs. These transformed formats are considered to be the archival versions, but the bit-wise copies are retained, so that someone can replicate what the center has done.

In some countries, there are intellectual property questions related to native versus transformed formats. According to Canadian Copyright Law, an author's rights are infringed if the original work is "distorted, mutilated or otherwise modified." After much discussion, the NLC decided that converting an electronic publication to a standard format to preserve the quality of the original and to ensure long-term access does not infringe on the author's right of integrity. However, this assumption has not been tested in court.

One of the paradoxes of the networked environment is that in an environment that is so dynamic and open to change, there is a greater and greater emphasis on standards. Those projects that have been archiving for a long period of time indicated that while they started out with a large number of incoming formats — primarily textual -- the number of formats have decreased. DOE OSTI began its project with a limited number of acceptable input formats, because there were so many different native formats. In the political environment of that time, it was difficult to gain support for the standardization of word processing packages. However, documents are currently received in only a few formats. Text is received in SGML (and its relatives HTML and XML), PDF (Normal and Image), WordPerfect and Word. Images are received in TIFF Group 4 and PDF Image.

The market forces have reduced the number of major word processing vendors. To a lesser extent, consolidation has occurred in the number of spreadsheet and database formats. However, there is less consistency in the modeling, simulation and specific purpose software areas; much of this software continues to be specific to the project. Therefore, the emphasis in these areas is on the development of standards for interoperability and data exchange, realizing that perhaps the market forces will not play as large a role here as with more general purpose software applications.

The previous life cycle functions that have been discussed are performed for the purpose of ensuring continuous access to the material in the archive. Successful practices must consider changes to access mechanisms, as well as rights management and security requirements over the long term.

Most project managers interviewed consider the access and display mechanisms to be another source of change in the digital environment. Today it is the Web, but there is no way of knowing what it might be tomorrow. It may be possible in the future to enhance the quality of presentation of items from the digital archive based on advances in digitization and browser technologies. NLM's Profiles in Science product creates an electronic archive of the photographs, text, videos, etc. that are provided by donors to this project. This electronic archive is used to create new access versions as the access mechanisms change. However, the originals are always retained. One of the most difficult access issues for digital archiving involves rights management. What rights does the archive have? How will the access mechanism interact with the archive's metadata to ensure that these rights are managed properly? Rights management includes providing or restricting access as appropriate, and changing the access rights as the material's copyright and security level changes.

Security and version control also impact digital archiving. Brewster Kahle raises many interesting questions concerning privacy and "stolen information," particularly since the Internet Archive policy is to archive all sites that are linked to one another in one long chain. Similarly, there is concern among image archivists that images can be tampered with without the tampering being detected. Particularly in cases where conservation issues are at stake, it is important to have metadata to manage encryption, watermarks, digital signatures, etc. that can survive despite changes in the format and media on which the digital item is stored.

References

Hodge, G.M. and Carroll, B.C. (1999), 'Digital Electronic Archiving: The State of the Art and the State of the Practice.' A Report Sponsored by the International Council for Scientific and Technical Information, Information Policy Committee and CENDI, 26 April 1999.

Moore, R., Baru, C., Rajasekar, A. et al. (2000), Collection-Based persistent Digital Archives. *D-Lib Magazine*, March and April 2000.

CEDARS Project. *Metadata For Digital Preservation The Cedars Project Outline Specification Draft For Public Consultation*, http://www.leeds.ac.uk/cedars/metadata.html

Friedlander, A. (2002), 'The National Digital Information In frastructure Preservation Program,' *D-Lib Magazine*, 8.4, April 2002, http://www.dlib.org/dlib/april02/friedlander/04friedlander.html

Hunolt, G. and Booth, A. (9/2001), *ESDIS Data Center Best Practices And Bench mark Report*, Science Operations Office, Earth Science Data and Information Systems Project, Goddard Space Flight Center, NASA Contract NAS5-00154.

Bibliography

Branschofsky, M. and Chudnov, D., (2002), *Dspace: Durable Digital Documents long term-preservation.* Proceedings of the Second ACM/IEEE-CS joint conference on Digital Libraries, Portland, Oregon, USA.

Carroll, B. & G. Hodge. (1999). "Digital Electronic Archiving: The State of the Art, the State of the Practice." [Online]. Available: http://www.icsti.org/Dig_Archiving_Report_1999.pdf

CEDARS Project. *Metadata For Digital Preservation The Cedars Project Outline Specification Draft For Public Consultation,* http://www.leeds.ac.uk/cedars/metadata.html

Faundeen, J. (2003b). "US Land Remote Sensing Archive." Presented at the ERPANET/CODATA International Archiving Workshop on the Selection, Appraisal and Retention of Digital Scientific Data held in Lisbon, Portugal, 15-17 December 2003.

Friedlander, A. (2002), 'The National Digital Information In frastructure Preservation Program,' *D-Lib Magazine*, 8.4, April 2002, http://www.dlib.org/dlib/april02/friedlander/04friedlander.html

Gilleland-Swetland, A. (2000). "Setting the Stage." In Introduction to Metadata: Pathways to Digital Information, M. Baca (ed.) [Online]. Available: http://www.getty.edu/research/institute/standards/intrometadata/2_articles/index.html

Hodge, G.M. and Carroll, B.C. (1999), 'Digital Electronic Archiving: The State of the Art and the State of the Practice.' A Report Sponsored by the International Council for Scientific and Technical Information, Information Policy Committee and CENDI, 26 April 1999.

Hunolt, G. and Booth, A. (9/2001), *ESDIS Data Center Best Practices And Bench mark Report*, Science Operations Office, Earth Science Data and Information Systems Project, Goddard Space Flight Center, NASA Contract NAS5-00154.

It's About Time: Research Challenges in Digital Archiving and Long-term Preservation. Final Report on a Workshop on Research Challenges in Digital Archiving, 12-13 April 2002. (2002), Washington, DC, Library of Congress.

Janes, Joseph. (1998). "The Internet Public Library: an intellectual history." *Library Hi Tech*, 16(2), 55-68.

Keller, M.A., Reich, V.A. and Herkovic, A.C. (2003), 'What is a library anymore, anyway?', *First Monday*, 8.5, May 2003, http://firstmonday.org/issues/issue8_5/keller/index.html

Ladner, Sharyn J., and Hope N. Tillman. (1993)."Using the Internet for reference". *Online*, 17(1), 45-51. January.

Levy, David M., (2000) "Digital Libraries and the Problem of Purpose." *D-Lib Magazine* 6, January.

Liu, Ying, and Anita S. Coleman. (2004)."Communicating Digital Library Services to Scientific Communities." *LIBRES* 14, no. 1.

Logoze, Carl, and David Fielding, (1998). "Defining Collections in Distributed Digital Libraries." *D-Lib Magazine,* November.

Lorie, R.A. (2002), *A Methodology and System for Preserving Digital Data.* Proceedings of the Second ACM/IEEE- CS joint conference on Digital Libraries, Portland, Oregon, USA.

Lund, William, (2001)."Digital Object Library Products", RLG DigiNews 5, no. 5.

Michelle Q. Wang Baldonado and Steve B. Cousins. (1996). Addressing heterogeneity in the networked information environment. *New Review of Information Networking*, 2:83-102.

Miller, Rush G., (2002)"Shaping Digital Library Content." The Journal of Academic Librarianship 28, no. 3 : 97-103.

Moore, R., Baru, C., Rajasekar, A. et al. (2000), Collection-Based persistent Digital Archives. *D-Lib Magazine*, March and April 2000.

OCLC/RLG Working Group on Preservation Metadata. (2002). "Preservation Metadata and the OAIS Information Model: A Metadata Framework to Support the Preservation of digital Objects." [Online]. Available: http://www.oclc.org/research/projects/pmwg/pm_framework.pdf

Preservation Metadata and the OAIS Information Model. A Metadata Framework to Support the Preservation of Digital Objects.A Report by the OCLC/RLG Working Group on Preservation Metadata, June 2002, http://www.oclc.org/research/pmwg/pm_framework.pdf

Research Libraries Group. (2002)."Open Archival Information System (OAIS) Resources." October 2002. [Online]. Available: http://www.rlg.org/longterm/oais.html

Rowlands, Ian, and David Bawden. (1999) "Building the Digital Library on Solid Research Foundations." *Aslib Proceedings* 51, September .

Schatz, Bruce R. (1997). "Information Retrieval in Digital Libraries: Bringing Search to the Net." *Science*, 17 January

Schwartz, Candy. (2000). "Digital Libraries: An Overview." *The Journal of Academic Librarianship* 26, November .

Trusted Digital Repositories: Attributes and Responsibilities. An RLG-OCLC Report, May 2002, http://www.rlg.org/longterm/repositiories.pdf

Index

A

Access management 189, 203
Administrative responsibility 123
Adobe systems 27
Archival community 118
Archival information 139
Archival storage 140
Archive architecture 100
Archive content development 115
Association of Moving Image Archives (AMIA) 11
Association of Recorded Sound Collections (ARSC) 11
Association of Research Libraries (ARL) 246
Audiovisual archives 3
Audiovisual documents 7
Audiovisual heritage 3
Audiovisual materials 5
Author supplied references 93
Auxiliary forms 127

B

Bibliographic control 108
British Library Research and Innovation Centre (BLRI) 155
Brochureware 158

C

Canadian Heritage Information Network (CHIN) 248
Cataloguing 268
Collection management 240
Computer-aided Design (CAD) 48
Conference of European National Libraries (CENL) 76
Content information 139
Content providers 153
Context information 139
Copyright statements 93
Courseware 158
Cryptographic keys 193

D

Data Encryption Standard (DES) 208
Data management 108
Database archiving 68
Dataware 158
Decomposition services 70
Descriptive information 140
Detailed cataloguing 9
Digital archives 11, 64
Digital environment, 52
Digital information 44, 47
Digital Libraries Federation (DLF) 90
Digital libraries implement 204
Digital library functions 47
Digital Media Projects Office (DMP) 71
Digital reference 72
Digital storage media 141
Digital technologies 89
Digitization Technology 18
Dissemination Information Package (DIP) 143
Document analysis 12
Document Type Descriptions (DTD) 31

E

Economic issues 97
Electronic libraries 72
Electronic records 187
Electronic reference library 76
Electronic technology 9
Electronic text creation 22
Electronic texts 12
Electronic-commerce transactions 187
Enhancement services 70

F

Financial sustainability 123
Fiscal commitment 188
Fixity information 140

G

Geographic information systems (GIS) 78
Graphical User Interface (GUI) 78
Guideware 158

H

HyperText Markup Language 32

I

Information technologies 42
Intellectual preservation 184
International Council on Museums (ICOM) 11
International Council on Traditional Music (ICTM) 11
International Development Research Centre (IDRC) 76
International Standards Organisation (ISO) 35
Internet Assigned Numbers Authority (IANA) 109
Internet Engineering Task Force (IETF) 109

J

Joint Information Systems Committee (JISC) 78

L

Library Systems and Services Incorporated (LSSI) 72

M

Machine-Readable Records (MARC) 77
Manage storage hierarchy 140
Markup Languages 25
Matrix structure 2
Medium preservation 172
Metadata issues 263
Migration strategy 141

N

Name Resolution Service (NRS) 109
National Science Foundation (NSF) 72
Navigation services 70
Networked resources 88
News websites 2
Non-proprietary markup 26

O

Online catalogue maintenanc 188
Online information services 153
Online Public Access Catalogue (OPAC) 76
Open Archival Information System (OAIS) 127
Organization viability 123
Organizational commitments 187
Organizational regimes 45

P

Packaging designs 142
Packaging information 140
Perpetual access 268
Personal computers (PCs) 73
Portable Document Format (PDF) 27
PostScript language 27
Potential readers 267
Preservation planning 111
Preservation policies 133
Preservation service 111

Preservation strategy 110
Preservation-oriented design 51
Primary Research and Training (CFPRT) 247
Procedural accountability 123
Procedural suitability 123
Programming language 27
Provenance information 139

R

Reference information 139
Refreshing mechanism 271
Registration services 69
Remote access 269
Remote harvesting 68
Resolution services 70
Resourceware 158

S

Searching services 69
Side bars 2
Smart-cards 197
Staged access 271
Standard Generalized Markup Language (SGML) 35, 49
Storage management 58
Submission Information Package (SIP) 103
System security 123

T

Technology preservation 184
Text Encoding Initiative (TEI 30
Threaded discussions 93
Transactional archiving 69
Transformation services 70
Tribal archives 2

U

Uniform Resource Names (URNs) 109

V

Video archives 10
Visual material 153

W

Web archiving 67
Web environment 71

X

XML documents 39